PRODUCTS LIABILITY

for Corporate Counsels, Controllers, and Product Safety Executives

PRODUCTS LIABILITY
for Corporate Counsels, Controllers, and Product Safety Executives

Warren Freedman

VNR VAN NOSTRAND REINHOLD COMPANY
NEW YORK CINCINNATI TORONTO LONDON MELBOURNE

Library of Congress Catalog Card Number: 83-19678
ISBN: 0-442-22493-1

Manufactured in the United States of America

Published by Van Nostrand Reinhold Company Inc.
135 West 50th Street
New York, New York 10020

Van Nostrand Reinhold Company Limited
Molly Millars Lane
Wokingham, Berkshire RG11 2PY, England

Van Nostrand Reinhold
480 Latrobe Street
Melbourne, Victoria 3000, Australia

Macmillan of Canada
Division of Gage Publishing Limited
164 Commander Boulevard
Agincourt, Ontario M1S 3C7, Canada

15 14 13 12 11 10 9 8 7 6 5 4 3 2 1

Library of Congress Cataloging in Publication Data

Freedman, Warren.
Products liability for corporate counsels, controllers, and product safety executives.

Includes index.
1. Products liability—United States 2. Product safety—Law and legislation—United States. 3. Actions and defenses—United States. I. Title.
KF 1296.F73 1984 346.7303′82 83-19678
ISBN 0-442-22493-1 347.306382

Preface

Today's headlines abound with details of Tylenol-caused deaths, Manville asbestos-induced disabilities, Ford automobile-caused injuries, Agent Orange-precipitated disabilities, and literally thousands of products which have allegedly caused personal injury, property damage, and economic loss. Even a defectively designed vitamin tablet allegedly caused comedian David Brenner to be hospitalized, for he could not swallow it! (He commenced suit in the federal district court in New York in February 1983 for pain and suffering!) From the sublime to the ridiculous, consumers have sued at the drop of a hat, seeking compensation from product manufacturers and others in the chain of distribution of the product. There is "an urge to sue" still rampant in the American marketplace.

According to the *New York Times* (Feb. 13, 1983) the Ford Motor Company is paying about $20 million as a result of lawsuits charging that defective automobile and truck transmissions caused deaths and injuries. As early as 1970 Ford was allegedly aware of the defect in millions of cars and light trucks "and could have corrected it for 3¢ a vehicle." The defect in the design of the transmissions caused the cars to jump into reverse after the driver had put the car in neutral. More than 1,000 persons have felt the "urge to sue" Ford. . . and are doing so today.

The Tylenol "scare" of 1982 which resulted in the deaths of seven persons who consumed the product laced with cyanide crystals brought "out of the woodwork" hundreds of "claimants" seeking compensation for alleged injuries. They argued that the packaging of Tylenol was unreasonably dangerous because of a failure to design the capsule, bottle, and box so as to preclude any tampering with the contents. But it will be difficult to persuade a jury to award damages against the product manufacturer where the *criminal* acts of third persons is the critical factor in the Tylenol deaths. Indeed, absolute protection against a determined poisoner is simply beyond reach. In the words of Food and Drug Administration Commissioner Arthur H. Hayes, Jr.: "There is no such thing as a tamperproof drug just the way there is no such thing as a hijackproof airplane."

Still another example of the "urge to sue" is the more than 1,800 products liability lawsuits filed against Pacor Inc., a Philadelphia-based firm which distributes and installs insulation in commercial and industrial settings. Approximately 20 percent of Pacor's annual expenses have been earmarked between 1977 and 1983 for legal expenditures to defend asbestos-caused injuries. Approximately 85 percent of Pacor's lawsuits were filed by former Naval Shipyard employees, and every day two more lawsuits are commenced against Pacor. Even their insurance coverage was cancelled in 1979 because of the asbestos problem! Some asbestos firms have filed for bankruptcy to withstand the onslaught of lawsuits. Another firm, Keene Corporation, estimates that of every dollar spent on asbestos litigation, about 70¢ goes to lawyers, 15¢ to insurance companies, and only 15¢ to those claiming injury. Yet the "urge to sue" continues. . . .

The Consumer Product Safety Commission periodically publishes the NEISS DATA HIGHLIGHTS; in 1980 kitchen drain cleaners were at the top of the list with a mean severity index of 160 involving more than 13,000 cases of injury. Next came liquid fuels, followed by lawn mowers, power saws, and ladders and stools. These five consumer products caused almost 300,000 cases of injury in 1980. The "urge to sue" apparently has solid roots upon which to grow.

Warren Freedman

Contents

Introduction

Safety is admittedly a relative term, although in theory one should be able to distinguish easily between a product which is safe and a product which is unsafe. But in terms of Products Liability it is the court (and/or jury) which determines, under the law and circumstances of the case, whether the product is safe or unsafe. The task of the Corporate Counsel, Controller, and Product Safety Executive is therefore a difficult one. . . .

This volume is designed to help the Corporate Counsel, Controller, and Product Safety Executive make those important decisions on Safety of Product. The author, a distinguished practicing attorney and scholar in the field of Products Liability, is former Counsel of Bristol-Myers Company, and has devoted more than 25 years to working with corporate officers and executives in solving the intricate problems of allegedly unsafe products.

Liability arises from the use as well as the misuse of a product. This book focuses upon the vulnerabilities of the product in the marketplace, and explains why product claims are increasing and why their defense is so costly. Safety factors are delineated amid new federal and state legislation. Economic issues involved in mergers are enumerated. Settlement techniques are explored. And even international products liability is observed in terms of the lack of uniformity of safety requirements.

The byword is Safety, and the product manufacturer, together with others in the chain of distribution of the product, profit thereby even to the satisfaction of the consuming public.

PRODUCTS LIABILITY

for Corporate Counsels, Controllers, and Product Safety Executives

Part I
Products Liability: Definitions, Principles, and Dangers to Business

THE URGE TO SUE: THE DEEP POCKET THEORY OF LIABILITY

A child died after drinking from a bottle of furniture polish (clearly labeled as poison) for the parents had neglected to store the bottle in a safe place. A factory worker lost a finger after he tried to increase his production rate by using a rag to tie down the safety mechanism on his machine. A woman is alive today because a certain antibiotic saved her life, *but* she is left without her hearing because her physician or the hospital failed to monitor her condition properly. A 10-year-old boy received minor injuries when he stood on the open door of an oven and the entire electric stove toppled over on him. A drunken automobile driver collided with a tree and was severely injured, but blames the design of the windshield of the automobile for his injuries.

These and other accidents involving products sold in the American marketplace, illustrate the 15 million injuries occurring each year. Although a relatively small number of these accidents have serious and/or long-lasting effects, at least *one million claims* will probably be made against American product manufacturers and/or product sellers this year. Of course, the mere fact that a product is involved in the accident does not necessarily mean that the product CAUSED the accident. There is the human factor, and indeed, *misuse* of the product may be the proximate cause of the injury; but that fact alone does not discourage the American accident victim from suing the product manufacturer or seller. Americans have an *urge to sue* because there is an excellent chance of a *financial* windfall, merely by filing and/or litigating a claim. Somebody must pay for the injury; someone owes the injured party monetary compensation; and the company which can afford to pay the poor accident victim must do so, for the *poor* victim must not be at the mercy of the *rich* product seller! The urge to sue is at the root of products liability in the United States; . . . "sue the bastards" is the name of the game for this social malaise. And the fact that plaintiffs' attorneys share in this money incentive by virtue of the contingent fee system simply increases the number of litigated matters. Of course, there are wholly justified suits filed on behalf of those severely injured by unsafe products. But the real prospect of monetary gain still encourages precipitant and frivolous actions to be filed by persons with *minor inconveniences* (or no injuries at all) who ask for big dollar judgments or awards!

Unfortunately, the courts in the United States have been most receptive to the claims of accident victims. The child who drank the furniture polish was entitled to compensation, and the product manufacturer was held liable because the bottle label did not *specifically* warn the parents against leaving the furniture polish within the reach of the child! Similarly, the family of the 10-year-old boy who stood on the open oven door won their case in the trial court, even though the state's highest court later reversed, holding that standing on an open oven door was "abnormal and improper use" of the electrical oven! The factory worker who lost a finger also won his case, even though he had intentionally bypassed the machinery's safety device, and by his own act had exposed himself to injury; that court said that the machinery manufacturer should have anticipated such misuse and should have precluded the nonoperation of the safety device. And the deaf woman successfully sued the drug manufacturer because her physician did not follow the official package instructions which accompanied the prescriptive drug product, so that to her, the prescriptive drug was defective! The drunken driver also succeeded in his suit against the automobile manufacturer because negligence in design of the windshield constituted a product defect, and furthermore, the car manufacturer knew or had reason to know that drunks drive automobiles! Whether a different windshield design would have averted the accident was deemed irrelevant! The automobile manufacturer was an insurer of the driver's safety!

The amount of the awards and the judgments in products liability situations has rapidly increased too. In 1965 the average award in a products liability suit was about $12,000; in 1973 the amount had risen to $80,000; and in 1983 too many verdicts and judgments range well into six and seven figures! In a growing number of work-related product injury cases, the employee can sue the product manufacturer and even his/her employer under the Dual Capacity doctrine—*after* the insured employee has collected from his/her employer under workman's compensation! Other factors conducive to high awards and judgments include: (1) no limitation on the amount of punitive damages; (2) the state of the art rule operating as of the time of the injury; (3) statutes of limitations commencing from the date of plaintiff's discovery of the injury; (4) the continuing liability of successor companies; and (5) newfangled theories of liability such as the "Market Share" concept which indicts an entire industry for perhaps the wrong of one product manufacturer! Also, children in many states are today entitled to compensation for "Loss of Parental Society" alongside the spouse's claim for Loss of Consortium—when one spouse is injured through the action or inaction of a tortfeasor!

What has happened and what is happening in the United States is the prevalence of the disease of "CONSUMERITIS" which is the coequal of MOTHERHOOD and RIGHTEOUSNESS. "Consumeritis" has three basic "UN-PRINCIPLES" (as in Alice in Wonderland): (1) "Injury begets liability," i.e., once there is an injury, someone other than the victim must pay for it; (2) a trial court is but a conduit to see that consumer juries and not courts decide *all* cases; and (3) the only guideline is the "Robin Hood syndrome" of robbing the rich so that the poor victim will be paid.

The *first* un-principle, that every injury begets liability, brings to mind the story of the little boy who found near his Christmas tree a bucket of defecatory matter; whereupon he jumped for joy and shouted, "Daddy must have bought me a pony for Christmas." Such illogical *deductive* reasoning explains why some lawyers are so pleased to find a serious personal injury, a substantial property damage, or a severe economic loss.

The *second* un-principle involves weak-kneed judges who conceive their roles as mere conduits to carry the case to the jury. Every question or issue is *factual,* and therefore the jury of consumers must decide. Furthermore, there is no need to expedite the trial of a lawsuit until the plaintiff has exhausted a very prolonged discovery procedure, has served countless and meaningless interrogatories directed to the culpable defendant, or has amended and amended the complaint ad nauseam. The plaintiff is entitled to a full day in court!

The *third* un-principle, or, the "Robin Hood syndrome," is a paternalistic expenditure of another's money. The "deepest pocket" must compensate for pain and suffering as well as for injury, for property damage, and for economic loss, and must willingly participate in a "structured settlement" for the benefit of the victim, regardless of fault or liability. A good example of this un-principle is found in the Texas case of *Rumsey* v. *Freeway Manor Minimax,* (423 SW2d 387, 1968), where an infant ingested some roach poison found in the home. The product was labeled in three places "poison," had a red skull and crossbones, and the labeling read as follows:

> "Give a tablespoon of salt in a glass of warm water and repeat until vomit fluid is clear. Have victim lie down and keep warm. Call a physician immediately! Warning: Cumulative Poison. Absorbed through the skin. Do not get in eyes, on skin or on clothing. Wash thoroughly after handling. Keep children and domestic animals away from baited areas and burn all pests killed."

OBVIOUSLY the parents had not heeded the obvious warning about keeping the product away from children, but nevertheless the guilty parents argued *successfully* that the labeling on the product was inadequate because it did not state that there was no specific antidote for the poisoning! The Texas Court of Civil Appeals agreed that the first aid instructions failed to warn that there was nothing truly effective that could be done once the child ingested the poison. The court reprimanded the product manufacturer for failing "to disclose the extent of the danger . . . and (failing) to disclose measures that may be taken to avoid fatal consequences." The court distinguished "first aid treatment" which the label recited, and a "specific" antidote which was not recited on the label: "if ingestion is discovered before absorption, first aid may suffice, but if not, then a specific antidote is necessary." The fact that the product manufacturer had complied with all federal and state marketing and labeling statutes for insecticides was insufficient because, said the court, there is a common law duty to warn the user, which duty transcends specific statutes. Even the infant's mother was found NOT GUILTY OF NEGLIGENCE for her failure to keep the poison beyond the reach of the infant because it did not appear that "she knew or should have known there was no specific antidote." The Texas court explained: "(E)ven though poison is known to the ordinary person to be inherently dangerous, there is a common law duty to warn of the full extent of the danger." AND YET THE COURT SAID NOTHING ABOUT THE NECESSITY FOR A FINDING THAT ADEQUATE WARNING SHOULD HAVE PREVENTED THE INJURY! Did the defendant prove that the INADEQUATE WARNING *CAUSED* THE INJURY? Defendant introduced no evidence to show that a warning of the proper kind would have been heeded by these parents and would have prevented the harm! The "deepest pocket" pays . . . almost regardless of fault.

TOYS and Liability for Injuries also illustrate the social malaise of the "urge to sue"; there are 750,000 injuries each year from the use and misuse of toys, and at least 100,000 lawsuits per annum result. A few examples are striking: a 14-month-old child was playing with a tiny figure in a pull-type vehicular toy when he put the figure into his mouth. The figure lodged in his throat and could not be removed by the child's parents. The toy figure had to be surgically removed at a hospital, but the anoxia which the infant suffered between ingestion and extraction left him permanently and severely brain-damaged. In *Cunningham* v. *Quaker Oats Co.* (Civ. Action #1973–343, U.S. District Court, Western District of New York at Buffalo) the jury on June 19, 1981 found the manufacturer Fisher-Price negligent in the design of the toy, and awarded $3.1 million to the infant and his parents. Plaintiffs had successfully argued that if the figure had been designed differently, perhaps larger, the child would have been unable to swallow it in such a manner. Apparently the jury was not interested in the failure of the parents to guard against such injuries; the "deep pocket'' was the toy industry which in fiscal year 1981 recorded retail sales of $7.35 billion!

The defendant helmet manufacturer admitted that 30 to 40 deaths occur each year from subdural hematomas received while youngsters are playing football; but the particular helmet which allegedly had an indentation at the point of impact when the plaintiff quarterback collided head-to-head with his own teammate during practice, was destroyed after the accident. Nevertheless, the Texas Court of Civil Appeals in *Rawlings Sporting Goods Co.* v. *Daniels* (619 SW 2d 435, 1981) affirmed a jury verdict of $1.5 million. The court reasoned that the particular helmet must have been defective! (Apparently no one came forward with any explanation of the injury.)

In January 1970 the Child Protection and Toy Safety Act amended the Federal Hazardous Substances Act by enlarging the definition of ''hazardous substance'' to include *toys* which present electrical, mechanical, or thermal hazards (Public Law 91–113). There is indeed an overreaching to protect children from the hazards of the marketplace.

The ''urge to sue'' frequently concerns *Wrong Defendants and Right Plaintiffs;* in *Racer* v. *Utterman,* the Missouri Court of Appeals in 1981 held the manufacturer (Johnson & Johnson) of a surgical drape strictly liable for failure to warn of the drape's flammability without any proof that the surgeon or hospital knew or should have known of the drape's flammability. It seems that during a D & C operation, plaintiff's body was covered by the surgical drape to provide a sterile field and block bacteria from the site of the operation. During surgery, the surgeon's hot cautery accidentally ignited a cotton gauze he was using as a sponge; he threw the smoldering gauze to the floor, but the gauze ignited the hanging end of the surgical drape, thereby inflicting severe burns on the plaintiff-patient. The Missouri Court of Appeals *affirmed* the jury award against Johnson & Johnson in the amount of $382,500 compensatory damages, but *reversed* the $517,500 punitive award. The court found that the surgical drape was an ''unavoidable unsafe'' product within the meaning of Comment K of Section 402A of the *Restatement of Torts Second* since there is no known method of making the drape fire resistant that does not adversely affect its function as a barrier against infection. *But* such a product is shielded from liability only when it is accompanied by an adequate warning of the danger, *which was not the case here!* Liability therefore arises out of the introduction of a defective product into commerce, regardless of the manufactuer's knowledge of the defect. (Punitive damages were disallowed because there was no proof that Johnson & Johnson was indifferent or showed callous disregard for the safety of others.) The hospital and the surgeon were the "right" defendants, but the product manufacturer presented the better target!

WHY PLAINTIFFS ARE FAVORED AND FLAVORED OVER DEFENDANTS

1. The Disappointed Consumer. The attitude of consumers toward products that they buy has changed. More and more people are dissatisfied with the goods and services they purchase. One reason is the higher expectation for proper product performance as a result of the Consumer movement. Another reason is that products are becoming more complex and technically sophisticated, so that consumers always expect the best. Also, more and more products are being introduced each year, greatly increasing the exposure of manufacturers and distributors. Furthermore, the American public has become accustomed to product defects by the recalls of millions of automobiles in recent years, and the large amount of publicity given other consumer product defect cases. The end result has been to create a mood in which the unsatisfied customer seeks to punish the product manufacturer as well as obtain compensation for any injury or loss suffered. Public awareness and antagonism toward business is also reflected in class action legislation, making it easier for dissatisfied customers to band together to file common lawsuits alleging defective products or fradulent selling practices.

The disappointed consumer of goods and services has pushed courts and legislatures into frantic activity since 1960 with self-serving phrases like "consumer protection" and "strict liability." It is a disturbing perception for consumers to portray a product as "evil," and this is a factor inviting courts to come to the aid of the plaintiff-consumer, not only to compensate for injury, damage, or loss, but to reimburse for disappointments in the performance of the product.

2. The Doctrine of Strict Liability, Favors and Flavors Plaintiffs. The popular vehicle for executing the paternalistic doctrine of the "deep pocket," i.e., giving credence to deductive reasoning that injury begets liability, and approving the conduct of weak-kneed judges who merely serve as conduits for the jury, is the doctrine of Strict Products Liability. Twenty-three years ago in the state of New Jersey, *Henningsen* v. *Bloomfield Motors,* (161 A2d 69) made the 1960 headlines by creating an illegitimate marriage between tort and contract. An automobile collision prompted suit not against the negligent driver but against the automobile manufacturer who *must* have produced a defective steering wheel because when the vehicle veers suddenly off the road into a tree, there must be something badly wrong with the steering mechanism of the car! (This same form of deductive reasoning promised a pony for the little boy at Christmas!) The doctrine of Strict Products Liability obviated the necessity of proving Fault or a finding of Negligence, and at the same time did away with the defenses of misuse and mishandling of the product. The automobile was deemed an unreasonably dangerous instrumentality, and therefore that automobile was "defective." The logic is that the injured user is entitled to compensation from the defective product manufacturer! The *Henningsen* case was indeed a radical departure from the tradition in law that Fault begets Liability! Here No-Fault was the basis for liability!

3. Impact of Legislation Benefitting Plaintiffs. The rising volume of claims has been nourished by new federal legislation (and regulations thereunder) such as the Occupational Safety and Health Act of 1970 (called "OSHA") and the Consumer Product Safety Act of 1972. OSHA focuses upon safety in the workplace, including materials, tools and equipment, and environment for the protection of employees. The CPSA covers products for use at home, in schools, for recreation, and for personal use or consumption. There is an inherent belief that something must be wrong with a given product!

4. Definitions and Other Considerations. "Liability" establishes a right of action for a civil wrong or tort by one party against another. The wronged party has the right to sue for injuries or damages or loss. Traditionally, liability was predicated upon fault. But today liability may not involve fault, for the compensatory system entitles any person who suffers injury, damage, or loss to compensation regardless of responsibility or negligence. The burden and cost of a no-fault compensatory system, in the final analysis, falls upon society as a whole.

"Strict Liability" is the doctrine imposing liability upon a party, regardless of fault, once the elements of "defect" proximately causing the injury, damage, or loss, and of "control by the product manufacturer" are proven.

"Warranty" is an allegation by the manufacturer or seller about the product; it may be oral or written, express or implied—and the breach of which calls for the imposition of liability.

"Privity" is the existence of a contractual relation between two or more parties such as buyer and seller. At one time, lack of privity was an effective defense, but "privity" today is meaningless except perhaps in the claim for economic loss.

"Third Party Action" describes the result whereby the first party who is injured and entitled to sue the second party or his employer actually sues a third party, such as the product manufacturer, for the injuries sustained in the course of employment.

5. Favoring the Plaintiff. Mr. Parry, a 58-year-old man, was shot in the head when a Daniel Boone-type flintlock rifle accidentally discharged. (He lost his left eye as well as hearing in his right ear.) He thereupon sued the gun's owner, who had been placing it in a truck near him when the gun fired. (Previously the rifle manufacturer and the retailer of the gun settled with Parry for $1 million, allegedly based upon proof that the gun was negligently designed, for it had no conventional safety catch and also had a soft-metal trigger that wore out prematurely.) A Florida jury now awarded Parry an additional $2 million from the gun owner, *Parry* v. *Allstate Insurance Co.*, Florida Circuit Court, Palm Beach County, #78–2856, 1982.

Liability can readily be predicated against others in the chain of distribution of the product. The nonmanufacturing seller is an easy target because he put the product into circulation; he is available for suit where the manufacturer may be out-of-state, and he can put financial pressure upon the manufacturer to defend or settle the claim. Retailers and wholesalers can be held strictly liable as illustrated by the California decision of *Vandermark* v. *Ford Motor Co.*, (391 P 2d 168) where the court ruled that the retailer as well as the manufacturer was liable to a consumer who was injured by a defect present in the Ford braking system. There was no evidence that the retailer had altered or worked on the defective part of the automobile, although Ford had delegated the job of final preparation to the dealer.

The court noted that retailers and wholesalers are an integral part of the overall marketing of the cars and should bear their share of the cost of injuries due to defective products.

An unusual claim against an airline arose out of the fact that an elderly mother, wearing KLM slippers given to her by her son who had been a first class passenger on KLM aircraft, fell on a noncarpeted area of a friend's apartment. The trial court dismissed the claim, and New York's highest court in *Gobhai* v. *KLM,* on October 12, 1982 affirmed: KLM was immune from liability since it did not manufacture, design, or sell the allegedly defective product, and the nature of the transaction was such that KLM had essentially performed a service, rather than supplied a product to the son and his mother.

Still another weird product claim was presented to CBS-TV and sponsors of a "World's Strongest Man Contest" by one Franco Columbu who alleged that as a result of his participation in the contest he sustained major injuries while running a 40-yard dash with an 8-foot high refrigerator strapped to his back. He claimed that the "back apparatus" was defective and had never been tested, and the California jury awarded him the sum of $1,036,760!

In September 1982 an Insurance Information Institute survey reported that a majority of both the American public and business executives think that products liability lawsuits are generally justified less often than more often, and that the amounts of money awarded to plaintiffs are usually "too high." A majority of those interviewed also were of the opinion that the judge and not the jury should determine the amount of the award.

SIZE OF THE AWARD AND/OR JUDGMENTS TODAY

The rising number of products liability lawsuits and the increased size of awards and/or judgments are of growing concern. In 1965 the average award in products liability suits was estimated at $12,000. By 1973 that average became $80,000, and today, in 1983, awards range well into six and seven figures. Obviously, such monetary awards, unless covered by insurance, have a serious impact upon industry and the public; some product manufacturers must go out of business, and the higher price for the product can discourage sales in a competitive market. The U.S. Commerce Department reported some years ago that nonwork accidents involving consumer products sold in the marketplace account for 20 million injuries a year! The cost to the product manufacturer is enormous—a $50,000 claim levied against an *uninsured* manufacturer with annual sales of $1 million would amount to a loss of 5 percent of sales, not to mention profits. If there are multiple claims or there is one really big judgment, the firm could easily go under!

1. Economic Loss. Plaintiffs sue for personal injuries, property damage, and for economic loss, which form of compensation is generally not available under the Strict Liability doctrine. Indeed, the majority of states have rejected Strict Liability for Economic Losses and consigned the parties to their contractual, sales, and warranty remedies under the Uniform Commercial Code. See *Purvis* v. *Consolidated Energy Products Co.,* (U.S. Court of Appeals for the Fourth Circuit, March 8, 1982, No. 81-1107) which case makes the point that tort theory is properly applicable to physical injury and property damage, while contract law protects expectation interests for Economic Losses when a qualitative product defect is involved.

In *Lowenstein* v. *General Motors Corp.,* the New York Appellate Division, Appellate Term, 2nd Dept., on April 9, 1982, unanimously reversed a judgment in favor of the plaintiff and dismissed the action because "an action to recover solely for *economic loss* is not maintainable in the absence of privity between the parties." The action was for breach of implied warranty by a consumer against a remote manufacturer to recover for a defective dashboard in her automobile. The contrary position in New York is *Schiavone Construction Co.* v. *Elgood Mayo Corp.,* (81 AD2d 221, 1st Dept., 1981), involving a truck hoist which was purchased through an independent distributor. The hoist did not break or cause property damage, but simply could not be used for the purpose for which it was designed and sold. The court allowed the contractor to recover its economic losses, to wit: "the cost of repairs to put the equipment into reasonably operable condition, and other economic loss due to downtime loss of production, additional labor incurred, and equipment rentals." The New York court lauded other decisions in which "courts were astute to find a remedy against the manufacturer. No reason appears why we should do less."

2. New Concepts for Measuring Liability. While working as a carpenter, the father of several minor dependent children was struck on the neck with a wooden beam which had slipped from the sling of a crane. As a result of the accident, the father had been hospitalized and paralyzed from the neck down. The minor dependent children in *Ferriter* v. *Daniel O'Connell's Sons,* Massachusetts Supreme Judicial Court, #79–795, dated September 9, 1980, brought suit for their Loss of Parental Society. They argued that the law recognizes the right of a spouse to recover the Loss of Consortium when her husband is negligently injured; and therefore the law should recognize the right of minor dependent children to recover for Loss of Parental Society. The court agreed that the children have a viable claim if they can show that they are minors dependent on their injured parent; this dependence must be rooted not only in economic requirements but also in filial needs for closeness, guidance, and nurture. The court recognized the shock to the children resulting from their visit to their father in the hospital immediately after the accident; and such emotional stress was compensable too! Indeed, emotional trauma suffered by a mere bystander can be compensable if directly inflicted. In *Johnson* v. *State,* (37 NY2d 378) the New York court allowed a recovery where a daughter had been mistakenly told of her mother's death, when in fact her mother was alive. The court ruled that the hospital owed a duty to the daughter and breached that duty, and the daughter's emotional injuries were the direct result of that breach of duty. And in California in *Mobaldi* v. *Board of Regents,* (127 Cal Rptr 720, 1976) at defendant's hospital, a foster mother was holding a child who was undergoing a diagnostic test, i.e., an intravenous pyelogram. The mother's presence was at the request of the doctor so as to calm the child. By mistake, instead of the doctor giving the child a 5% glucose solution, he was given a 50% mixture, and as a result the child started to breathe peculiarly and became spastic, convulsant, and finally, comatose. The plaintiff started to scream and by the time the doctors returned to the room, the child had received 150 cc. of the improper solution, and, suffering brain damage, became blind and a quadriplegic. As a result of witnessing the incident, plaintiff foster mother became severely depressed, lost 40 pounds, and suffered from insomnia, despair, and futility, and was under psychiatric care. The California Court of Appeals, in reversing a dismissal of her complaint and permitting the cause of action, held that for a plaintiff to recover for emotional trauma through injury to *another* person the following three factors must be considered: "(1) whether plaintiff was located near the scene of the accident as contrasted with one who was a distance away from it; (2) whether the shock resulted from a direct emotional impact upon plaintiff from the sensory and contemporaneous observance of the accident, as contrasted with learning of the accident from others after its occurrence; and (3) whether plaintiff and the victim were closely related, as contrasted with an absence of any relationship or the presence of only a distant relationship."

The court, in reversing the dismissal of the complaint stated:

> "We conclude that where, as here, the victim immediately injured and the plaintiff hold themselves out to the public as mother and child, the child is treated as a filial member of a foster mother's family, the child treats the foster mother as a mother, and the tortfeasor treats the two as mother and child, the relationship guideline is satisfied although the injured child is neither the natural nor adopted offspring of the emotionally traumatized foster mother."

Still another concept-expanding liability is the extinction of the Fellow Servant Rule which barred claims against the employer for injury by one employee when caused by another employee. In *Foley* v. *Clark Equipment Co.*, Philadelphia Court of Common Please, #5817, dated November 1981, two employees even "cooperated" to insure recovery by the injured employee against several defendants to the tunc of a jury award of over $18 million! Here plaintiff employee was struck by a forklift truck operated by another employee whose only excuse was that he did not see the plaintiff because his vision was obstructed by the design and the construction of defendant's carriage, mast, and hydraulic lifting apparatus. The obviousness of such an alleged defect to an experienced forklift driver should have constituted a patent and obvious defect so as to place liability solely upon the experienced driver. But the court itself did not recognize the patent and obvious defect!

Another troublesome element of damages is Pain and Suffering. How much should be paid to a sensitive person and how much to a nonsensitive, callous person? How much to a woman and how much to a man? Professor Jeffrey O'Connell in the University of Illinois Law Review (Vol 1981, No. 2) has proposed to abolish payments for pain and suffering in return for payment of claimant's attorney fees! He argues that the evil of recovery for pain and suffering is that it prompts the trivially injured person to bring a nuisance suit, keeping in mind that the insurer, to save money, will settle the claim, and the gain will be a windfall to the plaintiff. But pain and suffering remains an important ingredient in huge judgments and awards.

HOW TO CONTROL THE COST OF PRODUCTS LIABILITY: INSURANCE COVERAGE AND/OR IN-HOUSE PRODUCTS LIABILITY DEPARTMENT

1. Products Liability Insurance: delineates protection against claims arising out of the use, handling, or consumption of a product of the insured by any person not his employee, but only if the bodily injury or property damage occurs away from the premises of the insured and after possession of the product has been relinquished to others. (Employees are protected by workman's compensation insurance provided by the employer.) Products liability coverage is usually sold by property-liability insurers as a part of the Comprehensive General Liability (CGL) policy. Protection on the premises of the insured *before* possession of the product has been relinquished is provided as a part of the Owners, Landlords and Tenants (OLT) coverage or the Manufacturers and Contractors (M & C) coverage. It also is available in a package form such as the Commercial Multi-Peril (CMP) policy.

Note that the insurance policy insures an "occurrence" during the policy period which is ordinarily one year, but can cover much longer periods of time. Limits of liability are stated per occurrence and in the aggregate. For example, a policy may limit liability of the insurer to $500,000 for each occurrence and $1,000,000 for all occurrences within the policy period, less a deductible amount of $100,000 per occurrence. A fairly typical policy defines an "occurrence" as an accident, including continuous or repeated exposure to conditions, that results in bodily injury or property damage, neither expected nor intended from the standpoint of the insured, during the policy period.

Most product accidents (such as vehicle collisions or pressure vessel explosions) occur suddenly. The event alleged as the basis of the manufacturer's liability is clearly an "occurrence" under the policy for the period of time in which the accident happens. Thus, the coverage of that policy, including limitations and deductibles, applies. Although the product is alleged to have been defective since manufacture, it has been accepted that an "occurrence" does not happen until the defect results in bodily injury or property damage—perhaps a number of years later. This method of coverage has important practical consequences, to wit: when an insurer issues or renews a policy for a particular year, it assumes the risk of sudden occurrences involving products sold in prior years when the manufacturer may have been self-insured or covered by another insurer. These complex questions have been in recent years widely litigated in toxic tort cases.

The question is frequently asked: Why is products liability insurance generally so expensive and relatively unavailable? Part of the answer lies in the fact that:

> "The insurance dimensions of the product liability problems are somewhat different than those applicable to the medical malpractice. In the case of medical malpractice, the risk is concentrated on a relatively small number of doctors, hospitals, and other medical care facilities and is being underwritten by a small number of specialty insurers. By contrast, the premium base for product liability is very broad and the coverages are provided by a large number of insurers with varying degrees of sophistication in handling the loss exposure." *American Mutual Insurance Alliance, June 9, 1976*

2. Risk Management Within: Obviously, there is no single approach to risk management that is suitable to protect a company from its exposure to products liability, but risk management should include: identification of exposure to loss; determination of the importance of potential losses; and selection of the best techniques to handle the risks incurred.

Risk Avoidance means product redesign, for example; Risk Control means efficacious labeling; Loss Prevention means quality control; and Loss Reduction may mean product recall.

Risk Retention includes self-insurance and umbrella insurance with large deductibles.

Vulnerable areas for products liability may be summarized as follows: design errors; improper material selection; assembly errors; inadequate testing; inadequate or even improper instruction on product use; inadequate warning of latent dangers in product; insufficient or inadequate safety features; failure to anticipate foreseeable product misuse; or failure to take corrective action after discovery of product defect.

A firm under Risk Management should establish:

(a) *Design Review Committee,* reviewing all new products prior to marketing, and examining all old products for necessary change to keep abreast of products liability decisions. Documentation of the design process and full explanation of safety features must be preserved for possible litigation.

(b) *Quality Control Committee,* to check quality of components supplied by outside sources; testing of component parts is always advisable.

(c) *Record-Keeping Committee,* to issue regulations commensurate with the life of the product, and include samples of product.

(d) *Product Recall Committee,* to establish proper procedures and;

(e) *Labeling Committee,* to insure adequate warnings which are conspicuous and easily understandable.

The company Claims Handling Procedures must include responding to claimant, obtaining the allegedly defective product, compiling test reports, collecting advertising material, preserving production analyses, etc.

1. Establishment and operation of an in-house claims handling office should be the philosophy of management; the office must have liaison with all corporate departments, and use accident investigation techniques; pre-trial matters, including discovery and other preparatory procedures, etc., should be instituted.
2. Recruitment and training of personnel by the office must be planned.
3. Adjuncts of the office (attorneys, investigators) should be noted.
4. Relationship with top management and with other segments of the business must make reference to:
   a. Cost-effectiveness of in-house handling of claims; budgeting

and forecasting, which involves planning what activities are necessary; periodic status reports; early settlement of claims; and other considerations more significant than costs.

b. In all these considerations one must note the Attorney-Client Privilege and work product privileges which have been defined by the U.S. Supreme Court in *Upjohn Co.* v. *U.S.*, (449 US 383, 1981) as embracing the following: (1) the communications were made by corporate employees to corporate counsel upon orders of superiors in order for the corporation to secure legal advice; (2) the information sought and communicated concerned matters within the scope of the employees' corporate duties; (3) the employees were aware that the reason for the communication with counsel was so that the corporation could obtain legal advice; and (4) the communications were ordered to be confidential, and they remained confidential. Protection of record under the above privileges is a matter of company policy.

In summary, it is well to observe the classic work of Professor Lon L. Fuller, *The Morality of Law* (1963), in which he delineates an allegory about a hapless king who fails to make law for his subjects (pp. 38–39). The king's attempt to create and maintain a system of legal rules failed because (1) he failed to enact rules, so that every issue had to be decided on an *ad hoc* basis; (2) he failed to publicize or at least to make available to the affected party the rules that were expected to be observed; (3) he committed the abuse of retroactive legislation, which not only cannot itself guide action, but undercuts the integrity of prospective rules, since it puts them under the threat of retrospective change; (4) he failed to make the rules understandable; (5) he enacted contrary rules; (6) the rules required conduct beyond the powers of the affected party; and (7) he introduced frequent changes in the rules so that the affected party could not orient his action to them. Products Liability suffers from similar shortcomings, and indeed fails to make law in most respects. A jury or judge decides long after the product has left the manufacturer's control that the product was safe or unsafe. Decisions are necessarily made in hindsight . . . and seldom is a guideline born for future compliance by the product manufacturer.

Part II
Some Specific Products Liability Situations

Of the nine specific products liability situations hereinafter delineated, several may be classified under the heading of "toxic tort" cases, i.e., Asbestosis, "Agent Orange," DES (diethylstilbestrol), Environmental Contaminants, and Industrial Products. What these toxic tort cases have in common is the escalating number of toxic tort lawsuits in the courts today as well as the mounting costs inherent in the defense of the litigation. Industry has sought *legislative* relief principally in the form of compensation programs designed to obviate jury trials and the contingency fee system for attorneys representing the alleged victims. But the legislative process is very slow, and relief for the beleaguered manufacturers is doubtful in the foreseeable future. Several product manufacturers have resorted to bankruptcy under Chapter 11 of the United States Bankruptcy Code (11 USC Secs 1101 et seq, as enacted by the Bankruptcy Reform Act of November 6, 1978). Whether or not this route of bankruptcy is a panacea, only time will tell. But it is extremely doubtful that a product manufacturer, inundated with toxic tort litigations, will be able to effect discharge of future claims. Remedial legislation will be necessary to overcome the difficulty of consummating a plan of reorganization, as contemplated by the bankruptcy law.

ASBESTOSIS

An asbestos curtain in a theatre was once the symbol of safety and security against fire, but today asbestos is known to cause the disease of asbestosis. At least since 1960 (and arguably, before) asbestos has been incriminated as producing disease when it is inhaled; minuscule fibers of the material are drawn into the lungs.

The key question in an asbestos products liability lawsuit today is the *time* when the product manufacturer knew or should have known of the dangerous propensities of their asbestos-containing product. The asbestos industry argues that not until 1965 was there medical confirmation of the three primary diseases caused by asbestos fibers, to wit: asbestosis (both pleural and parenchymal); pulmonary (lung) cancer; and mesothelioma.

Probably the first asbestosis lawsuit was filed in 1968 in the federal court in Beaumont, Texas (*Potter* v. *Fibreboard Paper Products,* #6329, USDCED Texas); it was settled out of court, as was the very next suit. But the third case of *Borel* v. *Fibreboard Paper Products,* 493 F^{2d} 1076, resulted in 1973 in a written opinion by the U.S. Fifth Circuit Court of Appeals, finding the manufacturer liable as an expert who must keep abreast of scientific knowledge, discoveries, and advances. If the scientific knowledge is such that the manufacturer could reasonably foresee an unreasonable danger in the anticipated use of the products, the manufacturer is under a duty to adequately warn of the danger. In the absence of a warning, or if the warning is inadequate in the light of scientific information, liability for injury incurred in the use of the product exists—according to this leading case.

Today damage claims by workers exposed to asbestos (and by their families) constitute the largest and potentially most costly block of products liability litigation ever to confront American industry. As of July 1981, more than 25,000 people had filed more than 12,000 lawsuits against 260 companies! The numbers have increased in 1983.

A major issue is an insurance question, to wit: when a hazardous substance causes injury that takes years to manifest itself, can the manufacturer resort to insurance held throughout the time the victims were exposed OR only to policies of insurance held when the injury appeared? *Date of Exposure* vs. *Date of Manifestation* is the question. In *Eagle Picher Industries* v. *Liberty Mutual Insurance Co.,* (682

F^{2d} 12) the First Circuit U.S. Court of Appeals in 1982 chose the Date of Manifestation, i.e., insurance coverage was provided when the disease manifested itself years after exposure. New York cases, however, follow Date of Exposure, but the District of Columbia holds that insurance policies issued to manufacturers must cover *both* injuries that manifest themselves during the policy period *and* those that are caused by exposure during the policy period [*Keene Corp.* v. *INA*, (667 F^{2d} 1054, 1981)].

In late August 1982, the Manville Corporation, facing more than 16,000 products liability suits, filed for reorganization under Chapter 11 of the Federal Bankruptcy Code. The court was asked by Manville for protection from its creditors because of the financial drain in defending the thousands of products liability lawsuits. Manville identified about 52,000 potential lawsuits seeking more than $2 billion! In the meantime, Manville and other asbestos manufacturers are pressing the federal government to share in the financial and moral responsibility for the suffering caused by asbestos used at shipyards during World War II. The industry claims that the government specified the use of asbestos in ships and then failed to enforce federal laws designed to protect workers from occupational hazards, even though the government knew as much about asbestos as the industry did!

Certain pertinent questions can now be asked: (1) What did the asbestos industry know about asbestos in the 1930s? The evidence shows that the industry then was more concerned with minimizing discussion of its perils than exploring the real extent of the hazard. (2) Has asbestos a substitute? NO; no single fiber has been found which will provide the combination of strength, heat resistance, flexibility, and other characteristics of asbestos. (3) Which insurer pays? It depends upon its chosen criterion of Datc of Exposure vs. Date of Manifestation. (4) Should government contribute to a fund for asbestos victims? The industry says "yes," but the government is keeping its option open. However, there is no doubt that asbestos represents a major public health hazard, one that extends beyond the large group of people who suffer from occupational exposure. Every possible way should be found to remove asbestos from the human environment. But eliminating the substance from existing structures or from industrial applications may not be feasibile for sound technical, economic, or political reasons. There is still controversy about the amount of asbestos exposure that is compatible with good health.

Liability upon the asbestos manufacturer or distributor readily results from the mere existence of the disease and some evidence of exposure to asbestos. In *Dombroff* v. *Armstrong Cork Co.*, #79–14048, the Florida Circuit Court, Dade County, in 1981 considered the claim of a Maryland shipyard worker who had been exposed to various asbestos products between 1941 and 1945. It was alleged that as a consequence of this exposure the plaintiff-worker contracted mesothelioma and died in 1978, more than 3 years after exposure. But plaintiff's widow was unable to identify the particular asbestos-containing product that allegedly caused the death of her husband. On defendant's motion for summary judgment the Florida court ruled that plaintiff need not prove which product was the precise one that actually caused the injury, nor must proof be offered that exposure to asbestos can cause the injury. To establish liability the plaintiff must *only* prove by a preponderance of the evidence:

1. the product manufactured by each defendant sought to be held liable contained asbestos of a type that could have caused the decedent's injury;
2. the product manufactured by each defendant sought to be held liable was manufactured and distributed during the time decedent was allegedly exposed to its product;
3. the product manufactured by each defendant sought to be held liable was the kind customarily used in shipyards *in the relevant market area* in which the alleged exposure occurred, at the time of the decedent's alleged exposure;
4. the likely effect of exposure to the product manufactured by each defendant sought to be held liable, taking into account: (a) the manner in which the material was ordinarily used in shipyards *in the relevant market area* at the time of the plaintiff's exposure, and (b) the percentage concentration of harmful material in the product and its toxicity; and
5. the length of time the plaintiff's decedent worked in areas where he might have been exposed to the defendant's asbestos products. Once this evidence is presented, the burden of proof shifts

> to the defendant to come forward with proof that asbestos did not cause the injury. Damages are to be proportioned according to each manufacturer's share of the relevant market, with consideration given to such factors as the quality and quantity of the asbestos-containing product and the gross dollar amount of sales of the defendant.

There are defenses to asbestos litigation, and a glance in their direction will explain why the asbestos industry does not lose every lawsuit: (1) *Statute of Limitations:* Date of Manifestation of Injury or Date of Exposure; in *Wilson* v. *Johns-Manville,* the U.S. Court of Appeals for the District of Columbia on July 30, 1982 ruled that "the time to commence does not begin to run on a separate and distinct disease until that disease becomes manifest," and in *Porter* v. *American Optical Corp.* (641 F^{2d} 1128, 1981) the Fifth U.S. Circuit Court of Appeals adopted the Date of Exposure. (2) *No Collateral Estoppel:* once a case has been heard to a conclusion, similar cases on similar facts need not be tried to prove that fact found by court or jury; note *Borel* v. *Fibreboard Paper Products* (493 F^{2d} 1076, 1973), holding that once asbestos was found to be a defective product, that fact of liability would collaterally estop other manufacturers from contesting the fact of defectiveness. But *Hardy* v. *Johns-Manville Sales Corp.,* decided by the U.S. Fifth Circuit Court of Appeals, on July 26, 1982, ruled to the contrary. Otherwise all that claimant had to prove was exposure to the product, medical causation, and the amount of damages. (3) *Exclusivity of Workman's Compensation:* in *Kofron* v. *Amoco Chemicals Corp.* (441 A^{2d} 226, 1982) the Delaware Supreme Court ruled that employees who suffer from asbestosis are limited to worker's compensation as the exclusive remedy. The statute was held to apply to all compensable occupational diseases. (4) *Contributory Negligence:* in *Austin* v. *Raybestos-Manhattan,* a federal jury in Portland, Maine, on December 5, 1981, found that the employees had had respirators available, but did not wear such protective devices; and so the jury refused to make an award to the widow. (5) *No Product Identification:* in *Doan* v. *Eagle-Picher,* a Cleveland, Ohio jury on October 30, 1982 (after Manville filed for bankruptcy) cleared the product manufacturers of liability when it was shown that it was not their asbestos that caused the cancer. And (6) *Apportionment of*

Damages: in *Fischer* v. *Manville,* a 1982 jury in Elizabeth, New Jersey assessed 80 percent damages against Manville and 20 percent against another defendant manufacturer—thus apportioning the amount of damages between the named defendants.

Asbestos product manufacturers are also beginning to seek indemnity and/or contribution from various other allegedly responsible parties. The possible third parties include suppliers (mines, mills, the United States Government, other manufacturers), the United States Government (in its role as a specifier, supplier, employer, or other contractual relationship) and the asbestos unions (both local and international). However, in *Glover* v. *Johns-Manville,* #78–648–N, the federal district court for the eastern district of Virginia, on December 21, 1979, dismissed claims against the United States Government!

"AGENT ORANGE"

Latent disease lawsuits are perhaps best illustrated, in the dramatic sense of a "toxic time bomb," by the "Agent Orange" situation. In *In Re "Agent Orange" Product Liability Litigation* (MDL 381) the U.S. District Court for the Eastern District of New York (806 F Supp 762) had certified *all* Vietnam War veterans, their families, and survivors as potential plaintiffs in the class action suit against the manufacturers of the herbicide used as a defoliant in the war. But more than 50,000 potential plaintiffs were disappointed on November 24, 1980 when the U.S. Court of Appeals for the Second Circuit ruled that *state* statutes of limitations apply, and therefore the action was time-barred because most veterans had been exposed to the defoliant more than 15 years ago. However, in those states with "time of discovery" statutes of limitations, veterans would be able to sue.

Interestingly, the Governor of New York on June 3, 1982 signed legislation allowing "Agent Orange" suits in New York up to June 16, 1982, based upon injuries from military service between January 1, 1962 and May 7, 1975. However, there is another obstacle, to wit: *Feres* v. *United States,* (340 US 135, 1950) and *Stencel Aero Engineering Corp.* v. *United States,* (431 US 666, 1977), which decisions prohibit a member of the armed forces from suing the United States for injuries sustained incident to military service. Accordingly, suit would be brought against the chemical manufacturers who in turn would seek immunity from liability because they were following strict government specifications in producing the herbicide.

Indeed, on December 29, 1981 Dow Chemical Co., one manufacturer of "Agent Orange," found that the federal district court had dismissed its third party claims against the United States on the authority of the *Feres* and *Stencel* cases. Dow had argued that its products could not and did not cause the injuries; but, if plaintiffs can establish Dow's liability, then the United States must be held accountable for its fair share of the damages. The United States had promulgated the specifications for "Agent Orange," and had tested the herbicides for many years prior to use in Vietnam, according to Dow Chemical. But the court did not respond favorably.

Unfortunately, the Veterans Administrations has refused to complete until 1988 or 1989 its official study on whether exposure to "Agent Orange" damaged the health of Vietnam veterans and/or their offspring! In 1979 Congress had first directed the study! Hardly a week goes by without another poignant story of a veteran suffering health problems that the veteran associates with "Agent Orange." Few scientists doubt that "Agent Orange"—a mixture of two commonly used herbicides, 2,4,5-T and 2,4-D, plus dangerous contaminants known as dioxins—can be toxic. But nobody knows whether the average soldier on a one-year tour of duty in Vietnam got enough of a dose sprayed around him to produce an adverse health effect.

The defendants in "Agent Orange" cases assert the affirmative defense of compliance with governmental specifications in the manufacture of the herbicide, i.e., the government contract defense, to wit: the product was supplied to the government pursuant to a contract; the government had promulgated specifications for the product; the product met the government's specifications in all material respects; and it can be demonstrated that the government knew as much as or more than the defendant regarding the hazards associated with the use of the product. But courts have been slow to recognize this defense.

The dollars involved in such lawsuits are almost beyond contemplation. In August 1982 a jury in Edwardsville, Illinois awarded 47 railway workers the sum of $58 million after they were exposed to a solvent containing dioxin during the cleanup operations of a tank-car rupture. Many of the workers complained of the same symptoms as those described by Vietnam veterans. The railroad had argued that the dioxin involved amounted to only 22 parts per billion of the solvent! Suit was brought under the terms of the 1910 Federal Employee Liability Act which allows railway workers to bring personal injury actions into any court existing wherever the railroad's tracks go! Principal medical witness for the workers was Dr. Berthram Carnow, a professor at the University of Illinois School of Occupational Medicine in Chicago. He testified that exposure to dioxin was 200,000 times more deadly than exposure to cyanide, and that there is no safe exposure to it at any level! Plaintiffs' success in this toxic tort case will prompt other workers to join hands in products liability suits against any and all tortfeasors. But it should be noted that virtually all the health complaints by veterans against "Agent Orange" are widespread in the general population and have many different causes. Cancer is the cause of roughly 20 percent of all American deaths, and some 9 percent of all children born have at least minor defects, so one would expect to find many of these maladies among the veterans and their offspring anyway. At present more than 100,000 veterans have gone to the Veterans Administration for physical checkups, and more than 12,000 have filed claims of disability. At present the Veterans Administration attributes only one illness to "Agent Orange"—the skin condition chloracne.

DES AND BIRTH DEFECTS

The genesis of the drug DES (diethylstilbestrol) goes back to England, where in 1938, an Oxford scientist produced the first synthetic estrogen, thereafter donating his discovery to the world. Several American pharmaceutical companies in the market for new products, recognized this new find as a "breakthrough" which could be produced inexpensively for the purpose of providing estrogen replacement in women who were suffering menopausal symptoms. Moving quickly, 12 U.S. drug manufacturers, with the cooperation of the FDA, pooled their research literature and findings, and submitted individual new drug applications (based upon the cooperative effort of a committee organized by the drug companies), receiving FDA approval in 1941 for the use of DES in small dosages for certain women in menopause. Thereafter, more than 100 drug manufacturers became producers of DES, a generic synthetic hormone.

Shortly after approval by the FDA in 1941, several Boston researchers, on the basis of certain studies, concluded that DES could also prevent the miscarriage of a pregnant woman who had a risk history of spontaneous abortions. The dosage for this use was on an increasing graduated scale, with the peak being hundreds of times greater than the prior dosages for menopausal uses. In 1947, the FDA approved the use of DES for miscarriage purposes, clearing the way for widespread use by thousands of pregnant women who were then prescribed DES by their physicians.

Twenty years later, in 1967, the medical world was shocked when a prestigious medical journal published the findings of a Boston researcher who reported a possible link between DES and the vaginal cancer diagnosed in seven young women, all of whom were offsprings of mothers who had taken DES during their pregnancies. Four years later, in 1971, the FDA ordered the drug companies to cease the marketing of DES! It is estimated that 3 million women might have taken DES between 1941 and 1971. Perhaps 1 per cent of their daughters have reported a form of possible cancer. In *Sindell* v. *Abbott Laboratories,* (607 P2d 924) the plaintiff alleged that she developed a malignant bladder tumor as a result of her mother's ingestion of DES during pregnancy. Unable to identify which company manufactured the drug claimed to be responsible for her injuries, the plaintiff nevertheless brought an action against *eleven* drug companies and a number of other parties on behalf of herself and other women similarly situated. But the trial involved only five defendants: Squibb, Upjohn, Rexall, Abbott, and Eli Lilly. The trial court dismissed the action brought under several theories of liability on the grounds that the plaintiff could *not* identify which defendant had manufactured the particular DES which her mother had ingested so long ago!

On appeal the California Supreme Court in 1980 (607 P2d 924) *reversed* the trial court's dismissal of the claim, bringing victory to the plaintiffs. [The intermediate California Court of Appeals (85 Cal App. 3d 1) upheld both of plaintiff's theories of Alternate Liability and Concert of Action.] Judge Stanley Mosk of the California Supreme Court, in the majority opinion, held that once the plaintiff had proved the product DES to be dangerous and defective in formulation, the defendant manufacturers then had the burden of proving that they were not liable! The court ignored all the legal concepts of Fault, Causation, and Burden of Proof, *contrary* to Section 443 B of the *Restatement of Torts Second,* which reads as follows:

> "1. *Except as stated in subsections 2 and 3* the burden of proof that the tortious conduct of the defendant has caused the harm is upon the plaintiff. 2. Where the tortious conduct of two or more actors has combined to bring about harm to the plaintiff, and one or more of the actors seeks to limit his liability on the ground that the harm is capable of apportionment among them, the *burden of proof* as to the apportionment is upon each such actor. 3. Where the conduct of two or more actors is tortious, and it is proved that harm has been caused to the plaintiff by one of them, but there is uncertainty as to which one has caused it, the burden is upon each such actor to prove that he had not caused the harm."

Briefly, a look at the three theories of liability rejected by the California Supreme Court before accepting its own "Market Share Liability" theory (which Judge Mosk delineates at length later on in this book) is in order:

1. Alternate Liability is embodied in Section 443 B, Subsection 3 of the *Restatement of Torts Seconds:* "Where the conduct of two or more actors is tortious, and it is proved that harm has been caused to the plaintiff by only one of them, but there is uncertainty as to which one has caused it, the *burden is upon each actor* to prove that he has not caused the harm."

The theory is illustrated by *Summers* v. *Tice,* (33 Cal2d 80, 199 P2d 1, 1948): two hunters shown to be negligent in firing their guns were held jointly liable because it could not be determined which hunter had fired the shot which hit the plaintiff. But Judge Mosk decided that the rule in the *Summers* case was *not* applicable here because only 5 of 200 DES manufacturers, who would have been responsible for the harm to the plaintiff, were joined as defendants. (In *Nichols* v. *Nold,* (258 P2d 317, Kan 1953) three defendants were held liable when plaintiff could not identify the retailer, distributor, or bottler!)

2. Concert of Action is embodied in Section 876 of the *Restatement* *of Torts Second:* "For harm resulting to a third person from the tortious conduct of another, one is subject to liability if he (a) *does a tortious act in concert* with the other or pursuant to a *common design* with him, or (b) *knows* that the other's conduct constitutes a breach of duty and gives a substantial assistance or encouragement to the other so to conduct himself, or (c) *gives* substantial assistance to the other in accomplishing a tortious result and his own conduct, separately considered, constitutes a breach of duty to the third person."

The Concert of Action theory was given approval in *Bichler* v. *Eli Lilly Co.,* (436 NYS2d 625, AD, 1981, aff NY Ct. of A, 5/11/82), and *Abel* v. *Eli Lilly Co.,* (289 NW2d 120, Mich Ct. App. 1979). The California Supreme Court rejected this theory because there was no allegation that each defendant knew that the other's conduct was tortious, or that defendants had encouraged one another to test and warn inadequately; in short, there was no evidence of a common plan or concert of design of action. See *Lemmons* v. *Kelly,* (239 Or 354, 397 P2d 784, 1964) and *Bierczynski* v. *Rogers,* (239 A2d 218, Del 1968).

3. Enterprise or Industry-Wide Liability is embodied in the case of *Hall* v. *du Pont,* (345 F Supp 353, DCEDNY, 1972). Here substantially the entire blasting cap industry industry plus its trade association *were joined* in an action involving 12 separate blasting cap incidents which occurred in 10 different states. The federal court followed this line of reasoning: since there was evidence that the defendants had adhered to an industry-wide standard concerning the safety features, manufacture, and design of the caps, if the plaintiffs could establish that the caps were manufactured by one of the defendants, the burden of proof as to causation would shift to all of the defendants. *The industry-wide standard itself, therefore, became the cause of the plaintiff's injury.* Since each industry member had adhered to the standard, according to *Hall,* each member had contributed to the plaintiff's injury, and the New York federal court held:

> "The plaintiffs must show that there was a breach of duty as to them, some causal connection between the group-created risk and their injuries and that the harm has resulted from the conduct of someone and the tortious actions, and finally, that they must show by a preponderance of the evidence, that it is more probable than not that the caps involved in the accident were the products of the

named defendant manufacturers. That court went on to state that if the plaintiffs could meet these tests, they would be entitled to a shift in the burden of proof."

Judge Mosk of the California Supreme Court also rejected this theory by distinguishing the *Sindell* case from the *Hall* case on the facts: the blasting cap industry was composed of but 6 manufacturers, while there were 200 DES manufacturers; also there were no allegations, as in *Hall,* that DES manufacturers had delegated functions relating to safety to a trade association and therefore had jointly controlled the risk.

Judge Mosk thereupon simply fashioned his own theory of "Market Share Liability"; to wit: where there are fungible goods which can harm consumers but cannot be traced to the specific manufacturer, the known and unknown product manufacturers will *share liability* in proportion to their manufacture of the total industry production of the fungible goods. According to Judge Mosk:

> "Market share liability imposes only *several* liability upon the defendants. Each defendant will be held liable for a percentage of the judgment, as determined by that defendant's market share, *unless a particular defendant can demonstrate that it could not have made the DES which injured the plaintiff.* The plaintiff has the burden of joining in one action the *manufacturers of a substantial market share* of DES. Once the plaintiff has met her burden, the defendants may *cross-complain* against other manufacturers not joined in the action."

Note that "SEVERAL LIABILITY" is not *JOINT LIABILITY,* i.e., no defendant can be held liable for more than its share nor for more than 100 percent. BUT, can one defendant bring into the California action other nonresident defendants? That question is unanswered by the court. Also, plaintiffs are practically guaranteed to prevail on the Causation issue because the defendants are no more capable of disproving Causation than plaintiffs are capable of proving Causation! The dissent of Judge Richardson should be noted here: "The plaintiffs were not alive at the time of the commission of the tortious acts. They sue generations later. They are permitted to receive substantial damages from multiple defendants without any proof that any defendant caused or even probably caused plaintiff's injuries (at p. 938)."

Even the smallest of manufacturers are potential defendants as long as they have a "substantial" share of the market for that product; but Judge Mosk did not define "substantial," or "fungible," or "relevant market." In the ordinary tort case the defendant may be either insolvent or not amenable to process, but that defendant is still a nominal party, and his "market share" is a factor for the court to consider. Indeed, under Judge Mosk's opinion, not only are the plaintiffs relieved of matching the conduct of a particular defendant to their injury, but the rule "sprinkles the rain of liability upon all the joined defendants" (607 P2d at 939). Additionally, "market share liability" will fall disporportionately on those defendants amenable to suit in California.

One of the great evils of the *Sindell* case ruling is what the decision has done to scientific research and scientific progress: when a manufacturer prices its product, it must now consider the liability it may incur for its "fungible" product simply by being a member of the industry! One bad apple and the entire barrel of apples is ruined! Insurers are also troubled in that they are faced with the onus of answering for liability arising out of the conduct of *other* manufacturers! Professor Sheila Birnbaum in *National Law Journal (May 26, 1980)* cites still another problem:

> "Assume a plaintiff joins D1, who enjoyed 80% of the relevant market, and D2, who enjoyed 10%. Having met his burden of joining defendants with a 'substantial market share,' plaintiff's action would proceed despite the lack of proof of causation. Assume further that as the action proceeds, D1 is able to demonstrate it did not produce the injury-causing product, and is accordingly dismissed from the action. May plaintiff, having initially satisfied her burden, continue the action against D2? Does plaintiff's burden of joining defendants with a 'substantial' aggregate share of the market continue throughout the litigation, thereby permitting D2 now to move to dismiss the action?"

On October 14, 1980 the United States Supreme Court (449 US 912, 101 S Ct 285) REFUSED to review the *Sindell* case. Thus, the burden of proof in California is upon the defendants to prove that their product could not have been responsible for the harm. To review the elements of the cause of action under the "Market Share Liability" theory, note footnote 24 of the opinion: "1. There existed a sufficient industry-wide standard to safety as to the manufacture of the product. 2. Plaintiff is not at fault for the absence of evidence identifying the causative agent, but, rather this absence of proof is due to the defendants' conduct. 3. A generally similar defective product was manufactured by all the defendants. 4. The plaintiff's injury was caused by this defect. 5. Defendant's owed a duty to the class of which plaintiff was a member. 6. There is a clear and convincing evidence that plaintiff's injury was caused by a product made by one of the defendants. For example, the joined defendants accounted for a high percentage of such defective products on the market at the time of the plaintiff's injury. 7. All defendants are tortfeasors."

On May 13, 1981 the United States District Court for the District of South Carolina, Columbia Division, in *Ryan* v. *Eli Lilly, Rexall, Squibb, Upjohn, Abbott and McNeil,* REJECTED the *Sindell* holding in a lengthy opinion:

> "The market-share theory does not apply to this case. Plaintiff has neither alleged nor offered any evidence to show that the defendants before the Court accounted for a 'substantial share' of the relevant stilbestrol market. Thus, even if the theory of market-share liability could be reconciled with the plainly contrary law of the only state interested in this controversy, plaintiff has offered no basis for its application. The California court's market-share theory of liability represents market-share theory of liability represents a rejection of 'over one hundred years of tort law which required that before tort liability was imposed a 'matching' of defendants' conduct and plaintiff's injury was absolutely essential.' 26 Cal.3d at 616, 163 Cal. Rptr. at 147 (dissenting opinion). The courts of both Carolinas, however still adhere to this fundamental principle. The unequivocal law of South Carolina is the plaintiff in a negligence action has not only the burden of proving negligence but also the

burden of proving that the injury or damage was caused by the actionable conduct of the particular defendant."

Similarly, in *Mossier* v. *Adickes,* (251 S.C. 268, 161 S.E.2d 845, 1968), a judgment for plaintiff was reversed because "where the cause of plaintiff's injury may be as reasonably attributed to an act for which defendant is not liable as to one for which he is liable, plaintiff has failed to carry the burden of defendant's negligence. See also, *Elledge* v. *Pepsi Cola Bottling Company,* (252 S.C. 337, 113 S.E.2d 435, 1960). The Supreme Court of South Carolina has not carved out any exceptions to this traditional rule; the court places the burden of proof of proximate cause squarely on the plaintiff: "Application of this burden-shifting theory would violate established public policy and fundamental principles of tort law and procedure in this state in a variety of ways. This Court declines to apply this theory in the present case." Other recent cases "leaving the injury where it falls" because the product was not identifiable include *Gray* v. *United States,* (445 F Supp 337, SD Tex, 1978) involving DES; *Payton* v. *Abbott Laboratories* (-F Supp-, DC. Mass 1981); and *Namm* v. *Charles E. Frosst & Co.,* (427 A2d 1121, NJ AD 1981).

On May 11, 1982 the New York Court of Appeals had occasion in *Bichler* v. *Eli Lilly Co.* to consider a $500,000 jury award to a 17-year-old girl when it was determined that she was suffering from cervical and vaginal cancer attributed to her mother's ingestion of DES while pregnant with the plaintiff. The first trial was on the issue of product identification, and plaintiff lost; on the second trial plaintiff successfully argued that Eli Lilly Co. should be liable as a major producer of the drug. The highest New York court affirmed the jury award under the "Concert of Action" theory, i.e., the jury was permitted to infer an implied agreement between Lilly and other drug houses to market DES without prior testing on pregnant mice! In addition, the court stated that the jury could find that Lilly's failure to conduct such tests substantially encouraged or aided other companies to do the same even without an express agreement to do so. (Interestingly, the defendant in October 1982 sought to depose the jury about its verdict, but the court refused to permit same.) The same New York court in *Kaufman* v. *Eli Lilly Co.* on October 29, 1982 applied Collateral Estoppel to prevent the product manufacturer from relitigating the adverse jury findings that produced in the 1980 *Bichler* case a $470,000 verdict for the plaintiff! According to the court, "it is difficult to conceive of two cases which could be more similar from a factual viewpoint. . . In each case the plaintiff, a female, allegedly contracted cancer of the cervix upon reaching puberty, as a result of her mother's ingestion of DES in 1953 or early 1954 while pregnant with the plaintiff. In each case the plaintiff, because of the passage of time, is unable to identify the manufacturer of the DES her mother took. And in each case plaintiff seeks to recover on the basis of the same alleged wrongdoing by Lilly, and upon the same theory, i.e., concerted action." The court noted that Lilly had failed to raise any points to defeat the Collateral Estoppel application. The court concluded: "From the standpoint of avoiding the possibility of inconsistent results in the same jurisdiction, and the conservation of judicial manpower without unfairness to the parties, this is a logical and appropriate case in which to apply the doctrine of Collateral Estoppel."

ADVERSE REACTIONS TO PRESCRIPTIVE DRUGS

Perhaps 90 percent of today's prescription drugs involve drugs that were not even on the market 20 years ago. It is a herculean task for physicians to keep abreast of the latest information about the uses, effects, contraindications, and adverse reactions associated with those drug products. The Official Package Circular, or OPC, accompanying each prescriptive drug is designed to keep the physician up-to-date and thereby enhance the use of the product by the physician upon his/her patients. Suits against drug manufacturers generally allege failure to test the product adequately and thoroughly, and in doing so, failure to utilize scientifically sound test protocols and analyses of data, OR failure to design the safest effective formulation, OR omission of full and complete instructions for the use of the product, OR overpromotion and even distortion of data so as to misrepresent proper use of the product. The prescribing physician can be charged with failure to monitor the patient properly, OR not prescribing the drug of choice, OR simply administering the drug improperly and in the wrong dosage.

In *McNeary* v. *Lederle Laboratories,* a Washington Superior Court upheld a jury verdict of $1,100,000 on April 15, 1982 in favor of a

36-year-old woman who contracted polio from her infant daughter who had been vaccinated with the Sabin oral polio vaccine. Plaintiff alleged that her polio was caused by contact with her child's diapers! She argued that Lederle failed to give adequate warning and instructions concerning the risks of contracting polio from a vaccinee. She claimed that she should have been informed that Salk dead vaccine was a risk-free alternative to the live Sabin vaccine. And the jury agreed with her!

Prescriptive drug product *information* is usually the key issue in litigation involving pharmaceutical products, because drugs are simply not purified chemicals, but complex and often untested combinations of ingredients concerning which there is a paucity of positive information. Indeed, the product manufacturer has an obligation to test and determine the adverse effects of the drug, and then communicate that information to physicians who must make the decisions regarding drug choices and avoidance of harmful effects. Failure to warn is frequently the charge heard from victim's attorneys against both the drug manufacturer and the prescribing physician.

Pharmacological agents occur naturally, or are synthesized, or are a combination thereof. When one drug enhances the potency of another, the action is synergistic, and the synergistic effect of mixed or compounded drugs, and the potentiation effect of some other substance upon a drug, such as alcohol upon barbiturates, is of prime medicolegal significance. There are many inherent variables which cause desired and undesired effects (toxic and side effects), depending upon quantitative variations, like dosage, and qualitative variations, like the effects upon the person with known idiosyncracies. A given dosage can be too weak for some persons, correct for some, and too potent for others. For those for whom dosage is too potent, the effect is described as *toxic,* i.e., having a posionous effect upon living tissue. The side effects which vary with the person are both predictable and unpredictable, based upon the known or unknown hypersensitivity of the person and the individual's allergic or idiosyncratic reaction history.

In August 1982 the antiarthritic drug Oraflex, manufactured and distributed by Eli Lilly Co., was withdrawn from the U.S. market following reports of 61 deaths in Great Britain and 11 deaths in the United States associated with the use of Oraflex. Oraflex, or benoxaprofen, is one of a group of aspirin-like prescription drugs called nonsteroidal antiinflammatory drugs. The drug provides symptomatic relief from pain and inflammation associated with arthritis, but does not arrest the progression of the disease. On April 19, 1982 the U.S. Food and Drug Administration had approved Oraflex after more than two years of study, and Eli Lilly began to market Oraflex aggressively. Within 30 days 64,000 prescriptions had been written for sales totalling $1.3 million! But four months later the manufacturer withdrew the drug from the market. Since then it has been demonstrated that Eli Lilly Co. substantially underreported to the FDA the incidence of adverse reactions to Oraflex! This story of withdrawal of the prescription drug from the market will undoubtedly prompt a rash of lawsuits.

Indeed, injuries and deaths due to adverse drug reactions mount as pharmaceutical litigation seeks to impose full liability upon the pharmaceutical industry for its failures to test drugs, failures to design safe formulas, and for its overpromotion and distortion of scientific data concerning its products. The *New England Journal of Medicine* in January 1980 (p. 294) reported about the adverse effects of drugs which are often debilitating, and sometimes life-threatening, and how treating physicians are frequently misled in treating patients on drug therapy.

ALLERGIES AND THE PRODUCT

The term "allergy" describes unexpected and unanticipated reactions from the use of a product. These idiosyncratic reactions involve the antigen-antibody relationship. Indeed, allergy is the specifically acquired (or inherited) alteration in the capacity of the cells of the body to react to a product, perhaps as a result of previous exposure to the same product or to one structurally similar. It is generally stated that there is no product under the sun to which some person at some time will not react adversely! Indeed, there are no adequate means for determining in advance whether some untoward reaction will occur in a given person. There are no practical means of preventing an allergic reaction after contact with an offending product, such as desensitizing the person or altering his/her allergic potential. Liability is therefore predicated upon the knowledge of the product manufacturer as to the high incidence of sensitivity to the product, and upon the plaintiff's membership in that class of known persons who react adversely to that product.

The author's scholarly article which follows delineates the many problems of Allergy and the Law.

SMALL APPLIANCES AND MAJOR APPLIANCES

An appliance, whether small or major, must generally be deemed "defective" and "unreasonably dangerous" before liability can be predicated upon its use or misuse. But in *Edwards* v. *Mazor Masterpieces, Inc.,* (295 F2d 547, DC Cir 1961) the federal court held that the plaintiff, in an action for the wrongful death of her 12-year-old son, had stated a cause of action against the seller of a folding sofa bed for failure to warn of the dangers of a folding sofa bed that apparently closed on the child while he was sleeping, and suffocated him. (Since plaintiff had owned and used the folding sofa bed for about four years prior to the accident, it appears that she should have reasonably known that the bed could close if not fully opened into a "locked" position. Moreover, there was no allegation that the plaintiff-mother was lulled into believing otherwise by advertisements of the folding sofa bed.) Nevetheless the folding sofa bed was deemed "defective" and "unreasonably dangerous." Indeed, special concern must be given to injuries of minors from the use and misuse of the product. In *Strahlendorf* v. *Walgreen Co.,* (16 Wis2d 421, 1962) the minor plaintiff's grandmother purchased three small plastic toy airplanes mounted on a rectangular piece of cardboard from the defendant retailer. A small stick with an attached rubber band intended to be used as a catapult for launching the plane was also mounted on the card. The grandmother gave the card to her five-year-old grandson, and the boy and his father experimented with launching the plane. During the experimentation, the father discovered that the plane was dangerous because of its high speed and unpredictable course. So the father hid the plane, but the boy found it: and while launching the plane hit his sister in the eye with it. The injured sister and her father sued not the brother (or son), but the retailer, alleging negligence in selling an "inherently dangerous instrumentality" and in failing to warn of the product's inherent danger. The Wisconsin trial court directed judgment for the defendant retailer, although the jury had first awarded $8,625 to the plaintiffs. The Wisconsin Supreme Court, in affirming the dismissal of the claim, held that the "crucial factor" in causing the injury was "improper use, rather than any inherently dangerous characteristic of the plane." The court further ruled that any negligence on the defendant's part arising from its failure to warn of the dangerous propensities of the plane was obviated by the father's own admission that he, in fact, knew of the danger. But note that the grandson here was using the plane in precisely the way in which the toy was intended to be used! However, the father was contributorily negligent in not hiding the plane in a sufficiently safe place! The latter's negligence effectively insulated the defendant manufacturer from liability.

Misuse of a product is a recognized defense, as illustrated by *Procter & Gamble Mfg. Co.* v. *Langley* (422 SW 2d 773, 1967). Here the Texas Court of Civil Appeals reversed a $5,500 judgment for plaintiff and rendered judgment for the defendants. Plaintiff had purchased a home permanent wave kit, and upon applying the product to her hair, allegedly sustained hair breakage. Action for breach of implied warranties against the product manufacturer, the wholesaler, and the retail vendor resulted in a Dallas County jury finding in favor of the plaintiff, although the jury had found that the plaintiff (a) "failed to make a ten minute test curl to see if her hair could take a wave before applying the product"; (b) "after her hair felt sticky and gummy, she failed to use liquid neutralizer at once"; and (c) "she waved more hair after feeling strands of hair which were sticky and gummy." The aforesaid acts were clearly contrary to the instructions accompanying the product, but the jury inexplicably did not regard her acts as "negligent." Chief Justice Dixon, who carefully examined the testimony of the plaintiff, concluded that she had indeed failed to follow and had violated the above instructions. Furthermore, "Mrs. Langley did not keep or save any of the hair waving products which she claims in this instance damaged her hair. She disposed of them by throwing them away without having an analysis of them made." The court concluded that "there was not and could not be any direct testimony that the particular products she purchased were in any way defective or harmful if properly used. Neither do the circumstances constitute evidence to that effect.'' Accordingly, her MISUSE of the product ''constitutes a defense to her cause of action.''

Class Actions are frequently utilized as means to enable courts to handle multi-claimants. But in a 32-page opinion in *Feinstein* v. *Firestone Tire and Rubber Co.,* (USDCSDNY March 30, 1982), Federal Judge Haight refused to certify various suits seeking designation as a Class Action on behalf of millions of consumers for alleged defects in steel-belted radial Firestone tires purchased by such consumers. To do so would ''unleash a Frankenstein monster of unmanageability, weighted down with individual questions of fact and law which clearly predominate.'' Firestone, in 1978, had voluntarily recalled the tires, and Judge Haight stated that ''the majority of the tires'' sold by Firestone ''by doing what they were supposed to do as long as they were supposed to do it, clearly lived up to that 'minimum level of quality' which is all UCC Section 2–314(2)(c) requires.'' Furthermore, since the majority of the claimed class members had ''no legally recognizable claim, the action necessarily metastasizes into millions of individual claims'' which was ''fatal to a showing predominance of common questions.'' Judge Haight ruled that two decisive questions of fact, to wit: *existence of damage* and *proximate cause,* had to be decided for *each* purchaser, so as to ''preclude class certification.''

Earlier, on February 25, 1982 in *Avena, Silverman and Barnaba* v. *Ford Motor Co.,* the New York Appellate Division, 1st Dept., had laid down certain stiff rules for Class Action plaintiffs, including mandatory notice to putative members of the class. Here, a percentage of Ford automobiles, equipped with certain types of engines, were allegedly susceptible to developing a cracked engine block. Ford publicized an extended policy program, (notice of which was given by mail to each owner of that Ford vehicle) that Ford would pay 100 percent of the cost of any of these vehicles developing a cracked engine block. Three of the plaintiffs worked out a compromise of liability with Ford to discontinue the class action but without giving notice to the other putative members of the class. The court denied Ford's request for approval of the compromise, pointing out that the three plaintiffs were fiduciaries of the settlement, and the putative members of the class are owed adherence to ''uncompromising rigidity'' by which "the rule of undivided loyalty (has) been maintained." The discontinuance of the class suit was therefore without prejudice to the claims of other members of the class. But the court nevertheless found this procedure to be violative of New York CPLR Rule 908. (Ford's settlement with the three plaintiffs had been conditional upon NO NOTICE to the putative members of the class.) The court opined that "the potential for abuse by private settlement at this stage is also obvious and recognized. Fiduciary obligations should not be lightly assumed and cannot be lightly discarded." Nevertheless, the court offered no solution to the inordinate cost of the Mandatory Notice: "We have no occasion at this time to pass on what kind of notice would be adequate, or whether the individual plaintiffs would be free of their fiduciary obligations if they had applied to the court for class action certification or a determination of the property of class action status. . ." Indeed, the Class Action device has not yet been fully delineated.

ENVIRONMENTAL CONTAMINANTS

Toxic substances in our environment include not only asbestos, "Agent Orange," and nuclear radiation, but thousands of toxic killers ranging from arsenic, mercury, zinc, and benzene to such chemical agents as polyvinyl chloride (PVC), Kepone, and polychlorinated biphenyl (PCB). After a traumatic injury has occurred by contact with the toxic contaminant it may be years before there is any manifestation of injury; also, there is often little evidence of the causal relationship between the disease and the particular toxic substance. Potential defendants embrace the employer, the product manufacturer, the state, local, and federal governments, insurance companies, (for failing to conduct safety inspection), and the entire industry under the concepts of "enterprise liability" and "Market Share" liability. Furthermore, insurance coverage is not available for environmental contaminants under Exclusion (f) of the Comprehensive General Liability policy, OR under the Pollution exclusions: "This insurance does not apply: (f) to bodily injury or property damage arising out of the discharge, dispersal, release or escape of smoke, vapors, soot, fumes, acids, alkalis, toxic chemicals, liquids or gases, waste materials or other irritants, contaminants or pollutants into or upon land, the atmosphere or any water course or body of water; but this exclusion does not apply if such discharge, dispersal, release or escape is sudden or accidental."

The key words "sudden and accidental" were considered by a New York Supreme Court in *Evans* v. *Aetna Casualty & Surety Co.,* (435 NYS2d 953, 1981) where vandals broke a lock on a storage tank in plaintiff's gasoline facility, allowing the discharge of 18,000 gallons of gasoline into a creek which flowed into Lake Erie. The insurer denies coverage for the cleanup work, but the court, finding plaintiff strictly liable, ruled that the pollution was "sudden and accidental" and therefore the insurer was liable for the cleanup work. On the other hand, in *Barmet of Indiana, Inc.* v. *Security Ins. Co.,* (425 NE2d 201, 1981) the Indiana court held for the insurer. Here the plaintiff was engaged in the recycling of aluminum in a plant adjacent to an Indiana highway. On numerous occasions gases from this process traveled two or three miles and obscured visibility on the highway. Complaints had been received for many years, for indeed the pollution control system had malfunctioned regularly. There was no mechanism employed which could accurately predict when the emissions would escape. In 1978 a woman was driving on the highway and she was killed in an automobile accident. Suit against the plaintiff company by the victim alleged reduced visibility caused her death. The insurer refused to defend; and the court agreed that under the Pollution exclusion the discharge of the emissions was *not* "sudden and accidental" within the meaning of the policy.

Federal legislation in the area of environmental contaminants has been prolific: Federal Water Pollution Control Act Amendments of 1972 (FWPCA); Marine Protection Research and Sanctuaries Act of 1972 (MPRSA); Surface Mining Control and Reclamation Act of 1977 (SMCRA); Resource Conservation and Recovery Act of 1976 (RCRA); National Environment Policy Act of 1969 (NEPA); Clean Air Act of 1967 (CAA); and Clean Air Act of 1963 and 1965. A principal question is whether such federal legislation gives a citizen the right to sue for damages or injunctive relief on the basis of federal common law. The U.S. Supreme Court answered "no" in *City of Milwaukee* v. *Illinois,* #78-409 (April 28, 1981) and in *Middlesex County Sewerage Authority* v. *National Sea Clammers Assn.,*

#79–1711 (June 25, 1982). The highest Court further limited private causes of action in environmental litigation by its ruling in *California* v. *Sierra Club,* #79–1252 (April 28, 1981) where two citizens and the Sierra Club unsuccessfully sought to enjoin the construction and operation of water diversion facilities comprising a part of the California Water Project, alleging a violation of Section 10 of the Rivers and Harbors Appropriation Act of 1899 prohibiting unauthorized obstructions to a navigable waterway.

The Comprehensive Environmental Response, Compensation and Liability Act or "Superfund" Act of 1980 (42 USC 9601) requires a current site owner, regardless of his involvement with disposal of hazardous wastes on the site, to clean up the hazardous wastes *prior* to any adjudication of liability. He may then maintain a suit against the Superfund assets of $1.6 billion to recoup the cost of cleanup. Obviously even this procedure does not meet the needs of abating environmental contaminants. There must be funds available to meet the economic and medical needs of persons injured, and to compensate their loss of earnings, and their loss of property. Claims should be filed no later than three years after the claimant has discovered or should reasonably have discovered the injury or disease and its cause. The essential elements to establish a claim should consist of proof of exposure, proof of the injury or disease, proof of causation, and proof of compensable damages. (Proof of causation should include reliance on appropriate rebuttable presumptions.)

The settlement of lawsuits involving environmental contaminants is a prolonged and expensive process, and *Scenic Hudson Preservation Conference* v. *Federal Power Commission* 354 F 2d 608, CA2, 1965 and cert den 384 US 941, 1966; and 453 F2D 463, CA2, 1971, and cert den 407 US 926, 1972, followed by 330 NYS2d 71, 1972, 498 F2d 827, CA2, 1974, 499 F2d 127, CA2, 1974, and 587 F2d 549, CA2, 1978, is a good example. This 20-year litigation was finally settled by mediation. Here a coalition of citizen groups challenged FPC's grant of a license to build a hydroelectric plant on the Hudson River, based upon aesthetic, recreational, and conservation grounds. After the court granted plaintiffs the right to sue, the court voided the FPC-issued license because the FPC had failed to consider alternatives sufficiently, and had not weighed the need for preserving the unique beauty and historical signficance of the area. Later, the FPC, after proper finding, reissued the license and again plaintiffs challenged its findings. Plaintiffs then attempted to obtain relief in the New York courts, petitioning for reconsideration of the license based upon new evidence of threats to the fish resources of the Hudson River. Plaintiffs were successful in obtaining an injunction under Section 404 of the FWPCA prohibiting Con Edison from dumping rock and fill materials from the construction into the Hudson River without a permit from the Army Corps of Engineers. Finally, on December 19, 1980, 11 parties representing the federal government, conservation groups, and Con Edison executed an agreement which would settle all grievances and demands by balancing the cost-effective power plant with the protection of fish and aquatic resources. The agreement is to run for 10 years, until 1990.

Beyond such battles between environmental groups and public utilities, and without the aid and comfort of federal, state, and local legislation, injured parties have successfully sued for compensation. In *Alley* v. *Gubser Development Co.,* #80–Z–986, a federal jury in Denver on August 31, 1982, ordered four defendants to pay $560,000 to Mr. and Mrs. Alley who allegedly suffered health problems caused by exposure of formaldehyde fumes in their mobile home. The award consisted of $50,000 in compensatory damages *plus* punitive damages in the sum of $200,000 from the manufacturer of the mobile home; $150,000 from the wall paneling manufacturer; $150,000 from the manufacturer of the decking used in the mobile home; and $10,000 from the party who sold the mobile home to the plaintiffs. The injuries were hepatitis for Mr. Alley and respiratory problems for Mrs. Alley. It should be noted that the U.S. Consumer Product Safety Commission, in March 1982, had banned urea-formaldehyde foam insulation in both conventional and mobile homes.

Since there is apparently no provision in existing federal, state, and local legislation for recovery for personal injuries from hazardous waste, the citizen must resort to the common law actions based upon Negligence, Strict Liability, and Nuisance.

NUCLEAR ENERGY LIABILITY

The *New York Times* once described nuclear energy law as a body of law that runs from the invincible to the unthinkable! The noted scholar Dean Prosser in his *Law of Torts* (4th Ed., 1971, at p. 516) predicted that no court would refuse to recognize and apply to nuclear liability the principle of Absolute Liability, as found in cases like the 1865 English case of *Rylands* v. *Fletcher* (159 Eng. Rep 737) where the landowner who brought upon his land a vast quantity of water was held absolutely responsible for all consequential damages occasioned by the running of water off his land. Section 520(g) of the *Restatement of Torts Second* declared that "some activities, such as the use of atomic energy, necessarily and inevitably involve major risks of harm to others, no matter how or where they are carried on." However, in two recent decisions involving actions by utilities against builders and suppliers of nuclear facilities, the courts rejected the standard of strict or absolute liability. In *Nebraska Public Power District* v. *General Electric,* decided June 29, 1979 by Judge Urbom of the Federal District Court in Nebraska, the utility sought to recover damages for its building; the case was settled for 1 percent of ad damnum. In *General Public Utilities* v. *Babcock & Wilcox,* decided September 29, 1982 by the Federal District Court for the Southern District of New York (applying Pennsylvania law), settlement was achieved for 10 percent of ad damnum! Both courts applied to nuclear plants the same rules of liability that had been applied in the instance of conventional power plants and nonnuclear facilities.

On the other hand, in the protection of the public, comprehensive provisions for safety and risk allocation have been assured at the federal level. The Nuclear Regulatory Commission (NRC) is an independent agency that constantly monitors and updates a far-reaching set of safety standards. The Price-Anderson Indemnity Law of 1957 (which followed the Atomic Energy Act of 1954, which provided for a comprehensive licensing and regulatory program) had two prime objectives: (1) to insure that the public would be compensated if an accident did occur; and (2) to set a limit on liability of private industry in order to remove the roadblock to large-scale private participation in the development of nuclear energy. The act was amended or modified repeatedly over the next 20 years, but the limit of liability remains at $560 million. The 1966 amendment required insurance policies provided by the insurance pools to nuclear reactor operators, and indemnity was extended to them by government for losses in excess of the insurance, since legal defenses were waived in the event of a nuclear incident which exceeded criteria prescribed in NRC regulations.

Similarly subsidized is the coal industry, to the tune of $1 billion yearly in social security payments to miners who contract black lung disease. See the Federal Coal Mine Health and Safety Act of 1969, (30 USC 801–960) the Black Lung Benefits Acts of 1972, and the Black Lung Benefits Reform Act of 1977.

It should be noted that at least in New York the public utility is given added protection from liability by the rule in *Moch* v. *Rensselaer Water Co.,* (247 NY 160, 1928) which requires contractual privity before an injured person can recover against a utility for injury or damages. Recently in *Hernandez* v. *Consolidated Edison,* decided February 17, 1983 by the New York Supreme Court, New York County, two pedestrians were killed by an automobile during the July 1977 power blackout in New York City. (There had been a prior adjudication that Con Ed was grossly negligent in the blackout, by the New York Court of Appeals in *Food Pageant Inc.* v. *Consolidated Edison,* 54 NY 2d 167, 1981) but Justice Evans dismissed the complaint on the ground that there was no privity of contract between the utility and the decedents! Plaintiffs had failed to demonstrate what legal duty to their decedents, if any, Con Ed had breached. The court cited another New York Court of Appeals decision (*Tobin* v. *Grossman,* 24 NY 2d 609, 1969): "Every injury has ramifying consequences, like the ripplings of the waters, without end. The problem for the law is to limit the legal consequences of wrongs to a controllable degree."

Nuclear energy today supplies approximately 11 percent of national electricity requirements. There are about 70 nuclear operating permits issued by the federal government, and about 90 additional reactors have construction permits. A totally risk-free use of nuclear energy is impossible. But courts have been reluctant to take bold steps to deter nuclear accidents, as is illustrated by the 1979 shutdown of a nuclear generating plant known as "Three Mile Island Unit #2." General Public Utilities Corp. brought a $4 billion lawsuit against Babcock & Wilcox Co., which sold it the nuclear steam-supply system. But on October 4, 1982 the Federal District Court for the Southern District of New York dismissed the Strict Liability claim. Applying Pennsylvania law, Judge Owen noted that, while Pennsylvania courts "have not spoken precisely on the subject, I find every indication . . . that Strict Liability would not be applied." The court stated that the "rationale of deterence" did not extend to the purchase of a product as "specialized" as the nuclear steam-supply system . . . (And the parties) "are not a multi-million dollar automobile manufacturer and an ordinary member of the public, but are commercial enterprises contracting from positions of relatively equal bargaining power for a product designed to negotiable specifications and not furnished off the shelf." Of course, the plaintiff can still sue in Negligence and endeavor to prove fault on the part of the defendant!

INDUSTRIAL PRODUCTS AND OCCUPATIONAL DISEASES

The United States Government, in June 1977, published an invaluable booklet entitled "Occupational Diseases—A Guide to Their Recognition." Herein is a categorization of occupational dermatoses, pulmonary diseases, chemical hazards from plastics or synthetic resins, as well as an explanation of the means of contact and bodily entry of toxic agents, and the mode of action. There is also a listing of hazards and references to various occupations.

Generally, workman's compensation handles the problem of compensation for injuries to employees, but today, courts have gone far beyond what is reasonable to compensate the injured worker. In *Ziglar* v. *du Pont,* (280 SE2d 510, 1981) the North Carolina Appellate Court examined a du Pont insecticide, Vydate L. Oxamyl/Nematocide, which looks like water! Decedent's employer, a tobacco farmer, purchased the du Pont insecticide, and in a one-gallon container took it into the field. The product label warned "Danger—Poison" in red letters, and had a skull and crossbones; but the liquid resembled water. The decedent, a field laborer, drank the insecticide and died. The court reversed the summary judgment for du Pont, and pointed out that the jury could find that du Pont was negligent in marketing a toxic chemical that could easily be mistaken for water, without adequate precautions, such as using an opaque container and coloring the liquid. Also, the label warnings were not adequate as a matter of law because the product's resemblance to water and the foreseeability of its use around farm laborers mandated more prominent warnings. The court also pointed out that label instructions to administer salt water in case of ingestion were misleading in that the label focused upon salt water instead of urging vomiting by any means available.

In *Blankenship et al* v. *Cincinnati Milacron Chemicals, Inc.,* (433 NE2d 572, Ohio 1972) the Ohio Supreme Court ruled that an employee was NOT precluded by the exclusivity provision of the Ohio Worker's Compensation Act (nor by the Ohio Constitution) from enforcing his common law remedies against his employer for what the court deemed to be an *intentional tort.* Plaintiffs were eight current and former employees of the defendant, Cincinnati Milacron Chemicals, Inc., and they, and where appropriate, their spouses, brought a tort action seeking compensatory and punitive damages against Milacron and several individual employees. They alleged that while they were stationed at Milacron's chemical manufacturing facility, they were exposed to fumes and other noxious characteristics of certain chemicals (methyl chloride, stannic chloride, trimethylamine, and tin) within the scope of their employment, and that such toxic exposure factually and proximately caused them to be harmed by resulting chemical intoxication. Plaintiffs further alleged that despite the employer's knowledge that such hazardous conditions existed, defendants failed to correct the conditions or to warn the plaintiffs-employees of such dangerous conditions, and failed to report the conditions to various state and federal agencies as required by law. Plaintiffs charged that such failure (to correct, warn, and report) on the part of defendants was intentional, malicious, and in willful and wanton disregard of the health of plaintiffs, and factually and legally caused their injuries. Plaintiffs also asserted that notwithstanding defendants' knowledge that certain occupational diseases were being contracted, defendants intentionally, maliciously, and in reckless disregard of plaintiffs' interests, failed to warn plaintiffs and to provide medical examinations as required by law, thereby directly and proximately causing plaintiffs harm. On defendants' motion to dismiss plaintiffs' complaint on the basis of the exclusivity provision of the Ohio Constitution and the similar preclusion in the state's workers' compensation act, the trial court dismissed plaintiffs' action. The intermediate appellate court affirmed the dismissal, holding that the foregoing exclusivity provisions immunized the employer from tort liability for even intentional torts. But the Ohio Supreme Court *reversed* the dismissal of the complaint and held that a complaint charging the employer with an *intentional tort* was sufficient to withstand a motion to dismiss. The court stated that the exclusivity provision "shall be liberally construed in favor of employees and the dependants of deceased employees," and not bar a suit based upon an intentional tort.

Part III
Defenses to the Products Liability Situation

STATE OF THE ART AND COLLATERAL ESTOPPEL

In 1976 the National Machine Tool Builders Association reported that one out of every seven lawsuits against their members involved a machine that was 40 years old; one out of every four involved a machine that was 30 years old; and almost all the products liability claims involved machines more than 20 years old. Many of these machines had been sold, resold, junked, resurrected from the junkyard, and placed in operation in the plant of an employer of a person unfortunate enough to become permanently maimed by the use or misuse of the machine.

It is self-evident that the defense of claims for injuries from the use or misuse of such machines must involve the State of the Art. Is the machine manufacturer to be charged with a standard 40, or 30, or 20 years old—or is he to be held to a standard operative in the year that the injury occurred? The accepted definition of State of the Art is *the level of pertinent scientific and technological knowledge existing at the time the injury-producing product was designed and/or manufactured.* Too frequently courts confuse State of the Art evidence with industry standards or custom, existing statutes, or governmental regulations—all of which are current and not necessarily existent or in force when the product was designed and/or manufactured.

The term "State of the Art" was probably first used in a products liability situation in 1956 in the Illinois case of *Day* v. *Barber-Colman Co.,* (10 Ill App 2d 494). Here the plaintiff sued the manufacturer of an overhead door which fell on him and caused serious injury. The court rejected the argument that the manufacturer was negligent in the design of the door: "The design having evidently been found safe in the industry by experience and having been many times used safely by installers, the *state of the art* at the time and prior history of the use of the product would not have indicated or required any material change in the design or manufacture." Unfortunately the Illinois court did not clarify the definition to signify the then-existing technological capacity, the current custom of the industry, or the feasibility of a safer design. It is submitted that State of the Art is the point of scientific and technological advance with respect to a given product at the time of the manufacture and/or design of the product.

In *Dean* v. *General Motors Corp.* (301 F Supp 187, La, 1969) the plaintiffs alleged that their injuries were caused by negligence in the design of the GM ignition lock. But the court held for the defendant on a finding of nonnegligence, measuring the standard of care "by the knowledge available both at the time of design and manufacture." In 1961 the ignition lock system that GM used was deemed as good as or better than any other system in use at that time. But some courts in a Strict Products Liability situation have refused to recognize the defense of the State of the Art, because under Strict Liability, negligence is not an issue nor is a manufacturer's exercise of due care relevant. Only if State of the Art evidence is relevant to proof of defect or to proof that the product is unavoidably unsafe, will these courts admit such evidence. In *Boatland of Houston, Inc.* v. *Bailey,* (585 SW2d 805, Tex App., 1979, rev 609 SW2d 743, 1980), the deceased was operating a boat that hit a submerged tree stump and was thrown into the water; he was killed by the boat's propeller. It seems that the boat was not equipped with a "kill switch" which would have stopped the engine once the driver was thrown from the boat. At the trial, the defendant introduced State of the Art evidence to the effect that in 1973 when the boat was assembled, a "kill switch" was not within the existing technology of the boating industry. But the Texas Court of

Appeals ruled that such evidence should not have been admitted because the unavailability of "kill switches" at the time the boat was manufactured was irrelevant, because such evidence was directed at the care exercised by the defendant, and not whether the product was defective, which was the prime issue! The focus was upon the product, not upon the reasoning behind adoption or nonadoption of the design.

Failure to admit State of the Art evidence means that a once nondefective product can later be rendered defective in terms of the latest technology! It can be argued that where defendant's product was designed as safely as possible under the then-existing state of technology and scientific knowledge, that product should not be considered in a defective condition under Strict Liability at a later date.

The New Jersey Supreme Court in *Beshada* v. *Johns-Manville Corp.* (90 NJ 191) on July 7, 1982 dealt a blow to the manufacturer's defense of State of the Art by ruling that a manufacturer may be held liable for failure to warn of the dangerous nature of its product even though the danger may not have been discoverable under the State of the Art available when the product was marketed. Justice Pashman, writing for the court said: "Knowledge of the dangers of the product is imputed to the defendants. Plaintiff need not prove that defendants knew or should have known of its dangerousness. When the defendants argue that it is unreasonable to impose a duty on them to warn of the unknowable, they misconstrue both the purpose and effect of Strict Liability. By imposing Strict Liability (upon the asbestos product) we are not requiring defendants to have done something that is impossible. In this sense the phrase 'duty to warn' is misleading. It implies negligence concepts with their attendant focus upon the reasonableness of defendant's behavior. However, a major concern of Strict Liability—ignored by defendants—is the conclusion that if a product was in fact defective, the distributor of the product should compensate its victims for the misfortune it inflicted on them."

It is submitted that by precluding defendants from presenting State of the Art evidence to establish that the challenged product was not defective at the time of manufacture, the New Jersey Supreme Court has removed from the jury's consideration that very evidence that is necessary to maintain a distinction between Strict Liability and Absolute Liability. Products should be measured for defect according to the scientific and technical knowledge available when they were produced. We do not judge the Wright brothers' success with the "Kitty Hawk" in 1903 by the supersonic aircraft so common today! Perhaps the better approach toward recognition of the State of the Art defense is seen in the California federal case of *Pherson* v. *Goodyear Tire & Rubber Co.,* (590 F[2d] 757, CA9, 1978) wherein the jury instructions set forth the following "factors" in determining whether a defect in design existed when the tire left the control of the manufacturer: "One: The availability of an alternative design which would have prevented the injury. Two: The feasibility of the alternative design in terms of cost, practicality, and technology. A design may not be found defective when, under the present state of the art, alternative designs are unreasonable. A product need not be found defective simply because an accident occurred."

It should be observed that Sections 107(D) and (E) of the Model Uniform Products Liability Act of 1979 set forth a defense of "practical technological feasibility." Such a defense appears to be much broader than the State of the Art defense, but reflects the desired policy of allowing use of the State of the Art defense in all actions, including Strict Liability.

Closely related to the problem of the State of the Art defense is the evidentiary question of the admissibility of Post-Accident Design Changes. In *Caprara* v. *Chrysler Corp.,* (52 NY2d 114, 1981) the plaintiff was driving one of the defendant manufacturer's cars when on a downhill curve the wheel stuck, causing the car to swerve and crash, with resulting paraplegia to the plaintiff driver. An expert "implicated a defective lower front ball joint" supposed to carry the weight of the car. The car had gone only 9000 miles but the joint showed wear consistent with 10 or 15 times more travel. One of the defendant's engineers, called by the plaintiff, testified that *about four years after* the accident, the company modified the design by adding a plastic insert that would eliminate the play that caused wear. It was also shown that another manufacturer had introduced this modification *eight years before* the accident, and that the defendant knew about it. The higher New York court, by a 4–3 vote concluded that "the long-accepted proposition that, in a negligence suit, proof of a defendant's postaccident repair or improvement ordinarily is not admissible," should NOT be applied under Strict Products Liability.

The court stressed the "need to overcome the inordinately difficult problems of proof which face contemporary consumers who suffer at the hands of articles of commerce whose proclivities to injure are so often within the sole ken of those who design and manufacture them." The three dissenting judges suggested that the availability of evidence of the defendant's knowledge of its competitor's design change diminished the need for the plaintiff to rely exclusively on evidence of the defendant's own subsequent design change, which, as the dissent sees it, "will in almost all cases determine the result" in a jury's eyes. The dissent would save such proof for only that case in which the plaintiff has no other evidence available, in which event the plaintiff's need would outweigh the dangers of misuse. The dissent held that "(t)o admit evidence of subsequent change on a less limited basis (i.e., when other evidence is available) in strict liability cases generally is to make every manufacturer the insurer of the safety of his product." In the dissent's view, the majority, "while verbalizing the concept that a manufacturer is not an insurer, in effect makes him just that." It is submitted that both the majority and the dissenting opinions addressed the argument that a rule that punishes a manufacturer for taking a later step by always making it seem that he should have taken it earlier will be a deterrent to progress. But the majority felt that commercial self-interest is a sufficient incentive that neutralizes this deterrent. Note that the *Caprara* case dealt with a manufacturing flaw and not with design changes, which are often more subjective than objective, as in the instance of manufacturing defects.

A contrary position is taken in *Cann* v. *Ford Motor Co.,* (658 F2d 54, 1981). Here the injuries were sustained by a woman trying to get out of her husband's car at a gas station. With the engine running he shifted into "Park," but the lever slipped into "Reverse," and the car started to move; the wife was hurt trying to get out of the car. Plaintiffs were *not* allowed to present evidence that, after the accident, design changes were made to overcome the slippage problem. Under Federal Rules of Evidence Rule 407 entitled "Subsequent Remedial Measures," it is provided that "when after an event measures are taken previously would have made the event less likely to occur, evidence of subsequent measures is NOT admissible to prove negligence or culpable conduct in connection with the event." The U.S.

Second Circuit Court of Appeals refused to change that restrictive rule under Strict Products Liability.

This conflict of opinions is presumably resolvable under the doctrine of *Erie Railroad* v. *Tompkins,* (304 US 64, 1938) which requires a federal court to apply state law in a case in which federal jurisdiction is based solely upon the diversity of citizenship of the parties. The doctrine would prevent a party from undermining an important state policy by bringing his case or removing it to a federal court on the mere coincidence that diversity exists. However, it should be noted that Rule 407 of the Federal Rules of Civil Procedure "does not require the exclusion of evidence of subsequent measures when offered for another purpose such as proving ownership, control, or feasibility of precautionary measures, if controverted, or impeachment." Indeed, the primary rationale of Rule 407 is to foster the public policy of encouraging the making of repairs or changes or modifications or correction of defects which may have caused any accident. Other grounds for this exclusion are the total absence of probative value of such evidence in proving lack of due care, and the belief that such evidence is irrelevant and prejudicial. The U.S. Supreme Court in *Columbia & Puget Sound Railway Co.* v. *Hawthorne,* (144 US 202, 204, 1892) expressed the view: "Such evidence is incompetent because the taking of such precautions against the future is not to be construed as an admission of responsibility for the past, has no legitimate tendency to prove the defendant had been negligent before the accident happened, and is calculated to distract the minds of the jury from the real issue and to create prejudice against the defendant."

A unique position on this question was taken in 1979 by an Illinois appellate court in *Smith* v. *Verson Allsteel Press Co.,* (393 NE2d 598) where the court agreed that the defendant should be permitted to submit into evidence the precise reasons for postaccident changes if the court admits into evidence postaccident changes. Indeed, such precise reasons should not carry with them any admission of guilt concerning a deficiency in an existing product which may be the subject of the litigation.

Still another aspect of the same problem is Changing the Rule of Law. In *Wangen* v. *Ford Motor Co.,* (294 NW2d 437, Wis, 1980) a 1967 Ford was involved in a 1975 rear-end collision which propelled the car into a third car; the gas tank ruptured and fire ensued. Ford was sued on the "second collision theory," i.e., the car was defectively designed because it did not provide a reasonably safe environment in which passengers could encounter a *second* collision! In 1967, at the time the vehicle in question was designed and manufactured, the generally recognized rule of law was that an auto manufacturer had NO DUTY to design a vehicle which provided a "reasonably safe" environment for its passengers in the event of a *second* collision, *Evans* v. *General Motors Corp.* (359 F2d 822, CA7, 1966). Under the *Evans* rule the duty of the auto manufacturer was only to design a vehicle that was safe for its intended purposes, and those purposes did not include collisions! But in 1968, in *Larsen* v. *General Motors Corp.,* (391 F2d 495, CA8, 1968) a new rule was promulgated, to wit: since it is foreseeable that autos will be involved in collisions, their manufacturers have a duty to design them so that they are reasonably safe for their occupants when involved in a collision. In 1977 the *Larsen* rule was supported in *Huff* v. *White Motor Co.,* (565 F2d 104, CA7, 1977). QUERY: should Ford have recalled their 1967 car after the *Larsen* decision in 1968? Yet the *Larsen* decision gave the auto manufacturer nothing specific that could be transferred to a blueprint! There was no "defect" in the 1967 Ford—all that had happened was that a court had *changed the Rule of Law* between the time the product left the control of Ford and the time that the vehicle was subjected to judicial scrutiny! *Is the situation akin to an Ex Post Facto situation in criminal law? Changes in the Rule of law should be prospective, not retroactive.*

Still another aspect of the State of the Art defense for the product manufacturer is the doctrine of *Collateral Estoppel.* This doctrine seeks to terminate litigation by holding that once liability has been established in favor of or against a party, a later case involving the same product and the same liability issue need not be proven all over again! But there are basic factors before Collateral Estoppel can be invoked: (1) the issue in question must be identical with the issue of liability and determined in the prior action; (2) the issue in question must have been litigated and determined in the prior action; (3) the determination of the issue in question must have been necessary to reach the judgment or award in the prior action; and (4) the application of the doctrine of Collateral Estoppel is fair and equitable to the parties involved. Courts should also examine such matters as the competence and experience of trial counsel in the prior action as well as the size of the prior claim compared to the size of the present claim.

A smart defendant can use the doctrine of Collateral Estoppel to his/her advantage. In *Buckholt* v. *American Motors Corp.* the Nevada court was concerned with an Air Force officer who was severely injured in a Jeep CJ-5 rollover crash in 1976. After the 1982 trial, and before the trial court rendered its decision, the parties settled for $5.1 million. When the trial court finally made its decision, it ruled that its award, and not the settlement amount, controlled, but the Nevada Supreme Court on October 29, 1982 ruled otherwise. The reason why the successful defendant wanted the settlement and not the award was because the doctrine of Collateral Estoppel would bar relitigation in another case of the particular defect in the Jeep CJ-5. (The trial court had found that the vehicle was defective in its design because its rollover protection system was inadequate, its high center of gravity coupled with its short wheelbase and narrow track width made it unstable, it tended to oversteer and had become uncontrollable when fully loaded, and it failed to contain adequate warnings about the defects.)

The doctrine of Collateral Estoppel was also designed, inter alia, to curb frivolous lawsuits. It is neither a tool of the claimant, nor a shield to the product manufacturer. It is a doctrine of judicial finality which courts have sought to apply justly. It means that there will be but "one bite to the apple," as illustrated by *Flatt* v. *Johns-Manville* (488 F Supp 836, ED Texas, 1980) where the federal district court in Texas barred the manufacturer from contesting the issue of whether its asbestos product was unreasonably dangerous, because six years earlier in *Borel* v. *Fibreboard Paper Products Corp.,* (493 F[2d] 1076, 1974) the Fifth U.S. Court of Appeals had found such products to be unreasonably dangerous! But eight years later that same higher court in *Hardy* v. *Johns-Manville* (681 F[2d] 334, 1982) reversed its earlier thinking and placed limits on arbitrarily using Collateral Estoppel to streamline asbestos litigation. The 1982 court ruled that the nonparty defendants were not estopped, for they were not in privity with the party defendants simply because all were engaged in making asbestos products. Even those defendants who were parties to the earlier case could not be estopped from defending because: (1) the judgment in the prior action was ambiguous on key issues; (2) the presence of inconsistent verdicts (which defendants had won) made Collateral Estoppel improper and unfair; and (3) even without the above two reasons, a $68,000 liability in 1973 was not a foreseeably strong enough harbinger of multi-million dollar asbestos liability so as to avoid questions of full "incentive" in the prior litigation. The court in the *Hardy* case concluded that to do otherwise "would be to elevate judicial expedience over considerations of justice and fair play."

On the other hand, the New York case of *Kaufman* v. *Eli Lilly Co.,* decided October 25, 1982, dramatically illustrates the danger a manufacturer faces when the second case arises in the same jurisdiction as, and before the same judge who presided over, the first case. In its enthusiasm to apply Collateral Estoppel, the New York Supreme Court, New York County, ignored several facts: (1) at least six cases had been resolved in favor of the DES manufacturer, including some on the same liability issues; (2) the New York Court of Appeals had affirmed the prior case (*Bichler*) on procedural grounds, leaving unresolved the propriety of that trial court's application of that theory in DES cases; (3) Collateral Estoppel on the basis of *Bichler* had been denied in *Sardell* v. *Eli Lilly Co.,* (New York Supreme Court, New York County, October 15, 1982) on the grounds of inconsistent verdicts in other DES cases; and (4) the injuries involved in the two cases may not have been the same, to wit: cancer of the cervix. In *Baxter* v. *Fulton Ice & Cube Co.,* the New York Supreme Court, Kings County, Special Term, on February 10, 1983, refused to apply Collateral Estoppel in a personal injury action so as to limit the amount of damages that the plaintiff could recover to the amount awarded against a codefendant in an inquest following default. Justice C. Cohen observed that "the plaintiff at an inquest, particularly with respect to an uninsured defunct corporation, could hardly be expected to proceed with the same vigor as he would at a trial with a viable defendant." The inquest amount was $100,000; and the "two necessary requirements for the invocation of the doctrine of Collateral Estoppel" were *not* met, to wit: "there must be an identity of issue which has necessarily been decided in the prior action, and is decisive of the present action, and . . . there must have been a full and fair opportunity to contest the decision now said to be controlling."

Similarly, the Ohio Supreme Court in *Goodson* v. *McDonough*

Power Equipment, Inc., decided January 5, 1983, ruled that the doctrine could *not* be applied when the former adjudication of the issues arose out of a separate underlying incident. Here plaintiff sued the manufacturer of a riding lawn mower for injuries suffered by an infant. The Owner's Manual advised against "giving rides," and the infant lost a foot, allegedly because the lawn mower did not have a guard! Plaintiff moved for partial summary judgment on the grounds of Collateral Estoppel, to wit: the defendant lawn mower manufacturer had lost a similar suit in Florida before a jury! The Ohio trial court agreed that the plaintiff entered judgment on the issue of liability, and ordered a trial on damages only. The Ohio appellate court *reversed,* and the Ohio Supreme Court *affirmed,* ordering a new trial on *all* issues. The high court pointed out that "the common party (defendant) should not be deprived of his right to a jury trial." Indeed, the court raised the spectre of the first or early Florida decision as being an erroneous determination; fairness and fair opportunity to be heard are paramount: Collateral Estoppel could "result in a single jury, sitting in review of limited facts, entering a verdict which would establish safety standards for the entire country."

DISCLAIMERS OF LIABILITY

Another defense available to the product manufacturer, although of limited use, is the disclaimer or express warranty of nonliability—whether in advertising or in the labeling of the product.

In theory, at least, all warranties made with respect to a product may be disclaimed, not only by exclusion or modification, as under Section 2–316 of the Uniform Commercial Code, but also, as a matter of law, when the warranty is deemed unconscionable. Unfortunately, the UCC does not contain any definition of the word "unconscionable," but the term can be characterized as the absence of good faith, of diligence, of reasonableness, and of fair dealing. Under Section 2–317 of the UCC, an *express* disclaimer which is inconsistent with a warranty is enforceable if it is specific and conspicuously disclosed, and therefore can limit or restrict liability.

A product manufacturer has the right to disclaim liability for defects in the product, or at least to limit liability for damages to the replacement of parts. Where the manufacturer attaches a broad standard disclaimer, particularly if it is obscure, trying to limit his legal responsibility for defects in his product, he may find that the disclaimer will not help him.

Indeed, the courts will interpret it against him or will strike it down as a violation of public policy. The courts increasingly recognize that the buyer has no real choice to negotiate such terms in an ordinary retail sale. The sales promotion department tries to convince the buyer that the product is good, and the legal department tries to attach a disclaimer which will avoid liability if the impression created by the sales department is wrong. Justice requires flexibility here, and the disclaimer is simply declared null and void.

DATE OF EXPOSURE VS. MANIFESTATION OF INJURY: STATUES OF LIMITATIONS AS DEFENSES

A statute of limitations is designed to eliminate stale claims, especially where after many years it is difficult for the defendant to find old records and otherwise to defend his/her interests properly. Generally the injured person must commence his suit within three years after a personal injury. But *when* did the personal injury occur? In the case of asbestosis there can be a lapse of many decades between the victim's EXPOSURE to the asbestos and the MANIFESTATION of the injury. In New York, the highest court in *Steinhardt* v. *Johns-Manville Corp.*, #434, dated October 29, 1981, ruled that the date of injury was the date of the victim's *last* exposure to the invading substance. However, the majority of states adhere to the MANIFESTATION of injury date, i.e., the date of the first impairment, or the date the first X ray showed the abnormality; see *Locke* v. *Johns-Manville Corp.*, (275 SE2d 900, VA, 1981). A variation on the date of MANIFESTATION of injury is the Discovery rule, to the effect that the statute of limitations begins to run from the date the victim knew or should have known reasonably that he was injured from a particular cause or source; see *DaMato* v. *Turner & Newall, Ltd.*, (651 F3d 908, CA3, 198).

Criticism of the EXPOSURE date rule points out that the action could be time-barred before the injury becomes manifest. In *Garrett* v. *Raytheon Co., Inc.*, (368 So2D 516, Ala 1979) defendants had designed, installed, and maintained radar equipment prior to 1955 at

Fort Bliss, Texas. Plaintiff was a staff sergeant stationed there from 1955 to 1957 as an instructor in the use and maintenance of radar equipment. In 1975 plaintiff became ill, and in March 1977 his condition was diagnosed as radiation sickness. He commended suit in February 1978, more than 20 years after his last exposure to the radiation. Alabama had a one-year statute of limitations, and so the Alabama court dismissed his suit as time-barred, ruling that the statute of limitations began to run on the last day of his exposure to radiation in 1957! It was 18 years later that he first became ill! In another radiation case, *Cadieux* v. *International Telephone & Teleg.*, (593 F2d 142, CAL, 1979), an electronics technician died from cancer allegedly caused by exposure to radiation. The federal district court dismissed the plaintiff's wrongful death suit as being time-barred by Rhode Island's two-year statute of limitations for wrongful death. On appeal, the U.S. First Circuit Court of Appeals rejected the plaintiff's contention that the two-year statute of limitations should be read in products liability cases to mean, "two years from the date of discovery of the cause of death." The court concluded that the Rhode Island statute was very explicit in requiring the suit to be brought within two years "after the death."

The inherent unfairness of the EXPOSURE date is also seen in *Diamond* v. *E. R. Squibb & Sons, Inc.*, (366 SE2nd 1221, 1979). Here a woman and her parents brought an action in strict liability and negligence against a manufacturer of the drug diethylstilbestrol (DES). The plaintiffs brought the action after learning of the possible adverse effects of DES upon daughters of women who ingested the drug during pregnancy. However, the defendant's motion for summary judgment was granted on the ground that the action—commenced well in excess of 12 years after the last date of delivery of the drug—was time-barred. The Florida appellate court upheld the summary judgment for the drug manufacturer. In a similar case, *Hechtlinger* v. *Eli Lilly and Co.*, New York Supreme Court, New York County, dated October 16, 1981, Justice Fraiman adhered to the three-year statute of limitations for personal injuries, and dismissed the complaint of a daughter who sought to recover damages she allegedly sustained as the result of her mother's ingestion of DES before her mother gave birth in December 1957. The suit was commenced in November 1979, four years after she attained her majority of 18 years of age, but 22 years after her mother's exposure to DES. On the other hand, in *Reyes* v. *Anka Research Ltd.,* the New York Supreme Court, Kings County, dated November 24, 1981, did *not* dismiss the complaint brought against a physician for improper or negligent insertion of an intrauterine device for birth control purposes in 1973. The victim sustained an infection in 1978, and sued in July 1979. Justice Greenstein ruled:

> "In regard to the original insertion of the IUD, plaintiffs proceed under the theory that the IUD constituted a "foreign object" negligently inserted and/or left in the plaintiff-wife's body, so that the statute of limitations did not begin to run until the plaintiffs had or should have reasonably discovered the malpractice (*Flanagan* v. *Mount Eden Gen. Hosp.,* 1969, 24 NY.2d 427, 301 N.Y.S.2d 23). Under this theory, the applicable statute of limitations would be one year from the date of reasonable discovery, (CPLR 214–a), which plaintiffs claim was sometime in 1978–9. There is no claim by defendant that, if the one year rule is applicable, the action was not brought within the permissible time period."

> "The general rule is that the statute of limitations begins to run at the time of the medical treatment when the foreign substance e.g., a drug, is introduced into the body, and not at the time of discovery of the consequent injury or disease (*Thornton* v. *Roosevelt Hosp.,* 1979 47 N.Y.2d 780, 417 N.Y.S.2d 920). There is an exception to this rule, however, in the instance of a foreign object negligently left in the body, in which circumstances the action accrues at the time of reasonable discovery of the foreign object and the malpractice (*Flanagan, supra*). As the IUD is not a chemical compound, fixation device or prosthetic aid, it is not barred by statute from being classified as a foreign object, if appropriate (CPLR 214-a)."

> ". . . this court finds that the policy considerations stated in *Flanagan, supra,* lead to the conclusion in such circumstances that the cause of action did not accrue until the reasonable discovery of the malpractice (here seemingly in 1978–9). In addition, in this case, there was the alleged negligence of the defendant in failing to advise

the plaintiff of the recall of the particular type of IUD, which continued up to the time of reasonable discovery."

According to the U.S. Seventh Circuit Court of Appeals in *Neubauer* v. *Owens-Corning Fibreglass Corp.,* decided August 13, 1982, the statute of limitations for asbestos liability suits should begin to run when the plaintiff can first prove *through medical diagnosis* that he has the particular disease, and not when the disease first becomes noticeable to the plaintiff or when it impairs the plaintiff's health. Indeed, to give the claimant his day in court, courts have created "extensions," "exceptions," etc., and have used other devices to extend the time limitations or stop the running of the clock! In *Klein* v. *Dow Corning Corp.* (661 F[2d] 998) the Second U.S. Circuit Court of Appeals in 1981 ruled that plaintiff was not barred from commencing suit 13 years after a surgical implantation of a mammary prosthesis allegedly burst or ruptured. The court observed that there is no cause of action until the prosthesis breaks, and only then is there an injury!

The statute of limitations for personal injuries, in contrast to breach of warranty upon sale of the product, is generally shorter. In *McCarthy* v. *Bristol-Myers Co.,* the New York Appellate Division, 2nd Dept., on April 19, 1982, addressed itself to the claim of the plaintiff who in October 1971 was hospitalized with a kidney ailment in Pennsylvania. While so hospitalized she was treated with two prescriptive drugs, Kantrex and Keflin, the former being manufactured by the primary defendant. She alleges that as the result of these drugs she sustained severe injuries, including blindness. In October 1975 she sued the two drug manufacturers, but the New York court dismissed her causes of action in negligence and in Strict Liability under the three-year statute of limitations. But that court did not dismiss the breach of warranty cause of action which, arguably, was controlled by a four-year statute of limitations. During extensive discovery "facts developed . . . disclosed that Montefiore Hospital had made no direct purchases of either Kantrex or Keflin from defendants."

Justice Brown thereupon concluded that "there existed no direct contract of sale between either of the plaintiffs and the defendant manufacturers . . . no contract of sale existed." The court agreed to dismiss the surviving count of breach of warranty because "in determining the applicable Statute of Limitations the gravamen or essence of the action is examined, not merely its nomenclature . . . it is clear that the second cause of action while denominated one for breach of warranty, is in actuality one alleging strict products liability or negligence . . . Section 2–318 of the Uniform Commercial Code, as it existed at the time Mrs. McCarthy's cause of action accrued, required privity between a plaintiff and a defendant in a breach of warranty action . . . As the injured plaintiff was not in privity with the defendant drug manufacturers, she possesses only a cause of action sounding in tort under either a negligence or strict products liability theory . . . Her claim is therefore governed by the three year Statute of Limitations period . . . which began to run in 1971 at the time of injury . . . Since the cause of action under review was not interposed until 1975 it must be dismissed as time-barred. . ." Indeed, a persistent defense by the drug manufacturers utilized successfully the statute of limitations argument.

A contrary view similarly persistent is seen in *Lindsey* v. *Ullman and A. H. Robins Co.,* wherein the New York Appellate Division, 2nd Dept., on February 11, 1983, distinguished between "an intrauterine device which facilitates infection" and "dust, asbestos particles, a hazardous dye, or thorium dioxide substance which directly and immediately act upon the body causing injury." As a result of such a technical distinction, the court held that not the DATE OF INSERTION but the Date of Onset of Injury is "the accrual date to be used for computing the limitation of time for bringing suit." The New York court distinguished *Thornton* v. *Roosevelt Hospital,* (47 NY2d 780) a decision of the New York Court of Appeals: "It is well established in this State that when chemical compounds are injected into a person's body, the injury occurs upon the drug's introduction, not when the alleged deleterious effects of its component chemicals become apparent." (In the *Thornton* case, plaintiff's claim was interposed some 20 years after the injection.) The court in *Lindsey* rejected the argument: "The injection or inhalation of the harmful substance into the body constitutes the actionable 'invasion of the body' which *immediately* initiates the infection or disease process for which a negligent defendant is responsible," and concluded:

"But, that assumption is not valid or applicable to the facts of the case before us. *It cannot be said that there was injury at the time of the insertion of the shield because there is no basis in reason or in the record before us upon which to predicate an assumption that any infection or disease process began immediately upon insertion of the shield.* Unlike the harmful dust and chemical compounds, which were harmful in their very nature, i.e., they were the 'beasts themselves,' the shield was not, in and of itself, harmful. The beasts were the bacteria that availed themselves of the open highway created by the shield."

The court applauded the New York Court of Appeals decision in *Victorson* v. *Bock Laundry Machine Co.*, 37 NY2d 395, and reasoned as follows:

"The fact that Joyce Lindsey's injury came about because of an 'invasion' of the body by bacteria which was allegedly facilitated by a design defect in the shield invites comparisons with the inhalation or injection of harmful substances cases . . . Manifestly, if the shield were defectively designed in such a way that one of the spokes disengaged and punctured an organ or if its defective design enabled the braided string to entwine and constrict an organ then there would be no question as to the applicability of the general strict products liability accrual rule. In this case we see no justification for departing from the general rule stated in *Victorson* v. *Bock Laundry Mach. Co.* (37 NY2d 395, supra) and reaffirmed in *Thornton* v. *Roosevelt Hosp.* (47 NY2d 780, supra) simply because the shield facilitated infectious injury instead of causing direct physical injury. It must not be forgotten that we are dealing here with a product which was marketed for profit by Robins and we can perceive no sound reason why the policy behind the *Victorson* rule should not be applied to such product. Because of the nature of the shield, it was hidden from view after insertion in the body. But, why should that fact start the Statute of Limitations running immediately rather than when the object causes injury? Those cases applying the general rule spelled out in *Victorson* distinguish between the time the allegedly defective product is placed into the mainstream of

> commerce and the time when the cause of action arises. The cause of action comes into being only when the product causes damage or injury, that is, upon the breakdown of the device. In our view, this case is analogous to the breakdown cases (see *Klein* v. *Dow Corning Corporation,* 661 F 2d 998, injury at a time a mammary prosthesis broke and not the date of insertion; *Murphy* v. *St. Charles Hospital,* 35 AD 2d 64, injury at time prosthesis broke although it had been inserted years earlier). The 'breakdown' here would be at the point at which the shield's tail conducted infectious bacteria up into the uterus. The bacteria, an outside agency, caused an infection, inflaming the pelvic area, and causing plaintiff Joyce Lindsey's injury. The cause of action accrued when that injury occurred, not at some earlier date when the shield had been inserted, but had not yet had a harmful effect on Joyce Lindsey."

The statute of limitations defense was tested in another New York case where plaintiff was injured on September 28, 1978 by a Wascomat washing machine on the premises of Tumbler, operator of the laundromat. He sued Tumbler in January 1979, and in April 1980 Tumbler commenced third party actions against Wascomat and the distributor of the washing machine. The trial court concluded that "a tortfeasor may claim contribution from another person who may be subject to liability for damages for the same injury under any theory of liability that plaintiff could have asserted against that person but had not done so." But Wascomat argued that Strict Liability was not applicable, *as a matter of law,* because Tumbler was a nonuser and sought recovery for economic loss and not personal injury. Wascomat also contended that privity of contract was necessary for the breach of warranty cause of action. The New York Appellate Division, 2nd Dept. in *Doyle* v. *Happy Tumbler Wash-O-Mat Inc.,* decided on December 20, 1982, ruled that "the theory of liability was irrelevant" in face of "the fact of liability to the same person for the same harm," and furthermore privity of contract was not required in New York after September 1, 1975. The court, however, determined that the four-year statute of limitations for breach of implied warranty commenced AT THE TIME OF THE ORIGINAL SALE OF THE PRODUCT BY THE MANUFACTURER (which fact was not in the record). If the sale was prior to September 1, 1975 then privity of contract was required, and so the statute of limitations determined the outcome of the case.

A *Statute of Repose* is slightly different from a Statute of Limitations in that the former potentially bars suits BEFORE a cause of action accrues, while the latter bars suits AFTER a cause of action accrues. For example, the state of North Carolina in *Bolick* v. *American Barmag Corp.,* (284 SE2d 188, 1981) struck down a six-year Statute of Repose running from the date of sale of the product, as violative of Article I, Section 18 of the North Carolina Constitution, providing that "every person for an injury done him in his lands, goods, or reputation shall have remedy by due course of law." Here plaintiff-employee, in June 1977 caught his hand in a machine manufactured by the defendant, and brought suit in October 1979. But his employer had bought the machine from the defendant in April 1971, and so the employee's action against the product manufacturer was barred by the six-year Statute of Repose running from the date of sale. The trial court dismissed the action, but the appellate court *reversed* holding that the statute was "unconstitutional on its face." *The statute had in effect extinguished plaintiff's right before his injury had occurred.*

Other states which have held similarly are Florida, Kentucky, Wyoming, Hawaii, Illinois, Wisconsin, Minnesota, South Carolina, and Oklahoma on narrow issues such as an architect's continuing liability. But Massachusetts rejected a plaintiff's challenge to a Statute of Repose which precluded recovery for any injury that occurs more than six years after the performance or furnishing of the design, planning, and construction of improvements to real property. In *Klein* v. *Catalano,* decided July 7, 1982, the plaintiff was injured in 1976, more than nine years after the architect had completed all services to the MIT building. Justice Abrams entered judgment for the defendants because the statute not only precluded the plaintiff's tort action, but the warranty claims as well; to hold otherwise, where the architect had not only expressly guaranteed a specific result, would have defeated the statutory purpose.

Indeed, Statutes of Repose are generally constitutional and have become law in more than 30 states; they are based upon the life expectancy of the product rather than upon the accrual of a cause of action. For example, in Illinois (ch 83, Sec. 22.2(b)) the Statute of Repose provides that a strict liability case must be commenced within 12 years from the time of sale by the manufacturer, or 10 years from the sale of the product to the initial user, whichever occurs first. Several Statutes of Repose carry a presumption that products more than 10 years old have exceeded their *useful safe life,* and should not thereafter be the subject of litigation. The Oregon Supreme Court in *Johnson* v. *Star Machinery Co.* (530 p[2d] 53 at 56) in 1974 explained the rationale for Statutes of Repose:

> "In general, there are usually two reasons which are advanced as justification for the imposition of such statutes. The first concerns the lack of reliability and availability of evidence after a lapse of long periods of time. This rationale primarily protects defendants who, without prior notice of pending claims, would necessarily find it extremely difficult, it not impossible, to mount a defense because of the nonpreservation of evidence and the disappearance or death of witnesses after a long lapse of time . . . The second rationale concerns the public policy of allowing people after the lapse of reasonable time, to plan their affairs with a degree of certainty, free from the disruptive burden of protracted and unknown liability."

PRODUCT RECALL

Recall of products ranging from automobiles to small consumer products seems to be an everyday occurrence. The technique, and the government regulations thereunder, is a complex matter which in the final analysis is based upon finding, or belief in finding, a "defect" in the product. In court, proof of "defect" requires proof that the product was "unreasonably dangerous" or involved "unexpected dangers" or had an inadequate warning label. However, in simple terms, for a recall, a "defect" is the lack of something which is considered essential to the completeness of the subject matter involved. It can exist in physical characteristics or in functional performance; it can arise from design, faulty manufacture or assembly, or inadequate or improper maintenance and repair. "Defect" is a word of art, since the existence of a "defect" may in a given context carry with it dire financial responsibility. How is "defect" shown? It may be established by physical evidence, or it may, under certain circumstances, be inferred from proof of a functional failure of the product while in use. For example, in one case, a ceramic percolator coffee pot, while being used to pour coffee, broke about a year and a half after the percolator was purchased. Experts for both sides agreed that a small crack at the top of and inside the bowl had spread throughout a substantial portion of the bowl. A jury verdict was affirmed on appeal. Two judges concurring stated that the jury could have concluded from the thinness of the pot at the point of greatest stress that the pot had been defectively manufactured. The third judge said there was evidence from which the jury could have found that this type of pot would be filled from a faucet, and the defendant could foresee that the pot might be bumped, causing the initial crack. See *Toth* v. *Corning Glass Works,* (411 F2d 911, CA 6, 1969), for an analysis of "defect."

Occasionally the government may decide to use the *criminal* law to regulate product design or to correct a blatant defect in a product, either before or after a product recall campaign. Such a criminal trial took place in Elkhart County, Illinois, in 1978: the defendant was the Ford Motor Company and the product was a Pinto sedan. Attorney Malcom E. Wheeler of Los Angeles, who defended Ford, has set forth the *facts:*

> "On August 10, 1978, at about six o'clock in the evening, three teen-aged girls were driving a 1973 Pinto sedan south on U.S. Highway 33 toward Goshen, Indiana. They stopped for gas at a self-service station, filled up, and drove back onto the highway. The driver, however, had neglected to put the filler cap on tightly. It fell off and rolled across the highway, coming to rest near the curb in the northbound lane. The girls did a U-turn to retrieve the filler cap, pulled up where it lay, and drew to a stop in the right lane. They could not pull off the road, because it was designed with an eight-inch-high curb running its entire length, only inches from the traffic lane. Neither a shoulder nor periodically spaced turnouts existed to enable a vehicle in trouble to pull off for repairs. The curbed, shoulderless road was so dangerous that Elkhart County's Citizen Safety Committee had written a letter to the Indiana State Highway Department asking that the road be modified to provide safe stopping spaces for emergencies. The weather was clear; the road was dry; and visibility was unobstructed for more than a mile in both

directions. But, as the girls drew to a stop alongside the filler cap, a Chevrolet van weighing more than 4,000 pounds, modified with a rigid plank in place of the original front bumper, driven by a man carrying open beer bottles, marijuana, and caffeine pills, and travelling at some fifty-five miles per hour, bore down on them. Without touching his brakes, the van driver plowed squarely into the back of the Pinto, knocking it some 170 feet down the road, spinning it around, and causing it to jump the eight-inch curb with its left side wheels. The Pinto burst into flame. The two passengers died in the car, but the driver was partially ejected. She was rushed to the hospital and died several hours later. Before dying however, she told two of the hospital employees, an orderly, and a nurse, exactly what had happened. The police inspected the van immediately after the accident. They found the open beer bottles, the marijuana, and what they reported as capsules of speed.''

On these facts the county prosecutor charged Ford with reckless homicide and criminal recklessness, claiming that the cause of the deaths was the design of the PINTO and Ford's failure to *recall* the car from the market. According to Attorney Wheeler, his nine principal trial defenses were:

''1. In the 1973 model year, Ford was the only automobile manufacturer in the world that had voluntarily adopted a mandatory internal rear-impact fuel-system-integrity crash-test requirement.
2. The internal standard that had been adopted by Ford and met by the 1973 Pinto was a reasonable standard, the very one that had been proposed by the General Services Administrations in 1966, by the Canadian Government, by the National Highway Traffic Safety Administration in 1969, and by various private, non-manufacturer entities and researchers.
3. Any car manufactured in 1973, of any size and design, would have suffered a ruptured fuel system if hit by that van at that speed.
4. The 1973 Pinto was comparable in design, and the federal government's own statistics showed that it was comparable in safety performance, to other 1973 subcompact cars.

5. The 1973 Pinto had met all applicable governmental safety standards.
6. All of the key Ford engineering executives involved in the development of the Pinto had provided Pintos to their wives and children to drive, thereby demonstrating those executives' belief in the car's safety.
7. Even though Ford had believed the Pinto to have been reasonably designed, it had recalled the car in a manner that, during the relevant period, was accomplished as quickly as possible and under the guidance of the federal government.
8. The driver of the van had been the primary cause of the tragedy, but he was not even on trial.
9. The badly designed road had been the other cause of the tragedy, but its designers and the persons who approved it were not on trial."

The jury returned an ACQUITTAL on all counts. Indeed, *criminal* prosecution is no deterrent, and only increases the cost of the product without compensating the injured victim. In essence, criminal prosecution only gives a local prosecutor the power to try to use the criminal law to implement his individual notion of what is a desirable mix of product factors, without knowledge or training or expertise in that industry.

Product Recall, on the other hand, without the stifling effect of criminal wrong, is a voluntary withdrawal of the allegedly defective product from the marketplace, and can therefore serve as a defense or limitation on liability for the complying product manufacturer.

ASSUMPTION OF THE RISK, CONTRIBUTORY NEGLIGENCE, AND MISUSE

In theory, Strict Liability does not permit or accept the defenses of Assumption of the Risk and Contributory Negligence, because Fault, under that doctrine, is irrelevant. But there are recognizable defenses based upon plaintiff's conduct, to wit: (1) negligent failure to discover the defective condition; (2) use of the product after discovery of the defect; and (3) use of the product in a manner that could not reasonably have been foreseen by the product manufacturer. All three categories are embraced by Contributory Negligence, as illustrated by *Nelson* v. *Anderson,* (245 Minn 445, 1955) where plaintiff continued to use an oil burner that he knew was not functioning properly, and was injured when the oil burner exploded. The Minnesota court denied liability on the part of the manufacturer of the oil burner. More particularly, this second category of using the product after discovery of the defect may be delineated as *Assumption of the Risk,* and the third category of using the product in an unforeseeable manner is simply Misuse, another recognizable defense.

Under the doctrine of Strict Liability, Assumption of the Risk, Contributory Negligence, and Misuse are *not* recognized as defenses. And Comment *n* to Section 402A of the *Restatement of Torts Second* explains:

> "Contributory negligence of the plaintiff is not a defense when such negligence consists merely in a failure to discover the defect in the product, or to guard against the possibility of its existence. On the other hand, the form of contributory negligence, which consists in voluntarily and unreasonably proceeding to encounter a known danger, and commonly passes under the name of Assumption of the Risk, is a defense under this Section. . ."

And Comment *h* states:

> "A product is not in a defective condition when it is safe for normal handling and consumption. If the injury results from abnormal handling . . . or from abnormal preparation for use . . . the seller is not liable."

In *Martinez* v. *Nichols Conveyor & Engineering Company,* (243 Cal App 2d 795, 1966) the plaintiff was injured when the machine he was operating had a bolt shear off, causing an 800-pound weight to fall on his arm. Evidence was introduced at trial that the plaintiff's employee altered the machine in a manner contrary to the use sanctioned by the manufacturer and that the plaintiff knew of a recent failure of a bolt and the falling of a weight. The California District Court of Appeals held, *inter alia,* that plaintiff had failed to show that he was injured while using the product consistently with its intended use. Similarly, in

Ferraro v. *Ford Motor Company,* (423 Pa 324, 1966) the Pennsylvania Supreme Court recognized that the defense of Assumption of the Risk was available in an action based on strict liability in tort. The plaintiff in *Ferraro* was injured when the left front wheel of his new dump truck locked while he was making a left-hand turn. His conduct from which the jury might find that plaintiff knowingly assumed the risk, was his prior experience with similar failures of the truck. In *Robinson* v. *Reed-Prentice,* the New York Court of Appeals on February 14, 1980 considered an industrial accident involving a plastic molding machine manufactured by defendant and sold to plaintiff's employer. The mold on the machine consisted of two parts, called "platens." One platen was stationary and one was mobile. When the mobile platen was positioned next to the stationary platen, the mold was complete and the molten plastic was injected therein. After the molten plastic had assumed the shape of the mold, the platens would separate, thereby enabling the machine's operator to manually remove the finished product. The manufacturer of the machine designed it with a certain safety feature which blocked the operator's access to the platens while the molding process was ongoing. However, due to a peculiarity in its own manufacturing process, the plaintiff's employer did not find the design of this safety feature acceptable. The employer wished to mold items *on a continuous string,* whereas the machine was designed to mold items one at a time, in an *unconnected* fashion. Hence, for reasons of its own, the employer modified the safety feature in question, thereby allowing the operator to insert his hands near the platens, even while the molding process was ongoing. The plaintiff, while doing just that, caught his hands between the platens, thereby suffering injury. There was evidence in the record which indicated that the machine manufacturer knew, or should have known, that its safety feature was unacceptable to and would be altered by the plaintiff's employer. The manufacturer had sold molding machines to the employer on prior occasions, and the employer had made the same modifications on those machines as well. Although the manufacturer did not approve of this modification of its product (in a letter sent by the manufacturer to the employer it was stated that the employer had "completely flaunted the safeties built into the machine"), it had made it clear that it was not about to alter the safety guard's design, so as to accommodate the employer's desires. At the trial, the plaintiff's expert opined that it would have been possible for the manufacturer to modify this safety guard so as to accommodate the employer's peculiar manufacturing procedures—"without rendering the machine unreasonably dangerous." Thus, the manufacturer's position was that it could not be held liable because its product, which was reasonably safe and nondefective upon delivery, was *misused* by the employer when the modifications were made on its safety feature. The New York Court of Appeals noted that the "(d)efendants maintain that a manufacturer may not be held to answer in damages where the purchaser of its product deliberately destroys the functional utility of that product's safety feature. . ." Plaintiff argued that the injury was foreseeable to the manufacturer because the manufacturer knew of the modification of the safety feature, therefore the manufacturer had a duty to build a safety feature that was both functional and acceptable to the employer. But the court held that a manufacturer may *not* be liable if it sells a nondefective product which is rendered unreasonably dangerous only when it is subsequently modified and safety features are removed. Hence, subsequent modifications of a nondefective product cannot result in the manufacturer's liability when the modifications were the cause of the accident. The defense of MISUSE was affirmed:

> "Principles of foreseeability . . . are inapposite when a third party *affirmatively abuses* the product by consciously by-passing built-in safety features." (Emphasis added)

The rigor of the defense of Contributory Negligence in a Strict Liability situation is illustrated by *McGowne* v. *Challenge-Cook Bros., Inc.,* #80–2052, U.S. Eighth Circuit Court of Appeals. McGowne was killed after he fell into the charging hopper of a cement mixer while he was performing maintenance work. His family brought suit for wrongful death against the manufacturer of the cement mixer, under Strict Liability. The trial court precluded defendant from showing the Contributory Negligence of the decedent, and so the appellate court *reversed,* holding that Contributory Negligence was a valid defense under Strict Liability. The defense could show that the worker had voluntarily and unreasonably exposed himself to a known and appreciated danger.

COMPARATIVE NEGLIGENCE PRINCIPLES

It has been seriously questioned whether or not the principles of Comparative Negligence are truly defensive because the end result is to secure *some* compensation to the injured plaintiff, albeit the defense contribution thereto is diminished. But Comparative Negligence principles are readily applied to Strict Liability, as seen in *Dippel* v. *Sciano* (155 NW 2d 55) when the Wisconsin Supreme Court in 1967 stated: "A defective product can constitute or create an unreasonable risk of harm to others. If this unreasonable danger is a cause, a substantial factor, in producing the injury complained of, it can be *compared* with the causal contributory negligence of the plaintiff." There are a number of practical considerations that support the application of Comparative Negligence to Strict Liability cases: it provides a desirable vehicle for focusing on plaintiff's conduct and the contribution of plaintiff's conduct to his own accident and resulting injuries; and defendants should find products liability verdicts against them reduced by some share of negligence or fault attributed to plaintiff's conduct. Comparative Negligence permits the fair allocation of losses among codefendants by the invitation to the jury to allocate percentages of fault where fault can be found.

There are perhaps 30 states which have adopted the Comparative Negligence doctrine in general. Public policy calling for compensation to injured parties has been appeased to the extent that losses are apportioned between the parties according to their relative fault. Indeed, there are four categories or kinds of Comparative Negligence, to wit: "Virginal"; "Minor-Major"; "Less than 50%"; and "Less than 51%." In the "Virginal" category the plaintiff recovers no matter how much he was at fault, but his damages will be reduced proportionately by the percentage that the court or jury finds him to be at fault. For example, if plaintiff is found to be 50% negligent, he recovers 50% of his damages; if he is found to be 90% negligent, he recovers only 10% of his damages. In *NGA Li* v. *Yellow Cab Company,* the California Supreme Court on March 31, 1975 ruled that "in all actions for negligence resulting in injury to person or property, the contributory negligence of the person injured in person or property shall not bar recovery, but the damages awarded shall be diminished in proportion to the amount of fault attributable to that person."

The second category, "Minor-Major," requires the court or jury to compare first plaintiff's fault with defendant's fault so as to conclude that plaintiff's fault is "minor" and defendant's fault is "major," in which event plaintiff's recovery is reduced by the percentage which plaintiff's fault contributed to the injury or damage. For example, if plaintiff is found to be 10% at fault and defendant is found to be *more* than 10% at fault, then plaintiff may recover as much as 90% of his damages. But if plaintiff is found to be 50% at fault, there can be no recovery because plaintiff's fault is not "minor."

The third category, "Less than 50%," means that court or jury first determines whether plaintiff's fault was less than defendant's fault; and if so, then plaintiff can recover, although his recovery will be reduced proportionately by the percentage that the plaintiff was found to be at fault. For example, if plaintiff is found to be 50% at fault, plaintiff is barred from any recovery because his negligence is NOT "less than 50%." If plaintiff is 49% negligent and the defendant is 51% negligent, the plaintiff may recover 51% of damages.

The fourth category, "Less than 51%," requires the court or jury to determine whether or not plaintiff's fault is equal to or less than defendant's fault. If so, then plaintiff will recover, but his recovery will be reduced proportionately by the percentage he was found to be at fault. For example, if plaintiff is found to be 50% at fault, he may still recover 50% of damages; but if he is found to be 51% at fault, he recovers nothing!

These four categories of Comparative Negligence obviously will change from time to time as the states express their sovereign differences with respect to compensation for injured persons and damaged property. Recently in Oregon the trial court entered judgment finding the manufacturer and seller of a pickup truck 55% at fault, and the injured plaintiff driver 45% at fault, and so awarded the plaintiff a proportionately reduced amount of damages. The appellate court *reversed,* holding that a recovery of damages for injuries caused by a defective product is *not* reduced by plaintiff's *ordinary* negligence under the Oregon proportional fault statute (Sec. 18.470 Ore Rev Stat). The Oregon Supreme Court in *Sanford* v. *Chevrolet* (642 p[2d] 624) in 1982 *reversed* and held that the injured driver's *ordinary* negligence did constitute an offset against her products liability claim! On the other hand, in Minnesota in *Peterson* v. *Bendix Home*

Systems (318 NW 2d 50) in 1982 the jury determined that the plaintiff was 75% at fault while the defendant was but 25% at fault, and awarded damages for the difference between the value of the mobile home as warranted and the value as delivered, plus damages for installation and damages for physical harm to the mobile home, due to the formaldehyde fumes. But the Minnesota Supreme Court held that comparative fault was NOT applicable in a buyer's action against a manufacturer for damages to the product itself and incidental damages. Thus, a buyer's fault did NOT bar recovery for nonconsequential damages, and the plaintiff could recover for the full value of the mobile home, based upon the jury's finding that the home had no value after the tort was committed by the defendant.

WHY MARKET SHARE LIABILITY?

The question is posed not only for the purpose of reexamining briefly the *Sindell* case (pp. 26–27 herein) as a *defense ploy,* but also to see where the concept of Market Share Liability can lead American industry and the American consumer. The essence of Market Share Liability is that "We're all in this together, even though nobody knows whose product is at fault!" The theory is that manufacturers, distributors, and sellers of a specific class of products are jointly and severally liable to an injured person. The name of the game can be "concert of action," "alternative liability," or "enterprise liability"; the reasoning is that all these defendants can spread the risk of loss through insurance or by increasing prices of the products. But any insurance policy which could be purchased today to cover injuries which occurred decades ago would be so costly as to be of no practical value. The marketplace is not so perfect that manufacturers can pass these costs on to the consumers without any effect upon sales of their products. This is further complicated by the fact that many of the manufacturers may no longer produce the product involved, so that current users of other products must pay for the cost of such obsolete products. It does not seem equitable that the diabetic who requires insulin should pay a higher price if that life-preserving drug also happens to be manufactured by a DES defendant!

In *Gray* v. *United States,* (445 F Supp 337, 1978) the Federal Court for the Southern District of Texas entertained a claim by a daughter for injuries allegedly due to her mother's ingestion of DES during plaintiff's period of gestation. The claim was brought against one company, but that company soon established by deposition that no one could identify the product manufacturer. The court granted the company's motion to dismiss the complaint, holding simply that a plaintiff must prove that a defendant manufacturer actually made the particular product which caused the injury. Two years later in 1980 the *Sindell* case was decided, and it is interesting to raise the question of whether plaintiff *Gray* actually had her day in court! Today, under the Market Share Liability doctrine, *Gray* could choose the most attractive and financially well-off defendant or defendants and not worry about product identification! *Gray* would not even be concerned whether a defendant is insolvent or not in business any longer.

Asbestos is one product that apparently has not been given sanction under the "Market Share" liability concept. In *Related Asbestos Cases,* (543 F Supp 1152) the Federal Court for the Northern District of California in June 1982 observed that *Sindell* principles were not applicable because there were numerous factors that made it exceedingly difficult to ascertain an accurate division of liability along "Market Share" lines, to wit: the numerous varieties of asbestos fiber used in varying quantities by hundreds of manufacturers in their thousands of products; the numerous uses to which asbestos is put, creating difficulties in defining product and geographic markets; and the fact that exposures occurred over many years, during which time some defendants began or discontinued making asbestos products.

But DES is one product that always seems to fit the "Market Share" liability concept, particularly in California. In *Miles Laboratories* v. *Superior Court,* (184 Cal Rptr 98, 1982) the California District Court of Appeals held that even though a DES manufacturer marketed its DES exclusively for male use, it was still subject to joinder as a defendant with other defendants for injuries caused by ingestion of DES by a female! It should be noted that Miles marketed its DES product under the brand name Stilphostrol as a treatment for prostate cancer in males, and never for females as a miscarriage preventative. But the court point out that Miles knew or should have known that physicians often prescribed DES generically, and that pharmacists frequently filled prescriptions with any brand of DES they had in stock, and that Miles did nothing to prevent such use:

"The defendant gained a market share by acquiescence in the drug's use for an unintended purpose. Such conduct, if true, is certainly actionable under the logic and spirit of the *Sindell* decision."

A most unusual decision allowing a hospital to seek contribution from a DES manufacturer was *Helmrich* v. *Eli Lilly & Co.,* (455 NYS2d 460) decided November 9, 1982. Plaintiff sued the DES manufacturer and a hospital for injuries sustained as a result of her prenatal exposure to DES, and for the malpractice of the hospital in treating her. Her suit against the DES manufacturer was dismissed under the statute of limitations (451 NYS2d 1021). The hospital then asserted its answer—a cross-claim against the DES manufacturer for contribution. And the New York Appellate Division, 4th Dept., sustained the cross-claim since the plaintiff had sued each defendant for damages for the same injury. The court observed that the suit was not one for cancer and the other for aggravation of the cancer. Thus, potential liability for the same personal injury was the factor that permitted a claim for contribution under New York Law.

PUNITIVE DAMAGES

The question of whether punitive damages should be allowed in products liability litigation is a major one for manufacturers, their liability insurance carriers, the general public, and the courts. The punitive damages remedy, it is argued, performs an assortment of functions for both the individual and society by punishing monetarily the wrongdoing defendant, and deterring analogous conduct in the future. But before punitive damages are imposed, a flagrant disregard of the public safety by the wrongdoing defendant must be shown. A conscious or reckless indifference to the risk that a product may be excessively dangerous to the public merits condemnation in the guise of punitive damages, it is contended by advocates of punitive damages.

A review of cases involving manufacturing misconduct that courts have punished with punitive damages includes the following factors: (1) failure to warn of known dangers, both before and after sale, or use of totally inadequate warnings; (2) inadequate product testing (and little quality control) or no testing at all; (3) refusal to redesign or adopt feasible corrective measures, both before and after sale; (4) fraudulent conduct, such as deliberate concealment of substantial dangers in the product, or intentional deception concerning product safety; and (5) knowingly violating product safety standards.

The contrary view is that *civil* cases are not the proper vehicles for punishing what is described as criminal conduct, and that payment of monies to the victim will not deter future wrongdoing. The attractiveness of punitive damages to plaintiff is that it is open-ended in that the sky is the limit! But punitive damages should not be so grossly excessive "as to show by its very exorbitancy that it was actuated by passion," (*Nardelli* v. *Stamber,* 44 NY2d 500, 1978); nor should the amount be "big enough to be totally destructive" (*Faulk* v. *Aware Inc.,* 244 NYS2d 259, AD 1st, 1963).

The Uniform Product Liability Act (UPLA), recommended in 1979 by the U.S. Department of Commerce for use by the states, contains a remarkable compromise between those who urge the abolition of punitive damages in products liability and those who argue that "punitive damages serve an important function in deterring product sellers from reckless disregard for safety in the production, distribution, or sale of dangerous products" (Section 120). Subsection (A) requires "clear and convincing" evidence that there is justification for punitive damages; this standard is analogous to the criminal standard of "beyond a reasonable doubt." Plaintiff must show there was a conscious indifference on the part of the product seller to the safety of persons who might be injured by the product. Under subsection (B) the *trier* of fact, not the jury, determines the *amount* of punitive damages under the following guidelines: whether the wrongdoer was aware of the specific hazard and its seriousness; how profitable the misconduct was; how long the misconduct lasted, and if any concealment was involved; whether upon discovery of the misconduct the manufacturer moved quickly to discontinue the wrong, and whether the misconduct had been terminated; the financial condition of the defendant; other punishments imposed or likely to be imposed; and whether the harm suffered by the claimant was the result of the claimant's reckless conduct.

The state of California would readily allow recovery of punitive damages if there was any evidence of *Oppression, Fraud, or Malice.* See *Thompson* v. *Catalina,* (205 CAL 402, 271 P 198, 1928) and also *Silberg* v. *California Life Ins. Co.,* (11 Cal3d 452, 1974). Indeed, the state of California has codified the award of punitive damages in Section 3294 of the Civil Code, permitting punitive damages "for the sake of example and by way of punishing the defendant" where he is guilty of "oppression, fraud or malice." *Oppression* exists where one party dominates another so as to subject him to cruel and unjust hardships. An action for *Fraud* arises when "a material and knowingly false representation, made with intent to induce action, causes reasonable and detrimental reliance." Finally, "*(M)alice* in fact . . . denotes ill will on the part of the defendant. . ." In *Schroeder* v. *Auto Driveway Co.,* (11 Cal3d 908, 1974) California adopted a more liberal policy in favor of punitive damages by no longer requiring a personal ill will toward the plaintiff. Gross negligence is still not sufficient to evoke punitive damages. The defendant must know that his conduct is substantially certain to result in an injury, not that his conduct creates some risk of injury. Whether the injury resulted from a deliberate or nondeliberate act, *intent to injure* must be present. Therefore, courts must be careful to avoid simply characterizing conduct as "reckless" and then assuming that punitive damages are applicable. Although that term could be used to characterize conduct having a substantial certainty of causing injury, it could also characterize gross negligence; only the first characterization will justify punitive damages. Eight years later, in *Grimshaw* v. *Ford Motor Co.,* (174 Cal Rptr 348, 1981) the California Court of Appeals considered the problem of a Ford Pinto that burst into flames when rear-ended by another car on the highway. The driver suffered fatal burns, and the passenger, permanently disfiguring burns over the entire body. Suit was based upon the design defect, and the jury's verdict was for $125 million, including punitive damages. Later, the punitive damage portion was reduced to $3.5 million. The court held that the term "malice" as used in California Civil Code §3294 not only included an intent to harm, but encompassed conduct evincing callous and conscious disregard of public safety by those who manufacture and market mass-produced articles. Since in commerce-related torts, a manufacturer may find it more profitable to treat compensatory damages as a part of the cost of doing business, rather than to remedy the defect, deterrence of such "objectionable corporate policies" serves as one of the principal purposes of punitive damages, and such damages could be awarded in a products liability design defect action. Second, the court held that there was ample evidence of the defendant's malicious conduct and corporate responsibility, since, as a result of crash tests, the defendant, including its corporate officers, knew that the car's fuel tank and rear structure would expose consumers to serious injury or death in a low-speed collision. Furthermore, the defendant could have corrected the design defect at minimal cost, but deferred corrections after apparently engaging in a cost-benefit analysis.

However, the *majority* view in the United States believes that punitive damages impose an inappropriate burden on the *civil* justice system, and are a windfall to the plaintiff because such awards are for the purpose of sanction and not for the purpose of compensation. In *International Brotherhood of Electrical Workers* v. *du Pont,* (99 S Ct 2121, 2125, 1979) the U.S. Supreme Court described punitive damages as "simply not compensation for injury . . . they are private fines levied by civil juries to punish reprehensible conduct and to deter its future occurrence." Product safety is not necessarily promoted by imposing punitive damages upon the errant product manufacturer or seller. A jury could achieve the same result by simply increasing the amount of compensatory damages if an excessive award or judgment were certain to result in a safer product! Indeed, class actions and multiple claims against a product manufacturer can produce an "overkill," especially if multiple punitive damage claims are recognized in such civil cases. In *Roginsky* v. *Richardson-Merrell, Inc.,* (378 F2d 832, CA 2, 1967) the total punitive damages claimed exceeded the defendant's net worth! Even though a civil suit is not the best vehicle for deterring misconduct, punitive damages have been justified where the product defect was *deliberately* created for an *evil motive* or for a *desire to injure* for the sake of injuring. Such a situation simply does not arise in the typical products liability situation, no matter how crass and commercially callous a product seller is! It is unreasonable to believe that a product manufacturer would want to injure hundreds or thousands of customers; if there was a certainty of widespread injury known to the manufacturer, it is more likely that the product would be withdrawn from the market in order to avoid extensive compensatory damages. Punitive damages in civil law can only be based upon intentional infliction of injury.

The state of New York has refused to allow punitive damages in civil suits; in *Rosenfeld* v. *Isaacs,* (NYLJ December 11, 1980, p. 11 col. 5) the New York Appellate Division ruled that plaintiff's arguments for recovery of punitive damages "however appealing in logic and justice must be directed to the (State) Legislature," for the state "focused on monetary recovery for those who suffered from the tortfeasor's conduct, and not on the punishment of the miscreant"; also *Robert* v. *Ford Motor Co.,* (424 NYS^{2nd} 747, AD3, 1980). However, the legislature of New York, effective September 1, 1982, has authorized punitive damages in wrongful *death* cases (SB 8620 and AB 10924). The theory is that by permitting punitive damages where defendant's conduct has been outrageous, wrongdoing will be deterred, particularly in aviation cases. Punitive damages are supposed to be determined on the basis of the degree of the defendant's culpability and his ability to pay. The wealth of a defendant is admissible evidence in determining the amount of punitive damages to be awarded. At common law, punitive damages were always available in tort cases, but recoveries for wrongful death did not exist until the middle of the nineteenth century, when they were allowed by statute. The rule, fallacious or not, was based upon the "felony-merger" doctrine which had provided that when death was caused by a wrongful act it was a felony. The tort merged into the felony, the felon was put to death, and his property was forfeited to the Crown, so that nothing remained of the felon or his property on which to base a civil action. Based on this historical record, the English courts held that there was no right of action for wrongful death at common law. The felony-merger doctrine never existed in the United States. Nevertheless, American courts followed the English rule, and it was uniformly established in the United States that there was no right of action for wrongful death. In 1846, Lord Campbell's Act was enacted in Parliament, creating the first statutory right to sue for wrongful death, and state legislatures in the United States followed soon thereafter, by and large using Lord Campbell's Act as their model. The death law of most states today provides a right to the decedent's wife, husband, or next of kin to recover their pecuniary loss in the case of death. It was commonly stated that there having been no right to recover for wrongful death at common law, the new right to recover was purely *statutory,* and the elements of the recovery would be limited to the terms of the statute. On that basis there began to develop the principle that punitive damages would not be permitted in death cases, because the legislature had not spelled them out. The fact that the distinction between allowing punitive damages in personal injury cases and denying them in death cases was completely irrational did not occur to the courts. The result is that as of 1982 about half of the states in the United States deny punitive damages in death cases!

In New York, perhaps in anticipation of the September 1, 1982 statute authorizing punitive damages in death cases, the New York Court of Appeals on June 18, 1982 in *Sharapata* v. *Town of Islip* declared that punitive damages may not be assessed against the state or its political subdivisions. Here the minor plaintiff was injured while playing on a defective slide at the public park. Specifically, Section 8 of the Court of Claims Act does not authorize punitive or exemplary damages in its statutory waiver of sovereign immunity.

Admittedly, in summary, punitive damages are a windfall to the winning plaintiff because they are awarded for the purpose of sanction and not for the purpose of compensation. The imposition of punishment, and deterrence for wrongful conduct are properly the concerns of CRIMINAL, not civil law. Furthermore, there are no rules for prescribing the correct amount of punitive damages—indeed in a 1982 *University of Chicago Law Review* article, Professor Owen observed that "the increasing number and size of such awards may fairly raise concern for the future stability of American industry." Punitive damages, being criminal in origin, are not covered by insurance in most states unless specificallly included in the policy. Perhaps 20 states nevertheless have found coverage for punitive damages if assessed *directly* against the insured. A majority of states have not determined whether there can be insurance coverage for punitive damages assessed directly against the insured. At least five states (Louisiana, Massachusetts, Nebraska, New Hampshire, and Washington) do not permit punitive damages. See generally, Redden, *Punitive Damages,* Sc 7.6B (1980).

Part IV
Settlement Techniques and Alternatives to Litigation

An understanding of Settlement Techniques should begin with an attempt to define what it is that the techniques are designed to accomplish. Courts have isolated three component parts of a sustainable settlement, to wit: (1) Controversy, (2) Capacity, and (3) Compromise. Obviously, the Controversy preceded, but was the Controversy a valid one in the sense that the claim may have been time-barred, or was it frivolous and subject to dismissal? The point is that a settlement can be set aside on the basis of a lack of controversy. Then the parties consummating the settlement must have the Capacity legally to do so; an infant generally lacks the capacity to settle a claim without the approval of a court. Does a particular corporate officer have the authority to settle the case? The third element of Compromise is simply that there must be some evidence of a genuine concession on both sides; a settlement can be set aside if it is too one-sided. Even if the settlement embraces Controversy, Capacity, and Compromise, it may not be immune to attack, particularly upon the grounds of Fraud or Mutual Mistake.

The problems of Settlement can be very complex: *D'Ambrosio* v. *City of New York,* decided by the New York Appellate Division, 1st Dept., on January 29, 1981 is an example. Plaintiff was hurt by a metal disk sticking out of city sidewalk and sued the city of New York, which impleaded the owner of the property. Plaintiff did not amend his complaint to assert a claim against the owner. Plaintiff nevertheless settled with the owner for $22,500: plaintiff promising to repay the owner for any money that the owner had to pay the city. Plaintiff later received a jury verdict in the amount of $100,000 against the city, finding the city 65 percent at fault and the owner 35 percent at fault. Thus, the city had to pay the plaintiff the sum of $65,000, which amount the city then sought to collect from the owner—and which amount the owner would collect back from the plaintiff under the hold harmless agreement. Thus, plaintiff was relegated to the original settlement of $22,500 *plus* the recovery of $65,000 from the city of New York.

Still another example of the complexity of a settlement is seen in *Reynolds* v. *Morka Enterprises, Inc.,* decided by the New York Appellate Division, 3rd Dept., on August 7, 1981 (442 NY 2nd 664). P was an infant scalded by grease when a deep fryer fell at her family's concession stand in a park. The stand was operated by O, a corporation owned by her family. Her brother B was in charge of the stand at the time. The fryer was manufactured by M and bought from R. P sued O, M, and R. They cross-claimed among themselves and M impleaded B for contribution. A settlement was drawn up among P, O, and B, the family group, under which—as the settlement was approved by the court (CPLR 1207)—O paid $100,000 and agreed to pay up to $50,000 more, the gist of the agreement being that O would guarantee that P received at least $150,000 altogether. The action was to continue against M and R, and if it should produce less than $50,000 as M and R's share of P's damages, O would make up the difference. Should it reach or pass $50,000, O would not have to pay any more than the $100,000 it already paid. This arrangement is a form of a "Mary Carter Agreement," and so the settlement order dropped O and B defendants. M and R appealed from this settlement: they contended that under the terms of the settlement, O, in effect, retained a contribution right because O's total liability depended on how M and R fared in the action. The court rejected this reasoning, stating that the principal benefit that Section 15–108 of the New York General Obligation Law gives to nonsettling tortfeasors as a kind of "quid pro quo" for losing contribution rights against the settling ones is that the damages verdict in the action will be reduced by either the amount of the settlement, or the settling tortfeasors' share of the damages as found by the jury, whichever is the higher. In measuring the first entry in this comparison, the court stressed that M and R will have the benefit of a full $150,000 deduction, should the $150,000 turn out to be more than O and B's jury-found share of the verdict. Hence, under no circumstances will M and R lose their rights under Section 15–108 as a result of this settlement. Should the verdict be $200,000, for example, with M and R between them found responsible for 20 percent, and O and B responsible for 80 percent, $160,000 will be deducted, and M and R will face only a $40,000 judgment, their precise share. Should the M and R share be 50 percent, and the O and B share the same, M and R will have the benefit of a deduction of $150,000, the settlement figure (which in that event would be higher than the $100,000 jury-found share of O and B, and hence, be the deductible item under Section 15–108). To the extent that this arithmetic brings P less than $50,000 from M and R, O will have to make up the difference. The arrangement among P, O, and B is in any event no skin off the collective noses of M and R, and no violation of Section 15–108.

An examination of but a few recent cases illustrates indeed how complex settlements may be: in *Sochanski* v. *Sears Roebuck & Co.,* the Third U.S. Circuit Court on September 21, 1982, held that a pro rata agreement, releasing from liability the manufacturer of a defective tire, also released the secondary liability of a retailer that sold a cart on which the tire was mounted. A pneumatic tire explosion severely injured the plaintiff while he was repairing the tire. He sued both the tire manufacturer and the retailer. When he settled with the tire manufacturer, the retailer argued that it was also released, and the court agreed! In *Marchello* v. *Lenox Hill Hospital,* the New York Supreme Court, Bronx County, on September 21, 1982, granted plaintiff permission to seek rescission of a settlement of a prior action based upon an alleged mistake in fact, to wit: the doctors had misled all of the parties as to the seriousness of the injuries. In *McCarroll* v. *Kringstein,* New York Supreme Court, New York County, November 3, 1982, the plaintiff who gave his attorney "actual authority to settle" a dental malpractice case, cannot now repudiate the settlement based upon his claim that he did not "realize the legal import" of his authorization. And in *Condo* v. *Mulcahy,* New York Appellate Division, 2nd Dept., September 20, 1982, plaintiffs in a personal injury action cannot repudiate settlement agreements once they have given defendants general releases and stipulations of discontinuance but before defendants have made actual payment to the plaintiffs.

"MARY CARTER" AGREEMENTS

The name "Mary Carter Agreement," a type of settlement agreement, is taken from *Booth* v. *Mary Carter Paint Co.,* (202 So2d 8, Florida District Court of Appeals, 2nd District, 1967). Basically, it is an agreement between the plaintiff and one or more of the defendants who agree to settle the claim in exchange for a lesser amount, or for an interest in the outcome of the litigation; usually the settling defendant or defendants become "friends" of the plaintiff, and work against non-settling defendants. Generally, full exposure of the secret terms of the "Mary Carter Agreement" is required at trial by the court and for the benefit of the jury. Or course, inherent in the very agreement is that it will be kept *secret* from other defendants who have not settled! The settling defendant or defendants also agree to remain as a party or parties in the lawsuit, but on the side of the plaintiff, unbeknown to the other defendants. Plaintiff agrees to exercise diligence and good faith in prosecuting the action against the nonsettling defendants. Thus, in essence the "Mary Carter Agreement" is not a settlement or release because the plaintiff does not want to risk releasing all tortfeasors by releasing one tortfeasor. In *Taylor* v. *DiRico,* (124 Ariz 513, 606 P2d 3, 1980) the Arizona court warned: "Such agreeements, thus create situations ripe with temptation to act dishonestly and collusively. The courts must carefully monitor the proceedings to ensure that the parties honestly and vigorously contest the issues as they would have, but for the agreement." A "Mary Carter Agreement" may be very important to a plaintiff for it provides him with "front money" to proceed with renewed vigor against the nonsettling defendants!

The "Mary Carter Agreement" usually contains the following ingredients: (a) secrecy; (b) a contingent or guaranteed settlement amount with some pay-back feature that may or may not be enforced; and (c) a requirement that the settling defendant participate in the litigation in a manner materially inconsistent with its position before the settlement was effected. Many courts like in Nevada (*Lum* v. *Stinnett,* 87 Nev 402, 1971) and Wisconsin (*Trampe* v. *Wisconsin Telephone Co.,* 252 NW^{2d} 675) have voided such agreements as against public policy. But other courts have invalidated only the secrecy provisions and allowed the agreements to be enforced. Michigan, as illustrated by *Putney* v. *Haskins,* Michigan Supreme Court, September 1982, has declared that execution of the "Mary Carter Agreement" automatically disposes of all claims against all other defendants! Thus, the very purpose of the "Mary Carter Agreement" has been lost by the Michigan decision!

"STRUCTURED SETTLEMENTS"

"Structured settlements" is a fancy term coined by eager advocates for the plaintiff and for the defense in an effort to make the big settlement more palatable by reducing the down payment. Basically, it is argued that in it there is a long-term security to the claimant, tax-free benefits to both the plaintiff and the defendant, and a greater total settlement. There is even a Model Act for Periodic Payment of Judgments, promoted to provide for periodic payment of *all* court-awarded damages. It is estimated that in 1980 more than one-half billion dollars was paid by casualty insurance companies in "structured settlements." "Structured settlements" take advantage of both annuity contracts with life insurance companies and trust agreements based on government securities. Experience indicates that it is a rare client who does not appreciate the prospect of a tax-free lifetime income without the worry of investment management, in addition to a small lump sum payout at the time of settlement. Not only is this concept attractive to most claimants but it recreates the manner in which future income would have been received had the injury or death not occurred. A person or family is accustomed to receiving income on a periodic basis so as to manage living and household expenses, children's education, and the like. The extra burdens of managing and doling out the income annually are avoided by reason of the "structured settlement." Specifically, the *tax* advantage is clear, as set forth in *"Tax-Free Periodic Payment for Life,"* Revenue 79–220 of the Internal Revenue Service (July 23, 1979) which states:

> "Income Exclusions—Disability benefits—compensation for injuries or sickness—tort damages for personal injuries or sickness. Insurance company purchased and retained exclusive ownership in a single premium annuity contract to fund monthly payments stipulated in settlement of a damage suit. The recipient may exclude the full amount of the payments from gross income under Section 104(a)(2) of the Code rather than the discounted present value. Payments made to the estate after the recipient's death are also fully excludable."

The distinct feature of Management-Free Income, i.e., the management of the funds and the responsibility to provide guaranteed necessary income from present funds, is that it falls upon appropriate shoulders, i.e., the insurer, and not upon the recipient. The insurance company is well equipped to manage and invest its assets to provide the payout over the specified period. Usually this is done through the purchase of an annuity from a reliable life insurance company at the best rate available. An advantage to having a portion of the settlement paid out on an annuity basis is that the funds are not available to be squandered or dissipated, and such funds will stand in place of the lost future annual income of the injured party or the decedent. Trusts secured by U.S. government securities can also be designed to make payments for a given period of time.

It should also be noted that a casualty insurance company can provide a larger future payout with a smaller percent value lump sum. Hence, the benefit to the corporate defendant or its insurer is significant. The annuity portion of the "structured settlement" may reduce substantially the cost of achieving financial security and independence for the injured party or the survivors of the decedent. These savings, plus the nontaxability of future payments, can help close the otherwise unresolvable gap between plaintiff's demand and the insurance company offer. For example, in *Younger* v. *Stanford University Hospital,* a "structured settlement" achieved in October 1982 in San Jose, California, brought a brain-damaged infant $1.2 million plus a fund of $8.1 million which could pay out more than $122 million over the next 76 years! The child was born in April 1980. The three annuities provide the wherewithal for the total settlement at a lower present day cost.

The first known use of "Structured Settlement" occurred in 1958 in *M & P Stores* v. *Taylor,* decided by the Oklahoma Supreme Court. The jury had returned a verdict of $36,000, but added the following words to its verdict: "To be paid at $150 per month for 20 years." Neither side objected to this form of the verdict, and so the trial court accepted the verdict and discharged the jury. But the trial judge in entering the judgment struck out the extra words as surplusage. On appeal, the highest Oklahoma court reinstated the verdict as originally rendered by the jury: "The verdict should not have been rendered in this form, and should not have been received in this form. However, it was received and neither party now contends that the verdict was void, and under those circumstances this court will not of its own volition invalidate it."

"Structured settlements" are simply assessments of present worth of future payments; indeed, the cost to the defendant and/or its insurance carrier may be phenomenally small. For a $725,000 present cost, the plaintiff can receive $26 million over a projected life span. Should the claimant die at an age earlier than contemplated, the cost of the "structured settlement" would be considerably reduced. Lump sum settlements just cannot be bought as cheaply.

IRS Ruling 79–220 provides that if the defendant or its insurance carrier promises to pay a series of payments to the injured party and retains exclusive control over the annuity contract, the claimant never has constructive receipt or economic benefit of the lump sum annuity consideration, and therefore the investment gain is NOT taxable income to the claimant or to his estate. Section 104(a)(2) of the Internal Revenue Code enables a claimant to exclude from gross income the amount of any damages received as a result of bodily injury or property damages or economic loss.

The *Model Act for Periodic Payment of Judgments* is a piece of proposed state legislation designed "(1) to alleviate some of the practical problems incident to unpredictability of large future losses and to facilitate more accurate awards of damages for actual losses; (2) to pay damages as the trier of fact finds the losses will accrue; and (3) to assure that payments of damages more nearly serve the purposes for which they are awarded." But the bill has been bitterly opposed by plaintiffs' attorneys for many reasons, including the mandatory effect of the act if *one* party to the lawsuit has made "an effective election" to come under it.

ARBITRATION

The settling of disputes without legal action is at the core of arbitration, but the legal process is really not far away, not only in the procedure for arbitration but also in enforcement of the particular arbitration award. In an April 7, 1976 speech before the National Conference on the Causes of Popular Dissatisfaction with the Administration of Justice, the Chief Justice of the United States, Warren E. Burger noted: "Ways must be found to resolve minor disputes fairly and more swiftly than any present judicial mechanism makes possible; arbitration should be used more widely; ways must be found to compensate people for injuries resulting from the negligence of hospitals and doctors, without causing such severe distortions in the cost of medical and hospital care; and faster and less expensive ways must be found to compensate people for other people's negligence."

Consumers, government, and the business community have been concerned about the adequacy of existing legal procedures for the resolution of consumer grievances. The idea that arbitration might provide an excellent means of dealing with such disputes has been recognized by a number of business organizations which have adopted *voluntary arbitration programs,* and by the courts, which, in cooperation with the Federal Trade Commission, have regularly included arbitration provisions in consumer action consent decrees. *The Magnuson-Moss Warranty Act,* (15 USC 2301) which, since January 1975 has provided mandatory standards for consumer warranties, encourages fair and expeditious consumer complaint handling under informal dispute settlement procedures which meet minimum FTC requirements.

It has been suggested that *toxic hazard* cases can be handled by arbitration because scientists and businessmen better understand safety standards, and lawyers are often uncomfortable with relevant technology. These technological experts prefer to be not witnesses, but decision-makers, because of their expertise. The negotiating process, the normal technique used by our society for resolving controversies, can best be understood as a means through which participants attempt to erode the expectations of their adversaries. Voluntary dispute settlement systems such as mediation and arbitration do not seek to erode expectations and have proved effective because they strengthen and supplement the parties' ability to negotiate complex controversies. A mediator can be particularly helpful by bringing a unique technical expertise to bear upon such a problem, by providing innovative formulas for mutual compromises, and by explaining how each party can make minimum concessions for maximum gains. A mediator can facilitate a settlement by helping a negotiator "sell" a settlement to his particular constituency. In short, a mediator can contribute substantively and procedurally, by strengthening the negotiators' ability to settle. Arbitration is straightforward in its approach to dispute settlement: the representatives of the parties submit their facts and arguments to the arbitrators through witnesses or documents in whatever fashion seems best calculated to present the issue. The arbitrator manages the procedure and may ask for more information or for clarification. When both parties have had a fair opportunity to present their cases, the hearing is declared closed by the arbitrator, who must render a decision within 30 days, under American Arbitration Association rules. The arbitrator's award decides the dispute between the parties. The award does not establish general principles of law, and the arbitrator does not advise the parties as to other aspects of their relationship or business practices. The award will simply order one party to pay a certain sum or will deny a certain claim. Since the typical award does not establish precedents, the impact of the arbitration process is restricted to the parties involved. Their controversy is resolved. Industry practices may continue unchanged. This is viewed as an advantage by American businessmen who do not favor having their business decisions predetermined by the courts. Arbitration gives businessmen an opportunity to construct a self-contained, contractual system of dispute resolution. Business controversies can be channeled into private, non-precedent-making forums, avoiding the risks as well as the costs and delays that are always present in the courts. Sophisticated business lawyers take full advantage of this option; at any one time, millions of outstanding commercial contracts provide for arbitration under the rules of the American Arbitration Association.

Arbitration awards are generally reviewable by courts of law. Under Section 12 of the Uniform Arbitration Act, an award may be vacated by a court upon application of a party where "(1) the award was procured by corruption, fraud or other undue means; (2) there was evident partiality by an arbitrator appointed as a neutral, or corruption in any of the arbitrators, or misconduct prejudicing the rights of any party; (3) the arbitrators exceeded their powers; (4) the arbitrators refused to postpone the hearing upon sufficient cause being shown therefore or refused to hear evidence material to the controversy or otherwise conducted the hearing contrary to the provisions of Section 5 as to prejudice substantially the rights of a party; *or* (5) there was no arbitration agreement and the issue was not adversely determined in proceedings under Section 2 and the party did not participate in the arbitration without raising the objection." An award may be modified or corrected under Section 13 "(a) upon application made within 90 days after delivery of a copy of the award to the applicant . . . (in which event) the court shall modify or correct the award where (1) there was an evident miscalculation of figures or an evident mistake in the description of any person, thing or property referred to in the award; (2) the arbitrators have awarded upon a matter not submitted to them and the award may be corrected without affecting the merits of the decision upon the issues submitted; or (3) the award is imperfect in a matter of form, not affecting the merits of the controversy." But it should be noted that courts only reluctantly overturn or vacate or modify or correct arbitrators' awards. Courts simply do not want to vie with arbitration other than to do justice.

AUTOMATIC ACCIDENT COMPENSATION

In view of the rash of expensive litigation in the American products liability field, has the time come for an Automatic Accident Compensation law, perhaps modeled upon the Accident Compensation Act of New Zealand? Is such an act a viable proposition for modern corporations in modern society? Should not an expected loss have some degree of certainty and predictability for the corporation, for the insurance carrier, and for the injured consumer? Let us examine briefly what New Zealand has done to provide *administrative* remedies for injury, damage, and loss.

In the first place, New Zealand, since April 1, 1974, abolished the right to bring civil proceedings for damages arising out of personal injury or death; actions for loss of services and for loss of consortium are also abolished. (Non–New Zealand plaintiffs, however, can continue to sue New Zealand manufacturers in New Zealand courts!) Payments by the Accident Compensation Commission to injured persons are financed by taxation in the form of levies imposed on various sections of the community. Corporate responsibility for the injured consumer and the latter's comprehensive entitlement to care, treatment, rehabilitation, and compensation are inherent in the act, whose three purposes are the promotion of product safety, the rehabilitation of the injured consumer, and the prompt and realistic compensation of the injured consumer. But the act does NOT embrace sickness or disease which is the consequence of a self-inflicted injury. Otherwise, payment is automatic, and is based upon the fact of injury, regardless of fault. Personal injury includes physical, mental, medical, surgical, dental, or first aid misadventure; pregnancy, nervous shock, and mental strain are encompassed within the meaning of "bodily harm," and occupational disease is also covered. Generally, lump sums are payable, but workers may receive periodic payments; even funeral and transportation expenses are covered, but property damage is excluded. Benefits under the New Zealand act include (1) earnings-related compensation; (2) reasonable cost of medical and dental treatment; (3) reasonable cost of transportation to and from hospital and doctors; (4) reasonable cost of meals and accommodations to receive treatment; (5) damages for loss of clothing, spectacles, and other personal property; (6) reasonable cost of necessary continuous personal attention following injury; and (7) actual and reasonable expenses directly caused by the accident.

The operation of the New Zealand accident compensation program is handled by district liaison offices whose award determination is subject to the right of appeal, first to the Commission and then to the Appeal Authority; there is even a permissive right of appeal on questions of law to the New Zealand Supreme Court. Issues of entitlement, and not issues of tortious law, mostly occupy the attention of the judiciary in New Zealand today—a relief from the great burden of tort cases in the past.

Could a modern American corporation afford to operate a similar automatic accident compensation program for the benefit of its customers or consumers? The answer is "yes," particularly where the corporation faces the reality of the consumer who is ready to sue "at the drop of a hat" for costly sums of money. In September 1982 five airlines and the Aerospace Industries Association came up with a proposal for Automatic Accident Compensation that they hoped Congress would adopt. The Air Travelers Protection Act would provide a federal cause of action for all domestic plane crashes in which five or more persons are killed or injured, would establish a Compensation Pool funded by the aviation industry, and would do away with the plaintiff lawyers' contingent fee system. The act would exclude commuter flights or planes with 30 or fewer seats, private flights, military air transportation, and foreign air commerce, except when these flights are involved in an accident with a domestic airline: "The main objective of the act is to provide assurance of a prompt award to victims on a no-fault basis, and to protect the airlines and manufacturers from financial disaster." The courts would determine the fee for plaintiff's lawyer; the act also would eliminate punitive damages. H.R. 1027 was introduced in December 1981, but apparently has not yet received attention by the Congress.

"MINI-TRIALS" AND ALTERNATIVE DISPUTE RESOLUTION METHODS

In an effort to keep consumer disputes within the framework of the court system, recently efforts have been made to streamline court procedures that are frequently cumbersome. One of these efforts is "mini-trials" which allegedly bring business executives back into the dispute-resolution process. "Mini-trials" guarantee that management decision-makers are informed adequately about the dispute. "Mini-trials" give the business executive the psychological satisfaction of going through the gladiator phase of litigation and understanding what is likely to occur at a future court trial, if any. "Mini-trials" are also conducive to settlements. Some of the key elements of a "mini-trial" are: (1) top-level executives with decision-making authority participate on each side; (2) a "neutral advisor," perhaps a retired judge, law professor, or practicing attorney directs the questions and renders a nonbinding decision only if the parties do not settle on their own; and (3) lawyers for the parties negotiate an agreement on how the "mini-trial will proceed. The decision-making executives from both sides attend all sessions, and these executives then meet alone for the purpose of working out a resolution of the dispute. Any court proceedings are suspended by stipulation during the "mini-trial," and the parties agree that if no settlement is achieved, neither party will use in the court action any admissions or other concessions made by either party at the "mini-trial."

"Mini-trials" are especially useful after initial discovery when substantial legal fees and costly executive hours are forecast for the trial. "Mini-trials" thus can reduce management time, legal fees, and hasten the resolution of the dispute. California's "rent-a-judge" statutory procedure can also be employed: the disputing parties hire a retired judge and agree upon procedural rules; the judge's decision is as binding as a jury verdict or court judgment; the decision also may be appealed subsequently through normal appellate court channels. The advantages of this approach are flexibility and speed as well as economy.

"Mini-trials" and Alternate Dispute Resolution Methods would find Class Actions very difficult to handle. In the class suit the plaintiff asserts a claim on his own behalf and on behalf of other persons who have similar claims for damages or equitable or declaratory relief. Rule 23 of the Federal Rules of Civil Procedure, which governs prerequisites and procedure for conduct of class actions, would simply not be conducive to "mini-trials," for no hearing chamber could accommodate at one sitting all the corporate and business executives who would want to participate.

Probably the first "mini-trial" occurred in 1978 between Telecredit and the Cleveland-based conglomerate, TRW Inc. The plaintiff, Telecredit, charged that TRW had infringed upon its patents. Both sides agreed to a two-day secret hearing in which each side presented its case before a neutral adviser. The presentations were made by lawyers directly to the corporate executives involved. Thirty minutes were allotted for each argument, and then the top corporate officers worked out a compromise at an estimated savings of at least $1 million in legal fees! In 1982, TRW Inc. used the same approach in a $15 million suit filed by Automatic Radio; again the corporate parties were able to work out their differences without incurring huge legal fees.

Alternate Dispute Resolution Methods have been given great incentive by the nonprofit Center for Public Resources in New York City—which firm was the recipient in 1982 of a two-year grant of $285,000 from the Aetna Life & Casualty Foundation. A distinguished Judicial Panel serves private litigants, not only as fact-finders, but as mediators and even as consultants. Panel members are paid by the disputants who also must remit an administrative fee to the center.

Part V
Other Areas of Products Liability Significance

PRODUCTS LIABILITY EXTENSIONS OF WORKMAN'S COMPENSATION

Once workman's compensation is found applicable to an employee who is injured in the course of employment, benefits provided under the state statute are generally the *exclusive* remedy available to the injured employee against the employer. In recent years, however, employees have successfully bypassed the exclusive remedy bar by bringing tort claims against the employer and other parties on these theories, to wit: (1) the employer committed an *Intentional Wrong,* or (2) the employer occupies a *Dual Capacity* vis-a-vis the employee. Still another step that has been taken by the injured worker today is suit directly against the manufacturer of the product which allegedly caused the injury, or even suit against a supervisory employee, including a corporate officer, director, or stockholder, but only when that person was serving in a corporate employee capacity. (At least 16 states permit such circumvention of the workman's compensation law; see *Vittum* v. *New Hampshire Insurance Co.,* (369 A2d 184, 1977).

1. Dual Capacity. Under this doctrine, an employer normally shielded from tort liability by the exclusive remedy principle may become liable in tort to his own employee if he occupies, in addition to his capacity as employer, a *second capacity* that confers on him obligations independent of those imposed on him as an employer. The situation arises where an employer is also the manufacturer of a product used on the job site, e.g., the employee suffered personal injuries when the scaffolding on which he was working collapsed. In *Douglas* v. *Gallo,* (137 Cal Rptr 797, 1977) the California court held that plaintiffs may sue their employer based upon manufacturer's liability because the product had been manufactured by the employer for sale to the public rather than for the sole use of the employer in his business. The California court pointed out that employer who enjoys the cloak of immunity provided by workman's compensation law, does, upon engaging in the *dual capacity* of manufacturer of product for sale to the public, assume all the duties and liabilities of such manufacturer, and should be held to the standard of care of manufacturers for injuries sustained by employees in their use of such products: When an employee is hired, he assumes all hazards and risks of employment which naturally flow from that employment, but does not as employee give up rights as user against manufacturer. The California court also recognized that the "Worker's Compensation Act was adopted long before product liability became generally recognized by law. . . . We do not assume that the legislature in adopting the statute had an intent to withhold from an employee the protection the manufacturer's liability doctrine now requires. In electing to manufacture elevator scaffolding for the public, rather than obtaining it from a third party manufacturing firm, the defendant should be held to the standard of manufacturers generally."

In *Bell* v. *Industrial Van Gas, Inc.,* (30 Cal3d 268 1981) the plaintiff salesman was severely injured when a propane gas truck he was driving exploded as he was delivering flammable gas to a customer. After collecting worker's compensation benefits he brought a strict liability action against his employer, alleging that he was injured as a result of the dangerously defective condition of various items of equipment manufactured by his employer and used in making the propane delivery. The trial court dismissed the suit on the exclusivity of worker's compensation in California. But the California Supreme Court *reversed* because an employer is strictly liable in tort to an employee injured in the course of his employment as a result of defective products or defective equipment marketed by the employer to the public. Thus, the employer was involved in a "dual capacity" and can be sued as a products supplier by the employee. According to the court, an individual or a business entity can act in two or more different capacities, either simultaneously or sequentially, giving rise in law to distinct sets of obligations: "A coincidental employment relationship will not shield an employer from a common liability where the concurrent cause of the injury is attributable to the employer's separate and distinct relationship to the employee and which invokes a different set of obligations than the employer's duties to its employees."

The Dual Capacity doctrine was first recognized in California in 1952 in the landmark case of *Duprey* v. *Shane,* (39 Cal2d 781) where a nurse, injured in a work-related accident, was subsequently treated for the injury, albeit negligently, by her employer-chiropractor. The court upheld a recovery against the employer for malpractice, finding that the defendant, in treating the employee, was acting as an attending doctor rather than as an employer. The court noted: "It is true that the law is opposed to the creation of a dual personality, where to do so is unrealistic and purely legalistic. But where as here it is perfectly apparent that the person involved . . . bore towards his employee two relationships—that of an employer and that of a doctor—there should be no hesitancy in recognizing this fact as a fact."

But in Section 3602 of the California Labor Code, enacted September 13, 1982, California rejected the Dual Capacity doctrine: "The fact that either the employee or the employer also occupied another or dual capacity prior to, or at the time of, the employee's industrial injury shall not permit the employee or his or her dependants to bring an action at law for damages against the employer."

The U.S. Fifth Circuit Court of Appeals also rejected the Dual Capacity doctrine in a case based upon Louisiana law, *Darville* v. *Texaco, Inc.,* (674 F2d 446, 1982). And it would appear that at least 22 states have declined to adopt the Dual Capacity theory. The Massachusetts Supreme Judicial Court in *Longever* v. *Revere Copper & Brass, Inc.,* (408 NE2d 857) in 1980 declared:

> "Among the common law duties placed on an employer was the responsibility to provide a safe place to work as well as safe appliances, tools, and equipment for work. . . Nothing in the com-

pensation act altered the employer's duty to provide safe tools or machinery at work. . . . We think the duties of an employer who also manufactures equipment used in his business (and perhaps elsewhere) are not separate and distinct duties from the general obligations of employers."

In Michigan, in *Handley* v. *Wyandotte Chemical Corp.,* (325 NW 2d 447) in 1982, an employee was injured while lubricating a conveyor in an electrical generating plant. The entire plant, including the conveyor, had been constructed by the employer. In holding that the employer did *not* become liable under the Dual Capacity doctrine, the Michigan appellate court focused on the requirement that the employer's second capacity (as manufacturer) generates obligations independent of those imposed by its primary function, as employer. Therefore, no matter how different an employer's second function is from its primary function, no liability will arise when the action is, in reality, based upon the employer-employee relationship.

The state of New York also rejected the Dual Capacity doctrine in *Billy* v. *Consolidated Machine Tool Corp.,* (51 NY3d 152, 412 NE2d 934, 1980): "We would be seriously undermining the salutary social purposes underlying the existing workers' compensation scheme if we were to permit common law recovery outside of that scheme on the basis of such illusory distinctions." (p. 196). Similarly, the state of Delaware in *Kofron* v. *Amoco Chemicals Corp.,* (#80–139) and *Nutt* v. *du Pont,* (#80–288), both decided by the Delaware Supreme Court on January 6, 1982, ruled that employees were limited to worker's compensation as the only remedy for exposure to asbestos, despite their argument that defendants were guilty of gross negligence and intentional deceit. The court rejected the employees' argument that the scope of the workers' compensation act covered only accidental or negligent injury or death; indeed the act covered also nonnegligent injury or death.

2. Intentional Wrong. Many state workman's compensation statutes explicitly or by implication provide that if an *intentional* injury is inflicted upon an employee by his employer, the statute will not bar the injured employee from seeking another remedy at common law. The Ohio Supreme Court in *Blankenship* v. *Cincinnati Milacros*

Chemicals, Inc., (#81–402, filed March 3, 1982) permitted suit against the employer by employees who sustained injuries within the scope of their employment by exposure to noxious chemicals. Plaintiffs alleged that, although the employer knew of the employees' exposure to the poisonous chemical, it "failed to correct said conditions that existed, and failed to report said conditions to the various state and federal agencies to which they were required to report by law." The court refused to dismiss the complaint and concluded that the Ohio Constitution did not extend immunity to employers for intentionally tortious conduct. The Ohio Constitution provided:

> "For the purpose of providing compensation to workmen and their dependants, for death, injuries or occupational disease, occasioned in the course of such workmen's employment, laws may be passed establishing a state fund to be created by compulsory contributions thereto by employers, and administered by the state, determining the terms and conditions upon which payment shall be made therefrom. Such compensation shall be in lieu of all other rights to compensation or damages, for such death, injuries, or occupational disease, and any employer who pays the premium or compensation provided by law, passed in accordance herewith, shall not be liable to respond in damages at common law or by statute for such death, injuries, or occcupational disease."

The Ohio legislative scheme, according to the court, implementing this constitutional mandate, grants employers immunity from common law actions based on claims for damages arising out of "any injury, or occupational disease, or bodily condition, received or contracted by any employee in the course of or arising out of his employment." And so without express language in the Ohio Constitution or specific guidance from the Ohio legislature regarding the precise scope of employer immunity, the court turned first to the requirement in the Ohio Workers' Compensation Act that provisions in the statute be construed liberally in favor of employees, and secondly to general considerations of public policy. The liberal construction rule led the court to conclude that the language in the statute referring to injuries or disease "received or contracted by any employee in the course of or arising out of his employment" served first to limit the scope of compensability, and secondly to provide an area for judicial determination of "what risks are incidental to employment in light of the humanitarian purposes which underlie the act." The highest Ohio court reasoned that an injury caused by the intentional conduct of an employer was *not* an injury "arising out of the course of employment" within the meaning of the Workers' Compensation Act: "No reasonable individual would equate intentional and unintentional conduct in terms of the degree of risk which faces an employee nor would such individual contemplate the risk of an intentional tort as a natural risk of employment." The intentionally tortious conduct of an employer falls outside the parameters of the compensation scheme, and thus the employer will not enjoy the immunity from common law damage claims conferred by the statute. The court noted that this conclusion was fully consistent with one of the important societal goals underlying workers' compensation laws—to promote safe and injury-free working environment: "Affording an employer immunity for his intentional behavior certainly would not provide such an environment, for an employer could commit intentional acts with impunity with the knowledge that, at the very most, his workers' compensation premium may rise slightly."

Earlier, in 1978, the West Virginia Supreme Court in *Mandolidis* v. *Elkins Industries, Inc.,* (246 SE2d 907) also held that "the workers' compensation system completely supplanted the common law tort system only with respect to *negligently* caused industrial accidents" and that employers would not be immune from liability when their conduct was intentionally tortious. Thus, common law liability could be imposed only when the employer's conduct in maintaining unsafe work conditions rose to the level of "deliberate intention." But in California in *Johns-Manville Products Corp.* v. *Contra Costa Superior Court (Rudkin),* (27 Cal 3d 465) in 1980, suit was permitted against the employer only for *aggravation of the disease* attributable to the employer's *fraudulent* concealment of the condition and its cause. Plaintiff claimed that after he contracted an asbestos-related disease, the employer deliberately and fraudulently concealed from the worker, and from the doctors retained by the employer to treat him, that he was suffering from such disease and that it was connected to his employment, thereby aggravating the consequences of his illness. The employer also allegedly induced the worker to continue employment under hazardous conditions and prevented him from receiving proper medical treatment. The California court thereupon concluded that:

> "The policy of exclusivity of workers' compensation as a remedy for injuries in the place of employment would be seriously undermined by holding defendant liable for the aggravation of this plaintiff's injuries, since we cannot believe that many employers will aggravate the effects of an industrial injury by not only deliberately concealing its existence but also its connection with the employment. Nor can we believe that the legislature in enacting the workers' compensation law intended to insulate such flagrant conduct from tort liability."

Nevertheless, only a minority of states recognize this exception to the exclusivity of workman's compensation.

3. Direct Suits by Employees Against Product Manufacturers. Direct suit by an injured employee against the manufacturer of the defective equipment which injured him is also becoming more frequent today. More and more workers are turning to the product manufacturer for greater compensation for injuries. For example, an 18-year-old worker in a New Jersey plastics plant caught his fingers in the rollers of a pelletizing machine from which a protective guard had been removed. The New Jersey Supreme Court ruled that the manufacturer of the machine, Cumberland Engineering Co., Inc. could be held liable for the worker's injuries if, at the time the machine was made, it could have been reasonably foreseen that someone would remove the guard, and the manufacturer did nothing about it!

On the other hand, approximately 20 states permit an employer to commence a civil subrogation action under workman's compensation against the third party tortfeasor. See Section 29 of the New York Workman's Compensation Law; Section 3852 of the California Labor Code; and Section 34: 15–40 of the New Jersey Statutes Annotated. These statutes allow the employer to commence the third party action in the name of certain employees, i.e., those who after receiving compensation awards and appropriate notice fail to commence suit against those parties who may be liable for the damages they have suffered, and against whom the employer would otherwise have a statutory compensation lien. The amount recoverable by the employer, however, is limited by statute, with any recovery over and above the compensation payments going directly to the employee.

MERGERS AND ACQUISITIONS: LIABILITY OF THE SUCCESSOR BUSINESS

Years ago a corporation which acquired the assets of another company could be held liable for injuries caused by a defective product produced by its predecessor ONLY if it expressly or impliedly *assumed* such obligations, or if the sale was fraudulent or amounted to a true merger. The traditional rule regarding the liability of successor corporations is illustrated by *McKee* v. *Harris-Seybold Co.,* (264 A2d 98, aff 288 A2d 585, 1972) in New Jersey:

> "Where one corporation sells or transfers all of its assets to another corporation, the latter is *not* liable for the debts and liabilities of the former unless (1) the purchaser expressly or impliedly agrees to such assumption, (2) the transaction amounts to a consolidation or merger of the two corporations, (3) the purchasing corporation is merely a continuation of the selling corporation, or (4) the transaction is entered into fradulently to escape liability for debts."

But two years later, in 1974 in *Cyr* v. *B. Offen & Co.,* (501 F2d 1145, CA2, 1974) the federal court treated the business of the corporate defendant as a continuation of the business of its predecessor, and invoked liability upon it. Here, after the death of the owner, the employees had bought the business, assumed the company's obligations, but specifically declined to assume tort liability. Unfortunately, the new company did not notify any customers of the change in ownership. Several years later two men were killed in an accident involving a machine built and sold by the predecessor company, and the court deemed the structure of the sale of assets to be a continuation of the business. The successor company cannot render itself judgment-proof by virtue of the protective language in the purchase agreement which excluded the assumption of tort liability because, according to the court, it "cannot determine the rights of third parties when no effort to give notice of the change was made." Other reasons for imposing liability upon the successor company were: (1) the manufacturer is better able to protect itself and bear the costs; and (2) only the present manufacturer can improve the quality of the product:

> ". . . The very existence of strict liability for manufacturers implies a basic judgment that the hazards of predicting and insuring risk from defective products are better borne by the manufacturer than by the consumer. The manufacturer's successor, carrying over the experience and expertise of the manufacturer, is likewise in a better position than the consumer to gauge the risks and the costs of meeting them. . ."

Furthermore, even though the successor is not the party that sold the products, and thus implied their safety, sound reasons may apply for its liability, because it profits from and exploits the accumulated good will earned by the products. Therefore, the court held that the successor corporation was a continuation of its predecessor's sole proprietorship and was liable for injuries caused by products made and sold by the predecessor.

Three years later the California Supreme Court, in 1977, in *Ray* v. *Alad Corp.,* (560 P2d 3) also imposed liability on a successor corporation. Here, a ladder manufacturer sold to another corporation, for cash, its plant, equipment, inventory, trade name, and good will. The seller agreed to dissolve as soon as it could, and the purchaser assumed liability for paying for materials previously ordered by the seller, and for filling incompleted orders taken by the seller, in the regular course of its business. After the sale, and the dissolution of the seller, a workman fell from an allegedly defective ladder which had been produced by the seller. The workman brought suit against the successor corporation. The court justified its holding the successor liable because of these factors: (1) its acquistion of the seller's assets, and the seller's subsequent dissolution virtually destroyed the plaintiff's remedies against the original manufacturer; (2) as a result of acquiring the records of manufacturing designs and continuing to employ the seller's personnel, the successor "had virtually the same capacity as (its predecessor) to estimate risks of claims for injuries from defects in previously manufactured ladders for purposes of obtaining insurance or planning for self-insurance, and could pass the cost of such insurance on to its customers; and defendant's acquisition of the manufacturer's trade name, good will, and customer lists, and its representation of itself as a continuing business, made it an integral part of the overall producing and marketing enterprise which had to beat the cost of injuries caused by defective products:

> "We therefore conclude that a party which acquires a manufacturing business and continues the output of its line of products under the circumstances here presented assumes strict tort liability for defects in units of the same product line previously manufactured and distributed by the entity from which the business was acquired."

The New Jersey Supreme Court in *Ramirez* v. *Amsted Industries, Inc.,* (431 A2d 811, 1981) also imposed liability upon the successor by refusing to give credit to the exculpatory provisions in the sale agreement and by ignoring the lengthy period of 28 years between the initial sale of the allegedly defective machine and the date of injury to the plaintiff. The court held that a products liability cause of action accrues when the injury occurs, not when the product defect was created many years ago when the predecessor company was in control.

The contrary position is illustrated by *Bernard* v. *Kee Mfg. Co.,* (409 So2d 1047) where the Florida Supreme Court in 1982 dismissed a suit against the successor corporation. Here a person injured by a lawn mower sued the successor corporation which had purchased all of the assets of its predecessor for cash, but had not assumed liabilities or obligations; it had, however, continued the same manufacturing process. The Florida court was fearful of "the threat of economic annihilation that small businesses would face under such a rule of expanded liability," and felt that the responsibility for a defective product should be on the predecessor who actually placed the product in commerce.

Obviously, under these rules of liability a purchasing corporation should attempt to assure itself of *indemnity* from the selling corporation, and in the event the selling corporation is dissolved, to receive personal indemnity from its shareholders. Where insurance has been available to the seller, the coverage may apply to claims made after the acquisition for occurrences prior to the acquisition, and the seller and its shareholders, protected by insurance coverages, will be willing to assure indemnity for such claims. The seller will probably resist a requirement that it indemnify the buyer for claims arising from occurrences *after* the acquisition although caused by products manufactured prior to the acquisition, because the seller's insurance may only cover preacquisition occurrences. Some insurance policies are now written on a "claims-made" basis, which means there will be no coverage for occurrences prior to the acquisition unless the claim against the manufacturer is also made prior to the acquisition. Coverage by a "claims-made" insurance policy, of course, can be expected to affect the seller's willingness to agree to an indemnification provision. Also, where products liability insurance is prohibitively costly and has never been held by the seller, the seller and its shareholders can be expected to resist any indemnification. One solution to the impasse is for the seller to guarantee freedom from products liability claims for a definite number of years, secured perhaps by an escrow agreement of some portion of the purchase price. The gamble may be attractive to both parties at the time of the acquisition.

In *Holt-Howard Associates* v. *General Housewares Corp.,* the New York Supreme Court, New York County, in October 1982, ordered a successor company to indemnify its predecessor for injury damage to a customer. Here Holt-Howard was being sued in a personal injury action based on the sale of a product which was allegedly defective; the sale occurred *before* Holt-Howard sold its assets to General Housewares, but the injury occurred *after* Holt-Howard sold its assets to General Housewares. When Holt-Howard sold its assets the agreement provided that General Housewares would assume only *existing* liabilities. But the court termed the sale of assets as a "de facto merger rather than a mere sale of assets," and ordered General Housewares to indemnify Holt-Howard for all obligations arising out of the personal injury action: "Public policy requires that a purchasing party having received the benefit of a going concern should also assume the costs." Thus, the new business was a "mere continuation" of the old business, and the new business was liable as successor. To avoid successor liability the successor perhaps should change the name of the product, the physical location of the plant, the management of the business, and the personnel of the business, and also maintain the seller's existence for as long as possible!

The Nebraska Supreme Court in *Jones* v. *Johnson Machine & Press Co.,* in 1982 denied "successor" liability, pointing out that a corporation purchasing assets of another does not succeed to the liabilities of the seller unless certain exceptions are met. Public policy rules behind Strict Liability for those who create risk and obtain profit by placing defective products in the stream of commerce do *not* apply equally to successor corporations, according to the court. Similarly, the Washington Supreme Court in *Meisel* v. *M & N Modern Hydraulic Press Co.,* in 1982 found that the defendant was not a successor corporation for products liability purposes. Here plaintiff had injured her hand on an allegedly defective trim press made by M, a company dissolved many years ago. The defendant was a new corporation formed by the son of the original founder of M. The son inherited the land, buildings, and equipment as personal property and leased them to defendant corporation which began to manufacture a custom line of hydraulic presses. The court ruled that the defendant's use of the buildings was not a transfer of assets from M to the defendant, because the assets were inherited by the son personally and were the son's, not the defendant's, property.

CAN PRODUCTS LIABILITY DETER THE USE OF HANDGUNS?

This fascinating question of whether tort law can be used to control the use of handguns was raised in the November 1981 issue of *The Brief* (Tort and Insurance Practice Section of the American Bar Association), pp. 5–7 and 39–40. Can courts find handgun manufacturers and distributors as well as handgun owners liable for injuries caused by handguns, even where there is no defect in the particular handgun? Under the doctrine of Strict Liability it can be argued that handguns are so inherently dangerous that their misuse is not outweighed by any social utility or personal liberty; furthermore, handgun manufacturers, distributors, and handgun owners have generally failed to exercise that degree of care necessary to control the indiscriminate use of handguns so as to preclude handguns from falling into the hands of those persons who misuse handguns. The

California Supreme Court in *Barker* v. *Lull Engineering Co.*, (20 Cal[3d] 413) in 1978 opined: "A product may be found defective in design, even if it satisfies ordinary consumer expectations, if through hindsight the jury determines that the product's design embodies 'excessive preventable danger' or in other words, if the jury finds that the risk of danger inherent in the challenged design outweighs the benefits of such design." Recently, in *Parry* v. *Allstate Insurance Co.*, (#78–2856, Florida Circuit Court for Palm Beach County) a flintlock rifle manufacturer was charged with negligence for designing a gun without a conventional safety lock, and with a soft-metal trigger that wore out prematurely. A 58-year-old man was shot in the head when the .45 caliber flintlock rifle accidentally discharged in the hands of its owner who was placing the rifle in a truck near the plaintiff when the rifle fired! Before trial the flintlock rifle manufacturer and the Ohio gun retailer settled for $1 million. The Florida jury then returned a $2 million verdict against the owner of the flintlock rifle! The deterrent effect of that case is self-evident.

If handgun manufacturers, sellers, and owners can be held liable for injuries or death caused by handguns, *where there is no provable defect in the handguns,* it is submitted that the widespread misuse of handguns can be deterred. The basic premise is that handguns function as their manufacturers, sellers, and owners intend them to be used, to wit: as instruments of deliberate and intentional harm. These defendants devote little effort to minimizing the chances that handguns will fall into the hands of people who are apt to use them *criminally;* these defendants admittedly are not interested in restricting the distribution and sale of handguns. Products liability might also encourage the handgun industry to improve product safety as well, once legal responsibility for sale and distribution of guns becomes mandatory.

In Illinois in *Riordan* v. *Interarms, Ltd.*, (#81 L 27923, Circuit Court of Cook County) suit was filed by the widow of a former deputy police superintendent who was shot and killed in Chicago as he attempted to escort an unruly patron from a restaurant. She sought $10 million in damages against the handgun distributor who sold the unruly patron the deadly weapon. Her attorney argued that a gun is a per se dangerous instrumentality: that marketing it is like placing germs in food and having a patron get a disease! (Other potential defendants might be the unruly patron as well as the owner of the restaurant.) The theory of the cause of action is that the handgun industry is strictly liable because of the inherent danger of handguns, which hazard outweighs any social utility of the weapon. Similarly, all sellers and distributors of the handgun should be liable because they failed to exercise control over the handguns to prevent them from reaching persons who would misuse them and injure themselves or others. In *Franco* v. *Bunyard,* (261 Ark 144, 1977) the Arkansas Supreme Court ruled that a handgun seller should *foresee* that a buyer would fire the weapon in connection with a robbery and injure a store clerk, and therefore the court ruled that defendant seller was liable.

The "defect" in the product is not only a defective design that can make the safety catch less secure, but the "defect" can be in the very act of distribution and sale of the weapon to those persons who would misuse the handgun, to wit: the distributor did not take any necessary steps to prevent distribution to persons who would misuse it criminally. In *Moning* v. *Alfono,* (254 NW2d 759, 1977) the 12-year-old plaintiff lost an eye when he was struck by a pellet from a slingshot fired by his 11-year-old playmate. Suit was brought against the playmate, and the slingshot's manufacturer and the distributor, alleging in particular that the commercial defendants were liable because they were negligent in marketing the slingshot *directly* to children. The Michigan Court of Appeals agreed: "The issue in the instant case is not whether slingshots should be manufactured, but the narrower question of whether marketing slingshots directly to children creates an unreasonable risk of harm."

On June 21, 1982 the Eleventh U.S. Circuit Court of Appeals in *Decker* v. *Gibson Products Co.* held that the seller of a handgun could have foreseen that the buyer of the handgun would murder his former wife, especially since the buyer had not fully recovered from a mental illness. Furthermore, the handgun had been sold through improper legal procedures. Here the children and mother of the murder victim brought the negligence action against the seller of the handgun. The court reversed the trial court, stating that the plaintiffs were entitled to have a jury consider whether the defendant's sale of the handgun to a person known to have been convicted of aggravated assault was reasonable in light of the facts surrounding the transaction.

On the other hand, in *Scronce* v. *Howard Brothers Discount Stores, Inc.,* (679 F2d 1204) the Fifth U.S. Circuit Court of Appeals in 1982 faced a plaintiff who was injured when the rifle he was using at a shooting range exploded. The imported rifle had been purchased from an individual who had bought it at retail some years earlier. It was undisputed at trial that it was possible to have an explosion when the rifle was fired without a bolt head in place. However, plaintiff testified that when he arrived at the shooting range the bolt head was inserted in the rifle chamber and that he had not removed it. Experts for both sides agreed that the accident just could not have happened the way plaintiff told it! Hence there was no proof of causation, and the court dismissed the complaint for personal injuries.

Attorneys Biklen and Hemond of Hartford, Connecticut, in a letter published in the *ABAJ* for March 1982, (p. 244) recommended that every person who holds a handgun permit should be required to carry products liability insurance! The public would then be protected from injuries and losses caused by handgun misuse. Insurance would shift the cost of handgun violence from the victims to those who own handguns and those who profit from their sale and manufacture.

THE FRIVOLOUS LAWSUIT AND THE FRIVOLOUS DEFENSE

One of the real problems that constantly plague product manufacturers is the frivolous lawsuit, designed to force the manufacturer to settle the case by payment for perhaps "nuisance" value. The point is simply that it costs more to defend the nonmeritorious suit than to pay the undeserving plaintiff some small sum of money. Whether it is "blackmail" or simply shrewd business practice is irrelevant. Indeed, what can be done to frustrate frivolous lawsuits? A few examples in the field of *medical malpractice* may point the way to a solution.

How can doctors stop picayune lawsuits which are designed to be a nuisance and even a form of blackmail? Fortunately, there are several remedies: (1) The losing plaintiff or claimant can be made to pay attorney's fees, the costs of the action, and interest thereon, to the successful defending doctor or hospital; *or* (2) the doctor posits a COUNTERCLAIM, or COUNTERSUES the attorney and the patient, and seeks to collect substantial damages. On February 29, 1980 in *Peerman* v. *Sidicane,* the Tennessee Court of Appeals observed that a female patient had filed a complaint against the physician for *negligently diagnosing her ailment as gonorrhea!* The patient alleged that she suffered mental anguish because the physician had delayed the test results from a medical laboratory until he had obtained a "kickback" from the laboratory! The trial court granted summary judgment in favor of the physician, finding that the physician had, in fact, informed her after a physical examination that she *might* have gonorrhea, but seven days later had in fact told her that the tests revealed *no* gonorrhea. Suit for Malicious Prosecution was thereupon instituted by the doctor against the patient and her attorney who apparently had made no effort to ascertain the facts of the case. Her attorney did not interview any physicians regarding the standard of care, nor had he taken any depositions in the malpractice suit. Furthermore, the attorney had no knowledge as to whether the physician was or was not involved in a "kickback" situation! (The attorney merely *surmised* that a "kickback" *might* be involved.) The Tennessee jury returned an $11,500 verdict in favor of the physician ($3,000 compensatory damages and $8,500 punitive damages). The jury believed that the patient's attorney had entered, without his client's consent, allegations in the complaint based upon pure speculation, and had maliciously prosecuted the physician. Another successful countersuit by a physician was *Raine* v. *Drasin,* decided by the Kentucky Court of Appeals on March 21, 1980. The original plaintiff was a cardiac patient whose shoulder was injured while he was hospitalized. Suit was brought against the radiologist and orthopedist, seeking a total of $1,000,000 in damages. But weeks later the suit was dismissed *with prejudice* by the patient. Thereupon, these two physicians sued the two attorneys for the plaintiff, as well as the plaintiff-patient, for Malicious Prosecution. The jury returned verdicts in the amount of $37,500 compensatory and punitive damages against the *first* attorney, and $12,500 in compensatory damages against the *second* attorney. The Kentucky Court of Appeals ruled that the *initial* malpractice suit had been properly terminated in favor of the two doctors, but the court found reputational damage had been suffered by the two physicians because of the libelous statements in the complaint of the *initial* action. On the issue of MALICE, the court agreed that the *first* attorney who drafted the complaint had acted maliciously because he was aware of the *lack of any probable cause to sue* these physicians. (In fact, the *first* attorney had another hospital as a client and therefore had not even signed the complaint therein.) The court, however, dismissed the punitive damage awards, thereby reducing the award of compensatory damages to $15,000 against the *first* attorney only.

A Nevada case, *Bull* v. *McCuskey,* (615 P2d 957) decided in 1980 by the Nevada Supreme Court, raises an interesting problem: the physician had treated an 86-year-old woman for orthopedic injuries which she received in an automobile accident. The woman was hospitalized for three months in one hospital, then transferred to another hospital. She was depressed, uncooperative, and uncommunicative, the court observed. While in the second hospital, bed sores developed on her hips and heels, and her nephew brought suit, charging the physician in the second hospital with malpractice. Before filing suit, the nephew's attorney did not examine or obtain hospital records, or confer with a physician. Neither did he submit the complaint to a screening panel. Prior to trial, he offered to settle for $750. After a trial at which the attorney made several offensive comments about the physician, the jury returned a verdict in the physician's favor. The physician then countersued the attorney, claiming misuse of regularly issued process, or abuse of process. A jury awarded the physician $85,000, and the attorney appealed, but the highest Nevada court upheld the $85,000 award to the physician. The Nevada court said that compensatory damages in an action for abuse of process may include compensation for fears, anxiety, and emotional distress. The award of $35,000 compensatory damages was supported by the evidence, the court ruled; with respect to the *punitive damages* of $50,000, the jury could conclude that the suit was filed and the settlement offer made intentionally and with reckless disregard of the consequences. Such a conclusion would establish *malice* sufficient to support an award of punitive damages within the discretion of the jury, the court said.

The contrary view is shown in a Michigan case where a urologist sued two attorneys after their medical malpractice claim against him had been dismissed. Dr. Friedman's countersuit was based upon ABUSE OF PROCESS, MALICIOUS PROSECUTION, and NEGLIGENCE. The attorneys had evidently filed the malpractice claim *without being able to produce an expert medical witness,* according to Dr. Friedman's lawyer. They represented the husband of a patient who had undergone routine bladder surgery by Dr. Friedman. The woman had died on the operating table without apparent cause, but an autopsy later revealed that her death was caused by a rare blood condition (thrombocytopenic purpura) that is not diagnosable and is uniformly fatal. Despite their knowledge of the autopsy report, the attorneys still brought the claim against Dr. Friedman. But Dr. Friedman's case against the lawyers was dismissed at the trial court level; however, the Michigan Court of Appeals ruled that he had a cause of action for malicious prosecution, *Friedman* v. *Dozorc and Golden,* (83 Mich. App. 429, 1978). Dr. Friedman's lawyer in his countersuit was heard to say: "To an increasing degree, lawyers are going to be held responsible for their acts just like everyone else. These guys are proud of being hired guns, yet they're allowed to walk down the street and willy-nilly shoot anybody in sight." Both sides later appealed to the Michigan Supreme Court, but the highest Michigan court unfortunately ruled that the patient's attorney owed no actionable duty to the plaintiff physician, and therefore the attorney was NOT subject to liability for negligent conduct (412 MICH 1, 312 NW2d 585, dated November 23, 1982). Indeed, the creation of attorney's duty in favor of an adversary would be an unacceptable conflict of interest which would seriously hamper the attorney's effectiveness as counsel for his client. The Michigan Supreme Court pointed out that to recover upon the theory of Abuse of Process, plaintiff must prove "ulterior purpose" or an "irregular act"; on the Malicious Prosecution action the court reversed and found no proof of "special injury" (which requirement the dissenters would abolish). The decision was 4–3, and Justice Levin, who wrote the majority opinion for four justices, had to write on his own a concurring opinion joined in by one justice; there were two dissenting opinions in which one more justice concurred.

The state of Florida in 1980 enacted a statute which appears to have had a deterrent effect on patients filing frivolous claims against doctors and hospitals, because the unsuccessful plaintiff is required to pay the attorney's fees of the defendant doctor and hospital. (The Florida statute does exempt parties who are "insolvent or poverty-stricken.")

In summary, there are six criteria for a physician's *successful* countersuit for MALICIOUS PROSECUTION: (1) there was a commencement or continuation of an original civil or criminal judicial proceeding; (2) its legal causation was by the present defendant against the plaintiff; (3) its bona fide termination was in favor of the plaintiff; (4) there was an absence of probable cause for such prosecution; (5) there was *malice* on the part of the patient; and (6) damages conforming to legal standards resulted to the plaintiff. See *Field* v. *Goldstein,* (379 So2d 410, Fla App 1980). Other theories for successful countersuits by physicians include failure to reasonably investigate the claim; abuse of process (e.g., interference with personal freedom of the physician); intentional filing of a meritless suit; invasion of privacy, or damage to physician's reputation; and intentional infliction of emotional stress upon the physician.

There are many *unsuccessful* countersuits by physicians; in fact the *majority* view by the American courts is against such suits. In the case of *Tappen* v. *Ager,* (599 F2d 376, 10 Cir 1979), Dr. Ager brought an obstetrical malpractice and wrongful death action against Dr. Tappen for the latter's alleged misconduct at the birth of Dr. Ager's daughter. *Without waiting for the disposition of these cases,* Dr. Tappen brought a countersuit alleging, among other theories of liability, that Dr. Ager himself was negligent in failing to adequately investigate the suit prior to filing it, and was therefore guilty of Abuse of Process. The trial court dismissed Dr. Tappen's countersuit, and Dr. Tappen appealed. The federal court, applying Kansas law, *affirmed* the trial court's judgment, and held that there is no recognizable negligence tort which arises from merely prosecuting a lawsuit, since there is no duty running from plaintiff to defendant to use reasonable care in filing a suit. The court further found that Abuse of Process was inapplicable since there was no ulterior purpose in filing the malpractice action. The court also rejected Dr. Tappen's other counts and concluded that there is no actionable tort based upon the intentional filing of litigation without merit; that the filing of a suit, if free from malice, is privileged from liability for invasion of privacy. This in indeed the majority view in the United States today.

The Illinois Appellate Court in *Stopka* v. *Lesser,* (402 NE2d 781, March 18, 1980) affirmed the dismissal of the physician's malicious prosecution case against the patient's attorney. It seems that the patient was treated badly in the emergency room of the hospital, and a medical malpractice suit was filed against the hospital and a treating physician. Five months later, in an amended complaint, an inactive physician on the hospital staff was named as an additional defendant. This *inactive* physician was obviously not involved in the treatment of the patient, and it was not until 1 1/2 years later that the patient's attorney dismissed the *inactive* physician from the lawsuit! The *inactive* physician thereupon sued for damage to his reputation, mental anguish, and increased cost of insurance premiums. He alleged that the patient's attorney had breached a duty to him, thereby causing these damages. The trial court dismissed the suit upon the ground that the attorney owed no recognized legal duty to the *inactive* physician. The Illinois Appellate Court in affirming the dismissal pointed out that the *inactive* physician did not sustain a *special* injury beyond that of defending a malpractice lawsuit! However, the court indicated that it favored a reassessment of the "special damages" issued in Illinois—"(so as) to impose a meaningful duty upon attorneys to ascertain whether the party sued is possibly liable for the wrong committed." The court expressed the opinion that Illinois should "effectively deter meritless litigation by providing recovery from the attorney to the victim without the requirement of special damages."

Section 115 of the Uniform Product Liability Act, promulgated by the U.S. Department of Commerce on October 31, 1979, also seeks to penalize parties and their attorneys who bring frivolous lawsuits or who assert frivolous defenses, by providing that they pay for attorney's fees and costs. Unfortunately, this statute, proposed for adoption by the several states, does not substantively encompass the prima facie tort of intentional infliction of injury or damage or loss. It is submitted that the prima facie tort is the only meaningful cause of action which can curb the abuse of the frivolous suit and the frivolous defense in the fields of products liability and malpractice.

IMPACT OF FEDERAL AND STATE LEGISLATION UPON PRODUCTS LIABILITY

The Occupational Safety and Health Act of 1970, by seeking safety in the workplace, enhanced opportunities for other victims of even *misused* products to seek compensation. Indeed, if an injury follows a negligent plant inspection by OSHA, the injured person is entitled to sue the Federal Government under the Federal Tort Claims Act! OSHA has authority to promulgate generic labeling standards for hazardous products in the workplace. OSHA has excited interest in products liability.

The Consumer Product Safety Commission Act of 1980 deals directly with manufacturers whose products are sold in interstate commerce, issues product standards and required warnings, and even initiates product recalls. Its impact on products liability is self-evident.

The Product Liability Risk Retention Act of 1981 was designed to alleviate some of the financial burdens of procuring products liability insurance by approving the formation of risk retention groups.

The Uniform Product Liability act has been enacted in varying and sundry parts by the various states, all of which seem to disavow any uniform federal law on products liability.

Admittedly, the goal of other legislation in this field is Tort Reform, and a brief analysis thereof is in order: (1) statutes of limitations, to be shorter and based upon the time when the product left the manufacturer's control; (2) limitation on contingent fees collected by plaintiffs' attorneys, thereby reducing the size of judgments; (3) exemption from liability where the injury or damage was caused by subsequent modification, alteration, or misuse of the product; (4) elimination of the ad damnum clause exaggerating the injury or damage; (5) limitation on punitive damages; (6) restriction on recovery for pain and suffering; (7) recognition of industry standards and the prohibition of retroactive application of current industry standards; (8) utilization of split trials by trying the liability issue before assessing damages; (9) particular defenses for nonmanufacturers in the chain of distribution; and (10) creation of a unitary products liability cause of action replacing all other causes of action. The various states have enacted legislation to solve their particular problems, but little or no uniformity has resulted, for example, Kentucky (Rev Stat Ann Sec. 411.340), North Carolina (Gen Stat Sec. 99B–2) and Tennessee (Code Ann Sec. 23–3206) provide a defense for the seller when the product is sold in its original container. Nebraska (Rev Stat Sec. 25–21.181) prohibits suits against sellers on the basis of strict liability unless the seller was also a manufacturer. South Dakota (Comp Laws Ann Sec. 20.9–9) prohibits suits against sellers unless the seller is also the manufacturer or has actual or constructive knowledge of a defect. Arizona (Rev Stat Sec. 12–684) and Arkansas (Stat Ann Sec. 34–2806) provide for manufacturers' indemnification of sellers!

On October 1, 1982 the Product Liability Act of 1982 was reported out of its Senate Committee, and almost immediately opposed by plaintiffs' trial lawyers as an "unwarranted attack on the common law and the rights of states and injured victims." Even the American Bar Association showed its distrust for federal legislation which would set up uniform standards at variance with state standards.

INTERNATIONAL PRODUCTS LIABILITY

Products liability truly knows no boundaries in the sense that such lawsuits may be brought against American manufacturers in foreign jurisdictions and against foreign manufacturers in American jurisdictions. Traditionally, the liability of manufacturers, wholesalers, and exporters for defective products has been more restrictive abroad than in the United States, probably due to the fact that the consumer movement in foreign countries is less advanced, and the fact that conservative legal systems abroad: do not promote or perhaps have no jury trials; do not recognize damages for pain and suffering, or punitive damages; and do not operate on a contingent fee basis for lawyers representing claimants. But such tradition is beginning to change, not only from contact with the American products liability situation, but also due to the awareness that mass-produced products do have defects which can and do injure users, who, in the United States, receive large awards and judgments for personal injuries, property damages, and economic losses.

Because of potentially higher damage awards in the United States, foreign plaintiffs often try to sue American manufacturers in American Courts, even though their injuries occurred outside the United States. In *Dahl* v. *United Technologies Corp.,* (#79–2596/97/98/99) the U.S. Third Circuit Court of Appeals, on August 7, 1980, under the doctrine of Forum Non-Conveniens, affirmed the dismissal of a suit by Norwegian plaintiffs against an American manufacturer of a helicopter which crashed off the coast of Norway. The court ruled that both private and public interest militated in favor of jurisdiction by a Norwegian court, to wit: witnesses and materials were available in Norway, and Norwegian plaintiffs had no contact with American law, and it was therefore more appropriate to apply Norwegian law, and Norway's interest in helicopter accidents occurring over its territorial waters should be superior to American interest therein. (Incidentally, foreign plaintiffs with default judgments can readily enforce them in the U.S. courts against American companies under The Hague Convention on the Service of Judicial and Extrajudicial Documents in Civil and Commercial Matters. The U.S., along with Belgium, Denmark, France, Japan, Luxembourg, Holland, Sweden, and the U.K. ratified the Convention.) But foreign plaintiffs may successfully sue American manufacturers in the U.S. even where the foreign law does not recognize such a claim for relief. In *Uzcategui* v. *Minnesota Mining & Mfg. Co.,* New York Supreme Court, New York County, dated April 27, 1982, Justice Egeth refused to dismiss the products liability claim, brought on behalf of a Venezuelan infant by her father, for serious birth defects suffered by the infant whose mother was exposed to the defendant's floral adhesive while she was pregnant. The court noted defendant's argument that:

> ". . . Venezuela law is applicable since virtually all appropriately cognizable points of contracts are with Venezuela. Furthermore, the law of that country does not recognize any cause of action in strict tort liability. Defendant has submitted an expert affidavit setting forth its opinion as to the Venezuelan law in which it is contended that it is not clear that the courts in Venezuela would recognize a cause of action sounding in strict tort liability. As stated by James Otis Rodner, La Responsabilidad del Fabricante, Esqueme para su Fundamento en el Codigo Civil Venezolano: Ponencias Venezolanas al Decimo Congreso Internacional de Derecho Comparado, Budapest, published by the Central University of Venezuela, Faculty of Juridical and Political Sciences (1978), cited by defendant: 'In Venezuela, this liability of the manufacturer is a new topic. Neither doctrinal writing nor national court decisions have dealt with it to this date.' Venezuela is a civil law or Code jurisdiction. Although no Code provision has been been cited or relied upon to support a cause of action in strict products liability, proof of foreign law is essentially a factual matter. At this juncture, for the present motion, this court must determine that the proof adduced is inconclusive on the issue. It is wholly insufficient to justify

> granting the drastic relief of summary dismissal. Proof as to the viability of this claim under the foreign law should more appropriately await resolution at trial by the trier of facts after a full hearing as to the substantive provisions of the foreign law.
>
> Aside from the necessity of proof as to the foreign law to determine its applicability to the within action, there is an additional issue respecting conflicts of law or proper choice of law, which, under all applicable circumstances, presents a mixed question of law and fact. Requisite proof as to the place of manufacture of the allegedly defective product, place of injury, or other factors bearing upon the choice of law issues, may require the application of the law of one or more American jurisdictions in lieu of that of Venezuela. To facilitate a determination of this issue, it will be necessary that sufficient proof be adduced at trial to afford the trier of fact a rational basis to determine which jurisdiction has the most significant contacts as to the liability issues, in order to properly apply New York's governmental interest analysis approach to choice of law principles."

But the New York court did dismiss the causes of action for breach of warranty and for derivative claims of parents because the Venezuela statute of limitations was only three months! The court stated:

> "It is undisputed that both the father and the infant are citizens and residents of Venezuela, where both purchase and injury occurred and thus it is the jurisdiction where the cause of action accrued (*Martin* v. *Julius Dierck Co.,* 43 NY2d 583). Accordingly, under New York's borrowing statute (CPLR.202) the court must apply the shorter of the statutes of limitations applicable in New York or in the jurisdiction where the action accrued. The New York statute is three years for strict products liability and negligence. As discussed below, the Venezuela statute for breach of warranty is three months. Accordingly, the father's action, brought more than three and a half years after the birth of the child, is time-barred."

The American plaintiff may encounter difficulties in suing a foreign defendant in the United States, especially where treaties between the

U.S. and foreign countries apply. One example is *Kadoa* v. *Hosogai,* (608 P2d 68, 1980) where an Arizona court obstructed suit by the widow of an American citizen who was killed in an automobile accident in Arizona while he was a passenger in a car driven by a resident of Japan. After the accident, the Japanese driver returned to Japan to live with his family. The widow attempted to sue the Japanese driver, under the Arizona nonresident motorists statute, personally in Japan by a Japanese attorney, and by serving an attorney who acted on behalf of the Japanese driver when the Japanese driver was hospitalized in Arizona with brain damage as a result of the automobile accident. The Arizona trial court recognized only the service of process made under the Arizona nonresident motorists statute. The jury verdict went to the plaintiff, but the appellate court *reversed* and dismissed the complaint because the Arizona-sanctioned method of service of process was contrary to a treaty between Japan and the United States. The treaty in question is a multilateral international convention governing "Service Abroad of Judicial and Extra-judicial Documents," (see Rule 4 of 1980 Supplement of FRCP in USCA) to which the United States bound itself on February 10, 1969. Japan was one of the other countries to become bound by this convention. The treaty was intended to create a unitary approach to the problems involved in serving process abroad. Plaintiff argued successfully on appeal that the treaty provided the exclusive means by which to effect service in Japan. Articles 2 through 6 of the convention establish a system whereby each country agrees to establish a "Central Authority" to receive and attempt to satisfy requests from abroad for service upon persons within the country's borders. This is the primary method of service contemplated by the treaty. Other service methods were recognized, such as service via diplomatic or consular agents. But any contracting party may object, under Article 10, to the freedom to use postal channels for service of judicial documents, or to the use of officials in Japan to effect service, and Japan had expressly so objected. Thus, personal service by a Japanese attorney in Japan was ineffective service of process under the convention. A plaintiff attempting to serve a Japanese defendant should have served the "Central Authority" pursuant to Article 5 or some other means sanctioned by the treaty. The plaintiff's service upon the attorney or guardian ad litem was also ineffective for reasons of internal Arizona law.

A brief comparison of the differences between American and foreign products liability law is in order: punitive damages are not readily available abroad; extensive product safety and accident information is not readily available in foreign countries; American lawyers work under a contingency fee system, thereby financing the cost of litigation and encouraging more litigation and more claims; there is no national health insurance scheme in the U.S., and workman's compensation payments are sufficiently low to prompt juries to make big awards; the American plaintiffs' bar has a higher degree of technical expertise; pretrial discovery procedures are seldom utilized or even available abroad; and the lack of juries abroad results in a conservation of monies by serious judges not cognizant of community values and perspectives in a products liability situation.

In most foreign countries, changes in products liability law come about by *legislative* change such as consumer-oriented strict liability statutes and no-fault compensation schemes. For example, in September 1976, the European Economic Community Commission, consisting of 13 members appointed by agreement among member governments, submitted a proposed directive on products liability to the Council of Ministers. Drafted to achieve some uniformity among the Common Market member states (France, Germany, Italy, U.K., Netherlands, Belgium, Denmark, Ireland, and Luxembourg), it imposes tough strict liability laws on manufacturers, but has a monetary ceiling for awards and a ten-year statute of repose. If adopted by the Council of Ministers it would be binding on member states as to substantive law but not as to procedural law. On April 26, 1979 the European Parliament, consisting of 410 directly-elected members, voted to alter some of the pro-consumer provisions of the draft, but failed, for example, to change Article One which states, in pertinent part, that the "producer of an article shall be liable for damage caused by a defect in the article, whether or not he knew or could have known of the defect." In effect, this controversial section provides for no-fault liability by holding manufacturers liable for defects existing at the time the product was first put into circulation, even where the existence of the defect could not have been discovered by anyone, given the state of science and technology at that time. In turn, the EEC Commission rejected the European Parliament's suggestion that "those manufacturers who have taken timely steps to inform the public of defects of which they have become aware and who have taken all precautions which might reasonably aid in eliminating the injurious effect of the product'' be exempted from strict liability. In May 1980, the European Parliament called upon the EEC Commission to withdraw its proposed directive, and to date, there has been no final legislative result.

In terms of enacted legislation, West Germany passed a provision affecting pharmaceuticals. The ''Act on the Revision of the Law Relating to Pharmaceutical Products,'' which became effective in January 1978, marks a significant shift to expanded liability exposure for pharmaceutical producers in West Germany. Under section 84 of the act, pharmaceutical manufacturers are liable, regardless of fault, for ''nonnegligible'' damages arising from death or personal injury caused by the use of their products. However, there are several qualifications to the obligation to pay compensation. The drug product must have been put to its intended use in the amounts prescribed by the manufacturer, and the dangerous effects must have originated in the development or production of the product. The West German act does not address the question of whether or not a pharmaceutical product is ''defective.'' To this extent it does not fit into the typical mold of ''strict'' liability as that concept is generally understood in the U.S., nor does the act impose absolute liability. What is necessary for liability to attach is that damage occurs which goes beyond that which is ''acceptable in the light of results obtained by medical science'' and that this damage originates in the manufacturing or developing stage, or arises out of the manufacturer's failure to label the product properly. Although there is a monetary ceiling on damage awards (about $100,000 per person), this amount of compensation available under the West German act is quite high by European standards.

Appendices

Appendix 1
Model Uniform *Product Liability* Act*

DEPARTMENT OF COMMERCE

Office of the Secretary

Model Uniform Product Liability Act

Introduction

The Department of Commerce publishes herein its "Model Uniform Product Liability Act." It is offered for voluntary use by the states.

This Model Law will help to assure that persons injured by unreasonably unsafe products receive reasonable compensation for their injuries. It should also help to stabilize product liability insurance rates.

The Model Law, if enacted by the states, would introduce uniformity and stability into the law of product liability. This, in turn, would help stabilize product liability insurance rates. Uniformity and stability in this area are needed because product liability insurance rates are set on a countrywide basis. Thus, product liability law differs from medical malpractice, automobile, and other standard lines of liability.

The current system of having individual state courts develop product liability law on a case-by-case basis is not consistent with commercial necessity. Product sellers and insurers need uniformity in product liability law so they will know the rules by which they are to be judged. At the same time, product users are entitled to the assurance that their rights will be protected and will not be restricted by "reform" legislation formulated in a crisis atmosphere. Thus, the Model Law meets the needs of product users, sellers, and insurers.

Background of the Act

The Department of Commerce chaired an 18-month interagency study on the topic of product liability and published its final report[1] on November 1, 1977.

The genesis of the "Uniform Product Liability Act" can be traced directly to the

**Federal Register,* Vol. 44, No. 212 (Oct. 31, 1979)

[1] The "Final Report (cited as the "Task Force Report") of the Federal Interagency Task Force on Product Liability" (cited as the "Task Force").

Task Force study. The Task Force found that uncertainties in the tort-litigation system were a principal cause of the product liability problem. The "Task Force Report" noted that a few courts had come

> very close to holding that the tort-litigation system should provide a recovery for persons who merely proved that they were injured by a product (and that) while these cases appear to be relatively few in number, insurers have regarded them as quite important in their pricing practices.[2]

The "Task Force Report" called for improvement in insurer ratemaking practices but indicated that even if this were done, "the specter of these cases could still serve as an arguable justification for increasing premiums."[3] Decisions supporting this view continue to appear.

On the basis of the "Task Force Report," representatives from the Office of Management and Budget and the Domestic Policy Staff of the White House asked Commerce to prepare an options paper regarding what action, if any, the Federal Government should take to address the product liability problem. That paper was published in the Federal Register on April 6, 1978. 43 FR 14612 (1978).[4]

One of Commerce's recommendations was that a uniform product liability law be prepared. The overwhelming majority of public comment received in response to the "Options Paper" supported this recommendation.[5]

On July 20, 1978, the Administration announced its program to address the product liability problem. Included in that program as the principal long-range measure was the drafting of a model uniform product liability law.

On January 12, 1979, Commerce's "Draft Uniform Product Liability Law" was published in the Federal Register for public comment.[6] The written commentary received by Commerce regarding the Draft Law totals approximately 1500 pages, representing 240 separate communications.[7] The Department also made a special effort to bring the Draft Law to the attention of consumers. Working with its Director of Consumer Affairs and the Office of the Special Assistant to the President for Consumer Affairs and the Office of the Special Assistant to the President for Consumer Affairs, Commerce conducted consumer forums in Washington, D.C., Detroit, Los Angeles, and Atlanta.

In addition to meeting with consumer groups, the drafters of this Act met with representatives of product seller and insurer groups which expressed an interest in the proposal. The Draft Law was also reviewed at hearings before the Subcommittee on Oversight and Minority Enterprises of the House Committee on Small Business, and

---

[2] "Task Force Report" at p. 1–27.

[3] *Id.*

[4] Public comment on the "Options Paper" was later published in the Federal Register on September 11, 1978. 43 FR 40438 (1978).

[5] 43 FR 40443.

[6] 44 FR 2996.

[7] On file, Law Library, U.S. Department of Commerce.

before the Subcommittee on Consumer Protection and Finance of the House Committee on Interstate and Foreign Commerce.

The final version of the "Uniform Product Liability Act" has benefited substantially from its review by, and input from, the various groups affected by the product liability problem.

Other Sources of the Act

Apart from the public comment, this Act is based on the work products of the Interagency Task Force on Product Liability, including its "Final Report," its "Legal Study," its "Industry Study," and its "Insurance Study."[8] Also, a thorough review was conducted of all major case law and law review literature that had been published since the time of the Task Force's "Legal Study."

As will be apparent from the Act's section-by-section analysis, attention was given to:

(1) The findings of the extensive "Product Liability Closed Claims Survey" conducted by the Insurance Services Office in 1976–77;

(2) All product liability legislation enacted at the state level, plus major proposals introduced in state legislatures in the past two years;

(3) Congressional hearings on product liability and the Report of the House Subcommittee on Capital, Investment and Business Opportunities of the Committee on Small Business. *See* H.R. Report No. 95–997, 95th Cong., 2d Sess. (1978) (Honorable John J. LaFalce, Chairman); and

(4) Privately drafted model product liability legislation.

A bibliography of some of the major resources considered by the Department is set forth in Appendix A.

Criteria for the Act

The criteria[9] utilized in evaluating the provisions of the Model Law were:

(1) *To ensure that persons injured by unreasonably unsafe products receive reasonable compensation for their injuries.*

Many proposed alternatives in product liability law are primarily justified by the fact that they contain "cost-saving devices" for product liability insurers or their in-

---

[8]The Task Force's reports are available from the National Technical Information Service, Springfield, Virginia 22161 (Attention: Sales Desk). Reference should be made to the appropriate accession number, and a check made payable to NTIS in the proper amount should be enclosed:

Final Report—PB 273-220, $20.00 (1 vol.) (1977).
Selected Papers—PB 278-625, $17.50 (1 vol.) (1978).
Legal Study—PB 263-601, $31.25 (7 vol.) (1977) (The Research Group, Inc.).
Legal Study:
Executive Summary—PB 265-450, $8.00 (first of 7 vol.) (1977).
Industry Study—PB 285-542, $21.25 (2 vol.) (1977) (Gordon Associates, Inc.).
Insurance Study—PB 263-600, $9.00 (1 vol.) (1977) (McKinsey, Inc.).

[9]A more extensive discussion of these criteria appears in the "Task Force Report" at VII-29. The criteria are also set forth in Subsection 103(C) of the Act and are discussed in the corresponding section-by-section analysis.

sureds. However, these projected "cost savings" must be balanced against the responsibility of a product seller to provide reasonable compensation to persons harmed by unreasonably unsafe products. The cost of an accident should be shifted from a claimant to a product seller when there is a logical and articulated rationale for deeming it (as compared with the injured individual or society at large) "responsible" for the claimant's injuries.

(2) *To ensure the availability of affordable product liability insurance with adequate coverage to product sellers that engage in reasonably safe manufacturing practices.*

Product liability law should attempt to create a situation in which affordable product liability insurance is available to manufacturers that follow reasonably safe manufacturing practices. The law should not, however, be modified in order to provide such insurance to manufacturers who are unwilling or unable to follow reasonably safe manufacturing practices.

(3) *To place the incentive for loss prevention on the party or parties who are best able to accomplish that goal.*

Part of the product liability problem has been caused by unsafe manufacturing practices. Obviously, it is in the interest of all groups affected by the product liability problem to reduce the number of accidents caused by products. The Task Force study showed that product liability law can help bring about this goal. The threat of tort liability and product liability judgments has prompted manufacturers to make a greater effort to produce safe products. Nevertheless, existing state product liability law does not always place the incentive for loss prevention on the party or parties who can best achieve that goal.

The decision of where to place the incentive for loss prevention was not an easy one, and at least two factors helped determine the drafters' decision. One was based on pure economics—which party can prevent the loss at lowest cost? Economic analysis of preliminary drafts of this Act were helpful in this consideration.

A second factor focused on the question of who is in the best practical position to prevent a product-related harm. This consideration may be at counterpoint with pure economic analysis. Sometimes a product seller may be in a better practical position to implement a loss prevention technique although a product user could theoretically do so at a lesser cost.

(4) *To expedite the reparations process from the time of injury to the time the claim is paid.*

Delays in the reparations process do not serve any social interest. Seriously injured claimants can ill afford to endure long delays between the time of their injury and the time they are paid. Therefore, the Act has placed emphasis on arbitration and other means that will help expedite the reparations process.

(5) *To minimize the sum of accident costs, prevention costs, and transaction costs.*

The goal of minimizing accident, prevention, and transaction costs, while worthwhile, is not easy to fulfill within the tort-litigation system. For example, one can minimize "transaction costs" by abolishing trial by jury. However, this would be at the expense of other societal values which are particularly important in product liability cases, such as the need for the individualized judgment of cases and the experience of ordinary persons in making those judgments. Nevertheless, this consideration was significant enough to weigh in formulating the Act.

(6) *To use language that is comparatively clear and concise.*

Many product liability proposals that appear sound when stated in a broad and general manner break down when one focuses on the practicality of their implementation. In drafting the Act, practicality, together with conciseness and clarity of language, were important goals. The Act was drafted as a guideline for courts, not as a detailed legal contract between product seller and user.

Other considerations were utilized in the process of formulating each of the provisions. They are highlighted in the section-by-section analysis that accompanies the Act. Again, permeating the discussion of each provision is the concern that it is fair to all groups having in interest in the product liability problem.

It is important to understand the basic philosophy that underlies the Act. Product liability law is a branch of the law of torts. Its function is to shift the cost of an accident from a claimant to a defendant when the latter is deemed "responsible" for the claimant's injuries. This "responsibility" should be defined in terms that everyone can understand. Product liability law should indicate why a particular individual product seller was sufficiently blameworthy that it should bear the cost of that injury.

Tort law is not a compensation system similar to Social Security or Worker Compensation. A product seller should not, through the medium of tort law, be asked to pay merely because its product caused an injury. If a social judgment is made that product sellers are to bear the costs of all injuries caused by their products, it would be far more efficient to make purchasers of products third-party beneficiaries of product sellers' insurance policies as is the case with other compensation systems. Such systems also utilize cost-saving devices such as limiting recovery for lost earnings, eliminating recovery for pain and suffering, and abolishing the collateral source rule. In contrast, product liability law, with its full tort law recovery, reflects the social judgment that liability should be imposed only when it is fair to hold the individual product seller responsible for an injury.

This proposal is offered in the hope that it will stabilize product liability law and benefit product sellers and users alike.

C. L. Haslam,

General Counsel, Department of Commerce.

Victor E. Schwartz,

Chairman, Task Force on Product Liability and Accident Compensation.

Outline: Uniform Product Liability Act

(D) Product Liability Claim.
(E) Claimant
(F) Harm.
(G) Reasonably Anticipated Conduct.
(H) Preponderance of the Evidence.
(I) Clear and Convincing Evidence.
(J) Reckless Disregard.
(K) Express Warranty.
Sec. 103. Scope of this Act.
Sec. 104. Basic Standards of Responsibility for Manufacturers.
(A) Unsafe in Construction.
(B) Unsafe in Design.
(C) Warnings or Instructions.
(D) Express Warranty.
Sec. 105. Basic Standards of Responsibility for Product Sellers Other Than Manufacturers.
Sec. 106. Unavoidably Dangerous Aspects of Products.
Sec. 107. Relevance of Industry Custom, Safety or Performance Standards, and Practical Technological Feasibility.
Sec. 108. Relevance of Legislative or Administrative Regulatory Standards and Mandatory Government Contract Specifications.
Sec. 109. Notice of Possible Claim Required.
Sec. 110. Length of Time Product Sellers Are Subject to Liability.
(A) Useful Safe Life.
(B) Statute of Repose.
(C) Statute of Limitation.
Sec. 111. Comparative Responsibility and Apportionment of Damages.
(A) Comparative Responsibility.
(B) Apportionment of Damages.
Sec. 112. Conduct Affecting Comparative Responsibility.
(A) Failure to Discover a Defective Condition.
(B) Use of a Product With a Known Defective Condition.
(C) Misuse of a Product.
(D) Alteration or Modification of a Product.
Sec. 113. Multiple Defendants: Contribution and Implied Indemnity.
Sec. 114. Relationship Between Product Liability and Worker Compensation.
Sec. 115. Sanctions Against the Bringing of Frivolous Claims and Defenses.
Sec. 116. Arbitration.
(A) Applicability.
(B) Rules Governing.
(C) Arbitrators.
(D) Arbitrators' Powers.
(E) Commencement.
(F) Evidence.
(G) Transcript of Proceeding.
(H) Arbitration Decision and Judgment.
(I) Trial Following Arbitration.
Sec. 117. Expert Testimony.
(A) Appointment of Experts.
(B) Compensation.

Uniform Product Liability Act

Code

Preamble

This Act sets forth uniform standards for state product liability tort law. It does not cover all issues that may be litigated in product liability cases; rather, it focuses on those where the need for uniform rules is the greatest. The principal purposes of the Act are to provide a fair balance of the interests of both product users and sellers and to eliminate existing confusion and uncertainty about their respective legal rights and obligations. The fulfillment of these goals should help, first, to assure that persons injured by unreasonably unsafe products will be adequately compensated for their injuries and, second, to make product liability insurance more widely available and affordable, with greater stability in rates and premiums.

* * * * *

Analysis

Preamble

The importance this Act places on increasing the degree of certainty in the product liability litigation process is tempered by the recognition that, even with nationwide adoption of a uniform code, its application may vary from state to state on some issues. One of the Act's goals, the development of a fair balance of interests, has been achieved by applying the general criteria set forth in Subsection 103(C) of the Act and by revising the first draft of the Act (*see* 44 FR 2996 (1979)) in light of the public comment it generated. A second goal is to promote a greater degree of certainty than exists under the present system. This can be achieved if the Act is adopted by the states in which a substantial majority of product liability claims are brought.

* * * * *

Code

Sec. 100. Short Title

This Act shall be known and may be cited as the "Uniform Product Liability Act."

* * * * *

Analysis

Sec. 100. Short Title

This is the customary "short title" provision. It may be placed wherever state legislative practice dictates. If a state legislature introduces parts of the "Uniform

Product Liability Act'' as separate measures, the short title should be adjusted accordingly.

* * * * *

Code

Sec. 101. Findings

(A) Sharply rising product liability insurance premiums have created serious problems in commerce resulting in:

(1) Increased prices of consumer and industrial products;

(2) Disincentives for innovation and for the development of high-risk but potentially beneficial products;

(3) An increase in the number of product sellers attempting to do business without product liability insurance coverage, thus jeopardizing both their continued existence and the availability of compensation to injured persons; and

(4) Legislative initiatives enacted in a crisis atmosphere that may, as a result, unreasonably curtail the rights of product liability claimants.

(B) One cause of these problems is that product liability law is fraught with uncertainty and sometimes reflects an imbalanced consideration of the interests it affects. The rules vary from jurisdiction to jurisdiction and are subject to rapid and substantial change. These facts militate against predictability of litigation outcome.

(C) Insurers have cited this uncertainty and imbalance as justifications for setting rates and premiums that, in fact, may not reflect actual product risk or liability losses.

(D) Product liability insurance rates are set on the basis of countrywide, rather than individual state, experience. Insurers utilize countrywide experience because a product manufactured in one state can readily cause injury in any one of the other states, the District of Columbia, or the Commonwealth of Puerto Rico. One ramification of this practice is that there is little an individual state can do to solve the problems caused by product liability.

(E) Uncertainty in product liability law and litigation outcome has added to litigation costs and may put an additional strain on the judicial system.

(F) Recently enacted state product liability legislation has widened existing disparities in the law.

* * * * *

Analysis

Sec. 101. Findings

Chapters VI and VII of the ''Final Report of the Interagency Task Force on Product Liability'' (hereinafter cited as ''Task Force Report'') provide support for most of the findings made here. Additional support comes from the Report of the Subcommittee on Capital, Investment, and Business Opportunities, ''Product Liability Insurance,'' H.R. Rep. No. 95-997, 95th Cong., 2d Sess. (1978) (Honorable John J. LaFalce, Chairman) (hereinafter cited as ''LaFalce Subcommittee Report''). Among other things, the ''LaFalce Subcommittee Report'' called for clarification and simplification of ''present tort law relating to product liability by formulating Federal standards to be adopted by the States. . . .'' *Id.* at 76

Individual state studies on product liability conducted in Missouri (Report of the Senate Select Committee on Product Liability, 1977), Illinois (Judiciary I Subcommittee on Product Liability: Report and Recommendations—Part 1, undated), Georgia (Report of the Senate Products Liability Study Committee, 1978). Maine (Governor's Task Force, 1978). Michigan (Department of Commerce Task Force on Product Liability Insurance, 1978), and Wisconsin (Product Liability: An Overview, Wisconsin Legislative Council Staff, 1978) provide additional support for individual findings.

The Maine and Georgia reports emphasize that individual state tort reforms can do little to affect the product liability problem. This conclusion was reaffirmed in Governor Grasso's message vetoing a product liability tort bill passed by the Connecticut legislature in 1978, and Governor Brown's message vetoing a product liability tort bill passed by the California legislature in 1979. Both messages stressed that uncoordinated, individual state tort action will not stabilize product liability insurance rates.

More specific references to the findings of this Section appear in the following citations keyed to the various findings in each Subsection:

101 (A) (1) "Task Force Report" at V–19, VI–27–28.

(2) "Task Force Report" at VI–28–32.

(3) "Task Force Report" at VI–2–26.

(4) "Options Paper on Product Liability and Accident Compensation Issues," 43 FR 14612–14 (1978); "Georgia Report", Appendix B; Johnson, "Products Liability 'Reform': A Hazard to Consumers," 56 "N.C.L. Rev." 677 (1978): Phillips, "A Synopsis of the Developing Law of Products Liability," 28 "Drake L. Rev." 317, 388 (1979); Comment, "State Legislative Restrictions on Product Liability Actions," 29 "Mercer L. Rev." 619 (1978). *See also* "Federal-State Product Liability Legislation for Client and Counsel," Federal-State Reports, Inc. (1977–79).

101(B) "Task Force Report" at I–26–28, VII–15–17; "LaFalce Subcommittee Report" at 72; "Michigan Department of Commerce Task Force on Product Liability Insurance Report" at 6 (1978).

(C) Task Force "Insurance Study" at IV–88 (citing uncertainty); "Task Force Report" at V–48–49 (relationship of premium to risk).

(D) "Task Force Report" at I–28; "Maine Report" at 23.

(E) "Task Force Report" at VII–214–16; *see also* Insurance Services Office, "Product Liability Closed Claims Survey" (hereinafter cited as "ISO Closed Claims Survey") at 118–30 (1977).

(F) *See* "Federal-State Product Liability Legislation for Client and Counsel," Federal-State Reports, Inc. (1977–79); "Product Liability Trends," at 97–98, 104–05, 157–58 (The Research Group, Inc., 1978); "Business Insurance," July 23, 1979 at 31; *see also* "Wisconsin Report" at 29–37 (describing 25 separate bills on product liability introduced in one legislative session).

Code

Sec. 102. Definitions

(A) *Product Seller.* "Product seller" means any person or entity that is engaged in the business of selling products, whether the sale is for resale, or for use or consumption. The term includes a manufacturer, wholesaler, distributor, or retailer of the relevant product. The term also includes a party who is in the business of leasing or bailing such products.

The term "product seller" does not include:

(1) A seller of real property, unless that person is engaged in the mass production and sale of standardized dwellings or is otherwise a product seller;

(2) A provider of professional services who utilizes or sells products within the legally authorized scope of its professional practice. A nonprofessional provider of services is not included unless the sale or use of a product is the principal part of the transaction, and the essence of the relationship between the seller and purchaser is not the furnishing of judgment, skill, or services;

(3) A commercial seller of used products who resells a product after use by a consumer or other product user, provided the used product is in essentially the same condition as when it was acquired for resale; and

(4) A *finance lessor* who is not otherwise a product seller. A "finance lessor" is one who acts in a financial capacity, who is not a manufacturer, wholesaler, distributor, or retailer, and who leases a product without having a reasonable opportunity to inspect and discover defects in the product, under a lease arrangement in which the selection, possession, maintenance, and operation of the product are controlled by a person other than the lessor.

(B) *Manufacturer.* "Manufacturer" includes a product seller who designs, produces, makes, fabricates, constructs, or remanufactures the relevant product or component part of a product before its sale to a user or consumer. It includes a product seller or entity not otherwise a manufacturer that holds itself out as a manufacturer.

A product seller acting primarily as a wholesaler, distributor, or retailer of a product may be a "manufacturer" but only to the extent that it designs, produces, makes, fabricates, constructs, or remanufactures the product before its sale.

(C) *Product.* "Product" means any object possessing intrinsic value, capable of delivery either as an assembled whole or as a component part or parts, and produced for introduction into trade or commerce. Human tissue and organs, including human blood and its components, are excluded from this term.

The "relevant product" under this Act is that product, or its component part or parts, which give rise to the product liability claim.

(D) *Product Liability Claim.* "Product liability claim" includes any claim or action brought for harm caused by the manufacture, production, making, construction, fabrication, design, formula, preparation, assembly, installation, testing, warnings, instructions, marketing, packaging, storage, or labeling of the relevant product. It includes, but is not limited to, any action previously based on: strict liability in tort; negligence; breach of express or implied warranty; breach of, or failure to, discharge a duty to warn or instruct, whether negligent or innocent; misrepresentation, concealment, or nondisclosure, whether negligent or innocent; or under any other substantive legal theory.

(E) *Claimant.* "Claimant" means a person or entity asserting a product liability claim, including a wrongful death action, and, if the claim is asserted through or on behalf of an estate, the term includes claimant's decendent. ''Claimant'' includes any person or entity that suffers harm.

(F) *Harm.* ''Harm'' includes: (1) damage to property; (2) personal physical injuries, illness and death; (3) mental anguish or emotional harm attendant to such personal physical injuries, illness or death; and (4) mental anguish or emotional harm caused by the claimant's being placed in direct personal physical danger and manifested by a substantial objective symptom. The term ''harm'' does not include direct or consequential economic loss.

(G) *Reasonably Anticipated Conduct.* ''Reasonably anticipated conduct'' means the conduct which would be expected of an ordinary reasonably prudent person who is likely to use the product in the same or similar circumstances.

(H) *Preponderance of the Evidence.* ''A preponderance of the evidence'' is that measure of degree of proof which, by the weight, credit, and value of the aggregate evidence on either side, establishes that it is more probable than not that a fact occurred or did not occur.

(I) *Clear and Convincing Evidence.* ''Clear and convincing evidence'' is that measure or degree of proof that will produce in the mind of the trier of fact a firm belief or conviction as to the allegations sought to be established. This level of proof is greater than mere ''preponderance of the evidence,'' but less than proof beyond a reasonable doubt.

(J) *Reckless Disregard.* ''Reckless disregard'' means a conscious indifference to the safety of persons or entities that might be harmed by a product.

(K) *Express Warranty.* ''Express warranty'' means any positive statement, affirmation of fact, promise, description, sample, or model relating to the product.

Analysis

Sec. 102. Definitions

(A) *Product Seller.* ''Product seller'' includes any party in the regular commercial distribution chain. It does not include the occasional private seller. This is in accord with the ''Restatement (Second) of Torts'' Section 402A. Comment f (1965). The term also includes lessors (except finance lessors) and bailors of products, in accord with the majority of decisions that have addressed the issue. *See* Annot., 52 ''A.L.R.3d'' 121 (1973); ''Francioni v. Gibsonia Truck Corp.,'' 472 Pa. 362, 372 A.2d 736 (1977) (finance lessor); Fraser, ''Application of Strict Tort Liability to the Leasing Industry,'' 34 ''Bus. Law.'' 605 (1979).

The Act excludes the seller of real property from its coverage, except for a builder-vendor engaged in the mass production and sale of standardized dwellings, including modular homes. *See* ''Schipper v. Levitt & Sons,'' 44 N.J. 70, 207 A.2d 314 (1965); ''Berman v. Watergate West, Inc.,'' 391 A.2d 1351 (D.C. 1978) (extending ''Schipper'' to cooperative apartments); ''Fuqua Homes, Inc. v. Evanston Bldg. & Loan Co.,'' 52 Ohio App. 2d 399, 370 N.E.2d 780 (1977) (modular homes). *But see* ''Wright v. Creative Corp.,'' 30 Colo. App. 575, 498 P.2d 1179 (1972) (rejecting ''Schipper''). The potential liability of sellers of real property not engaged in such large-scale operations is left to each state's laws governing real property transactions. However, all sellers of building materials, furnishings, appliances, and other products made part of improvements to real property are not exempted from the coverage of the Act. *See* Maldonado, "Builder Beware: Strict Tort Liability for Mass Produced Housing, 7 Real Estate L. J." 283 (1979).

The Act also excludes from its coverage the provider of professional services when a product is utilized or sold as part of the rendition of such services. *Compare* "Barbee v. Rogers," 425 S.W.2d 342 (Tex. 1968), *with* "Newmark v. Gimbel's, Inc.," 54 N.J. 585, 258 A.2d 697 (1969) (differentiating "sales-service hybrid transaction" of a beautician from "professional ministration" of a physician or dentist). The majority of current decisions look to the factual circumstances of each case and generally exclude persons exercising professional judgment within their legally authorized scope of practice. Thus, in the absence of any product preparation or modification, of any representation by service providers that the products are their own, or of warranty, the courts have generally not applied product liability doctrines where the provider is called upon to exercise such professional judgment. However, appropriate remedies may be available to injured parties under other theories of law, including malpractice. *See* "Batiste v. American Home Prods. Corp.," 32 N.C. App. 1, 231 S.E.2d 269 (1977).

Consequently, it is the intent of the drafters of this Act that professionals, such as pharmacists, physicians, optometrists, and opticians, should *not* be considered product sellers in those circumstances where they are selling a product while acting within their legally authorized scope of professional practice. *See* "Bichler v. Willing," 5 App. Div.2d 331, 397 N.Y.S.2d 57 (1977); "Batiste v. American Home Prods. Corp.," *supra.* In addition, pharmacists or other professionals, employed by and working within the scope of their employment for a hospital or other health-related facility, would *not* be considered product sellers within this context since they would be rendering a part of the overall services of such facilities.

On the other hand, a pharmacist or other professional who is engaged in a commercial, non-professional sales transaction, such as the sale of perfume or photographic film, *would* be considered a product seller. Thus, the Act states that a party shall be considered a product seller when the sale of a product is the principal part of the transaction and when the essence of the relationship between the buyer and seller is *not* the furnishing of a professional skill or service. *See* Annot., 2 "A.L.R.3d" 1425 (1970).

With respect to non-professional services, when the sale of a product is the principal part of the transaction, and the essence of the relationship is not the furnishing of judgment, skill, or services, the non-manufacturer product seller is responsible under Section 105 of this Act. Therefore, when a non-professional service, such as application, installation, or dealer preparation, is an incidental part of the overall transaction of sale of a product, the provisions of Section 105 govern the entire transaction. *See* "Newmark v. Gimbel's, Inc.," 54 N.J. 585, 258 A.2d 697 (1969); "Winters v. Sears, Roebuck & Co.," 89 "A.L.R.3d" 196, 554 S.W.2d 656 (Mo. 1977). However, when the non-professional service is the predominent element of the transaction, or when the service and sale elements are clearly distinguishable or contracted for separately, the Act does not apply to such non-professional service. Instead, it is governed by other applicable law of the state. *See* "Nickel v. Hyster Co.," 97 Misc. 2d 770, 412 N.Y.S.2d 273 (1978). *See also* Brook, "Sales-Service Hybrid Transactions: A Policy Approach," 28 Sw. L.J. 575 (1975); and Greenfield, "Consumer Protection in Service Transactions—Implied Warranties and Strict Liability in Tort," 1974 "Utah L. Rev." 661.

It is also the intent of the drafters that this Act include manufacturers and other product sellers of new or remanufactured products, but not ordinary commercial sellers of used products. In this context, the commercial seller of used products is one who resells a product after it has been used by a consumer or other product user and is in essentially the same condition as when it was acquired for resale. Thus, the commercial seller of used products may be differentiated from sellers of fully *rebuilt or remanufactured* products that are included within the definition of "manufacturer" under Subsection (B). The slight majority of decisions indicate that product liability law does apply to sellers of used products; however, such sellers are not held to the same standards as are sellers of new products, due to the different nature and condition of the used product at the time of sale. Therefore, the issue of the potential liability of sellers of used products is left for resolution not under this Act, but rather under the other law of the state. *See* "Tillman v. Vance Equip. Co.," 596 P.2d 1299, 286 Or. 747 (1979); "Mickle v. Blackmon," 252 S.C. 202, 166 S.E.2d 173 (1969) (manufacturer); "Peterson v. Lou Bachrodt Chevrolet Co.," 61 Ill. 2d 17, 329 N.E. 2d 785 (1975) ("as is" sale by dealer).

(B) *Manufacturer.* The term encompasses those product sellers who initiate and carry out the process of production. It also includes manufacturers of component parts, "private labelers" who hold themselves out to the public as manufacturers, and those product sellers who rebuild or remanufacture products for resale in "like new" condition. It does not include independent product designers whose services are contracted for by product sellers, if such designers are not otherwise engaged in the business of selling products. *See* Subsection (A) (definition of "product seller"). Unless they actually engage in some element of manufacture, traditional wholesalers, distributors, and retailers are excluded from the definition. However, if they do participate in the actual manufacturing process, they are deemed manufacturers, but only to the extent that they engage in such activity. They do not become manufacturers of the product as a whole.

This definition is drawn in part from Arizona's product liability law. *See* "Ariz. Rev. Stat. Ann." Section 12-681 (1) (Supp. 1978). Its greatest import within this Act is in regard to the responsibility of a manufacturer for defective products, as contrasted with that of other product sellers. *See* Section 105, "The Basic Standards of Responsibility for Product Sellers Other Than Manufacturers."

(C) *Product.* "Product" means property which, as a component part or an assembled whole, is movable, and possesses intrinsic value. Therefore, included are all goods, wares, merchandise, and their components, as well as articles and commodities capable of delivery for introduction into trade commerce.

The definition follows existing case law by including movable dwellings, such as mobile homes, campers and similar vehicles. *See* "Morrow v. New Moon Homes, Inc.," 548 P.2d 279 (Alaska 1976) (mobile home). Also included are water, natural gas, and electrical energy provided by public utilities or other product sellers. *See* "Moody v. City of Galveston," 524 S.W.2d 583 (Tex. Civ. App. 1975) (water); "Harris v. Northwest Natural Gas Co.," 284 Or. 571, 588 P.2d 18 (1978) (warnings regarding gas); "Ransome v. Wisconsin Elec. Power Co.," 87 Wis. 2d 605, 275 N.W.2d 641 (1979) (electricity). However, human biologicals, such as blood and other bodily tissues or organs, are expressly excluded from the definition. In addition, representations of value, such as money or choses in action, are excluded, although the physical document and the ink or any other material used in printing the document do fall within the definition. *See 72 C.J.S.* "Product" (1951), and Sections 85–82 (Supp. 1975); 63 "Am. Jur.2d" "Products Liability" Section 5 (1972).

In a specific case, the particular product with which this Act is concerned is the "relevant product" which actually gave rise to the product liability claim. The "relevant product" may be the product as a whole or the particular component part or parts which gave rise to the product liability claim.

(D) *Product Liability Claim.* An important purpose of this Act is to consolidate product liability actions that have, at times, been separated under theories of negligence, warranty, and strict liability. This approach was suggested by the Task Force's "Legal Study" as well as by the "LaFalce Subcommittee Report." While an argument may be made that negligence theory is qualitatively different from strict liability and, therefore, should be preserved, product liability theory and practice have merged into a single entity and can only be stabilized if there is one, and not a multiplicity of, causes of action.

"Product liability claim" embraces express as well as implied warranty actions.

(E) *Claimant.* Living persons and those claiming through or on behalf of an estate in wrongful death or survival actions are both included within the meaning of the word "claimant."

Although the "Restatement (Second) of Torts" leaves open the question of whether persons other than product users should be included within the compass of product liability claims, subsequent case law has been almost uniform in ruling that *such persons should be included. See* "Giberson v. Ford Motor Co., 504 S.W.2d 8 (Mo. 1974) (collecting cases). *See also* Annot., 33 "A.L.R.3d" 415 (1970). The definition follows this line of decisions. *See* "Guarino v. Mine Safety Appliance Co.," 25 N.Y.2d 460, 255 N.E.2d 173, 306 N.Y.S.2d 942 (1969) (rescuer).

(F) *Harm.* Section 402A of the "Restatement" includes physical harm to persons and property. This Act provides that harm may manifest itself as damage to property, disability, including personal physical injuries and illness, death, and mental anguish or emotional harm attendant to such disability or death. It also includes mental anguish or emotional harm in circumstances in which the claimant is actually placed in personal danger, and the mental anguish or emotional harm is accompanied by substantial objective symptomatology. *See* "Wallace v. Coca-Cola Bottling Plants, Inc.," 269 A.2d 117 (Me. 1970).

The term also includes damage to the product itself. There is strong case law support for leaving direct economic loss cases to the field of commercial law. "Hawkins Constr. Co. v. Matthews Co., Inc." 190 Neb. 546, 209 N.W.2d 643 (1973); "Dennis v. Willys-Overland Motors, Inc.," 111 F. Supp. 875 (W.D. Mo. 1958); "Price v.

Gatlin," 241 Or. 315, 405 P.2d 502 (1965). Courts that have allowed recovery in tort where the purchased property is "destroyed," but not where there is "mere loss of the bargain," have had difficulty applying this distinction where the product is wholly ineffective. *See* Anthony v. Kelsey-Hayes Co.," 25 Cal. App. 3d 442, 102 Cal. Rptr. 113 (1972); "States Steamship Co. v. Stone Manganese Marine Ltd.," 371 F. Supp. 500, 504–505 (D.N.J. 1973) (collecting cases). For this reason and the fact that loss of the bargain damages are in essence a part of commercial law, claims for direct economic harm have been left to the "Uniform Commercial Code" ("U.C.C.").

The Act also does not include damages for consequential economic losses. Almost all courts have been in accord with "Seely v. White Motor Co.," 63 Cal. 2d 9, 403 P.2d 145, 45 Cal. Rptr. 17 (1965), on this issue and have left claimants with whatever rights they have under the "U.C.C." Pursuant to Section 103, the Act follows the weight of authority in this regard, and does not preempt such recovery under the "U.C.C." *See* "Brown v. Western Farmers Ass'n.," 268 Or. 470, 521 P.2d 537 (1974); "Eli Lilly & Co. v. Casey," 472 S.W.2d 598 (Tex. Civ. App. 1971); "Paul O'Leary Lumber Corp. v. Mill Equip., Inc.," 448 F.2d 536 (5th Cir. 1971).

The insurance costs of extending consequential economic losses beyond parties to a contract would be enormous. It is much less expensive and more efficient for the product purchaser to obtain insurance against consequential economic losses caused by business stoppage. Also, most courts believe that a commercial purchaser should be charged with the risk that the purchased product will not match its economic expectations unless the manufacturer agrees that it will. *See* Note, "Economic Loss in Products Liability Jurisprudence," 66 "Colum. L. Rev." 917 (1966).

(G) *Reasonably Anticipated Conduct.* The definition is based in part on Arizona product liability law. *See* "Ariz. Rev. Stat. Ann." Section 12–681(4) (Supp. 1978). "Anticipated" conduct includes occurrences which are expected, ordinary, usual, and familiar. The definition focuses on the class of persons which the product seller knows is likely to use the product. *See* "Thibault v. Sears, Roebuck & Co.", 395 A. 2d 843 (N.H. 1978). The concept of "reasonably anticipated conduct" should be contrasted with "foreseeable conduct." Almost any kind of misconduct with regard to products can be "foreseeable"—especially if the trier of fact is permitted to use hindsight, *e.g.*, that a soda bottle will be used for a hammer, that someone will attempt to drive a land vehicle on water, that perfume will be poured on a candle in order to scent it. *See* "Moran v. Faberge, Inc.," 273 Md. 538, 332 A. 2d 11 (1975). This same conduct may not be reasonably anticipated by a potential product litigant, or by the trier of fact.

The Act's reliance on the concept of "reasonably anticipated conduct" places incentives for loss prevention on both product sellers and product users. It also helps to ensure that the price of products is not affected by the liability insurance costs that would spring from providing coverage for abnormal product use.

(H) *Preponderance of the Evidence.* Unless otherwise stated, the standard of evidence under this Act is the standard utilized in most civil litigation—a preponderance of the evidence. This standard requires a showing that it is more probable than not that a fact occurred or did not occur. *See* 30 "Am. Jur.2d" "Evidence" Section 1164 (1967).

(I) *Clear and Convincing Evidence.* Proof that is "clear and convincing" not only carries with it the power to persuade the mind as to its probable truth or correctness of fact, but also has an additional element of clinching such truth. The term is best understood in context. It requires more proof than does the preponderance of the evidence standard (the ordinary standard under this Act), but does not require proof beyond a reasonable doubt. *See, e.g.,* "Aiello v. Knoll Golf Club," 64 N.J. Super. 156, 165 A. 2d 531 (1960); "Cross v. Ledford," 161 Ohio St. 469, 120 N.E. 2d 118 (1954); "Brown v. Warner," 78 S.D. 647, 107 N.W. 2d 1 (1961).

(J) *Reckless Disregard.* As Prosser has indicated, "reckless disregard" occurs where the actor

> has intentionally done an act of an unreasonable character in disregard of a risk known to him or (one that was) so obvious that he must be taken to have been aware of it, and so great as to make it highly probable that harm would follow.

W. Prosser, "Torts" 185 (4th ed. 1971).

The term denotes aggravated conduct which represents a major departure from ordinary negligence.

(K) *Express Warranty.* This definition is based on its counterpart in the "Uniform Commercial Code" and includes any positive statement, affirmation of fact, promise, description, sample, or model relating to the product. *See* "U.C.C." Section 2-313; 63 "Am. Jur. 2d" "Products Liability" Section 93 (1972). The product seller may give an express warranty orally or in writing, or through any other actions intended as a communication. *See* "Alan Wood Steel Co. v. Capital Equip. Enterprises, Inc.," 39 Ill. App. 3d 48, 349 N.E. 2d 627 (1976); "Larutan Corp. v. Magnolia Homes Mfg. Co.," 190 Neb. 425, 209 N.W. 2d 177 (1973). It should be noted that an action based on a violation of an express warranty must include the element of reliance, and the breach must relate to a misrepresentation of material facts. *See* Subsection 104(D).

* * * * *

Code

Sec. 103. Scope of This Act

(A) This Act is in lieu of and preempts all existing law governing matters within its coverage, including the "Uniform Commercial Code" and similar laws; however, nothing in this Act shall prevent the recovery, under the "Uniform Commercial Code" or similar laws, of direct or consequential economic losses.

(B) A claim may be asserted under this Act even though the claimant did not buy the product from, or enter into any contractual relationship with, the product seller.

(C) Whenever this Act does not provide a rule of decision, reference may be made to other sources of law, provided that such reference conforms to the intent and spirit of this Act as set forth in the following criteria used as guidelines for its development:

(1) To ensure that persons injured by unreasonably unsafe products receive reasonable compensation for their injuries;

(2) To ensure the availability of affordable product liability insurance with adequate coverage to product sellers that engage in reasonably safe manufacturing practices;

(3) To place the incentive for loss prevention on the party or parties who are best able to accomplish that goal;

(4) To expedite the reparations process from the time of injury to the time the claim is paid;

(5) To minimize the sum of accident costs, prevention costs, and transaction costs; and

(6) To use language that is comparatively clear and concise.

*   *   *   *   *

Analysis

Sec. 103. Scope of This Act

(A) The Act consolidates all product liability recovery theories into one. The approach taken is in accord with the Task Force's "Legal Study." While some have argued that for trial tactics purposes, it is useful to retain the negligence and breach of warranty causes of action as distinct from strict tort liability, a claimant's attorney can retain the essence of this utility by showing the basic wrongfulness of the product seller's conduct under Sections 104 or 105.

The Act explicitly preempts the "Uniform Commercial Code" ("U.C.C.") and similar laws in instances where such laws have governed matters within the Act's coverage. The purpose of this provision is to prevent conflicting product liability rules and remedies. *See, e.g.,* "Swartz v. General Motors Corp.," 378 N.E.2d 61 (Mass. 1978). Although the Act eliminates breach of warranty as a separate cause of action in product liability cases, express warranties continue to play an important role in the Act. *See, e.g.,* Subsections 102(K), 104(D), 105(B), 106(B)(4), 107(E)(4), 110(A)(2), 110(B)(2)(a).

Because the Act does not provide remedies for purely economic losses, Subsection (A) ensures that the Act does not prevent recovery under commercial law for loss of the use of a product. Thus, product liability actions for personal injury, illness, death, or damage to property (other than the product itself) are governed by this Act. On the other hand, recovery under the "U.C.C." or similar law for economic losses is not precluded by this Act.

(B) The Act is in accord with the "Restatement (Second) of Torts" in that it is unnecessary for the claimant to be in contractual privity with the product seller in order to recover for harm. *See* "Restatement (Second) of Torts" Section 402A, Comment I.

(C) The Act and its accompanying commentary do not purport to be an exhaustive compilation of the entire subject of product liability law. Rather, they focus on subject matter areas that the "Task Force Report" suggested have created the most problems and are of major importance.

The interstices of the Act will be filled by statutory or common law additions of the individual states. Some of these interstitial issues will be pointed out in the section-by-section analysis. Others will be discovered in the course of litigation under the Act.

It is the intent of Subsection (C) that these additions of statutory or common law should enhance, rather than conflict with, the basic purposes of this Act. Those courts or legislatures that make such additions should keep in mind the "Criteria for the Act'' set forth in this Subsection. A full explanation of the criteria is set forth in the Introduction to the Act. In regard to these criteria, it is essential to note that this Act does not intend to set up a compensation system similar to Worker Compensation. Rather, the purpose of the Act is to impose liability ''only where it is fair to deem the product seller responsible for an injury.'' ''Introduction,'' p. 14, *supra.*

* * * * *

Code

Sec. 104. Basic Standards of Responsibility for Manufacturers

A product manufacturer is subject to liability to a claimant who proves by a preponderance of the evidence that the claimant's harm was proximately caused because the product was defective.

A product may be proven to be defective if, and only if:

(1) It was unreasonably unsafe in construction (Subsection A);

(2) It was unreasonably unsafe in design (Subsection B);

(3) It was unreasonably unsafe because adequate warnings or instructions were not provided (Subsection C); or

(4) It was unreasonably unsafe because it did not conform to the product seller's express warranty (Subsection D).

Before submitting the case to the trier of fact, the court shall determine that the claimant had introduced sufficient evidence to allow a reasonable person to find, by a preponderance of the evidence, that one or more of the above conditions existed and was a proximate cause of the claimant's harm.

(A) *The Product Was Unreasonably Unsafe in Construction.* In order to determine that the product was unreasonably unsafe in construction, the trier of fact must find that, when the product left the control of the manufacturer, the product deviated in some material way from the manufacturer's design specifications or performance standards, or from otherwise identical units of the same product line.

(B) *The Product was Unreasonably Unsafe in Design.*

(1) In order to determine that the product was unreasonably unsafe in design, the trier of fact must find that, at the time of manufacture, the likelihood that the product would cause the claimant's harm or similar harms, and the seriousness of those harms outweighed the burden on the manufacturer to design a product that would have prevented those harms, and the adverse effect that alternative design would have on the usefulness of the product.

(2) Examples of evidence that is especially probative in making this evaluation include:

(a) Any warnings and instructions provided with the product;

(b) The technological and practical feasibility of a product designed and manufactured so as to have prevented claimant's harm while substantially serving the likely user's expected needs;

(c) The effect of any proposed alternative design on the usefulness of the product;

(d) The comparative costs of producing, distributing, selling, using, and maintaining the product as designed and as alternatively designed; and

(e) The new or additional harms that might have resulted if the product had been so alternatively designed.

(C) *The Product Was Unreasonably Unsafe Because Adequate Warnings or Instructions Were Not Provided.*

(1) In order to determine that the product was unreasonably unsafe because adequate warnings or instructions were not provided about a danger connected with the product or its proper use, the trier of fact must find that, at the time of manufacture, the likelihood that the product would cause the claimant's harm or similar harms rendered the manufacturer's instructions inadequate and that the manufacturer should and could have provided the instructions or warnings which claimant alleges would have been adequate.

(2) Examples of evidence that is especially probative in making this evaluation include:

(a) The manufacturer's ability, at the time of manufacture, to be aware of the product's danger and the nature of the potential harm;

(b) The manufacturer's ability to anticipate that the likely product user would be aware of the product's danger and the nature of the potential harm;

(c) The technological and practical feasibility of providing adequate warnings and instructions;

(d) The clarity and conspicuousness of the warnings or instructions that were provided; and

(e) The adequacy of the warnings or instructions that were provided.

(3) In any claim under this Subsection, the claimant must prove by a preponderance of the evidence that if adequate warnings or instructions had been provided, they would have been effective because a reasonably prudent product user would have either declined to use the product or would have used the product in a manner so as to have avoided the harm.

(4) A manufacturer shall not be liable for its failure to warn or instruct about dangers that are obvious; for "product misuse" as defined in Subsection 112(C)(1); or for alterations or modifications of the product which do not constitute "reasonably anticipated conduct" under Subsection 102(G).

(5) A manufacturer is under an obligation to provide adequate warnings or instructions to the actual product user unless the manufacturer provided such warnings to a person who may be reasonably expected to assure that action is taken to avoid the harm, or that the risk of the harm is explained to the actual product user.

For products that may be legally used only by or under the supervision of a class of experts, warnings or instructions may be provided to the using or supervisory expert.

For products that are tangible goods sold or handled only in bulk or other workplace products, warnings or instructions may be provided to the employer of the employee-claimant if there is no practical and feasible means of transmitting them to the employee-claimant.

(6) *Post-Manufacture Duty to Warn.* In addition to the claim provided in Subsection (C)(1), a claim may arise under this Subsection where a reasonably prudent manufacturer should have learned about a danger connected with the product after it was manufactured. In such a case, the manufacturer is under an obligation to act with

regard to the danger as a reasonably prudent manufacturer in the same or similar circumstances. This obligation is satisifed if the manufacturer makes reasonable efforts to inform product users or a person who may be reasonably expected to assure that action is taken to avoid the harm, or that the risk of harm is explained to the actual product user.

(D) *The Product Was Unreasonably Unsafe Because It Did Not Conform to an Express Warranty.* In order to determine that the product was unreasonably unsafe because it did not conform to an express warranty, the trier of fact must find that the claimant, or one acting on the claimant's behalf, relied on an express warranty made by the manufacturer or its agent about a material fact or facts concerning the product and this express warranty proved to be untrue.

A "material fact" is any specific characteristic or quality of the product. It does not include a general opinion about, or praise of, the product.

The product seller may be subject to liability under Subsection (D) although it did not engage in negligent or fraudulent conduct in making the express warranty.

* * * * *

Analysis

Sec. 104. Basic Standards of Responsibility for Manufacturers

No single product liability issue has generated more controversy than the question of defining the basic standards of responsibility to which product manufacturers are to be held. *See, e.g.,* Epstein, "Products Liability: The Search for the Middle Ground," 56 "N.C. L. Rev." 643 (1978); *see also* Vetri, "Products Liability: Developing a Framework for Analysis," 54 "Or. L. Rev." 293, 310 (1975); Henderson, "Judicial Review of Manufacturers' Conscious Design Choice: The Limits of Adjudication," 73 "Colum. L. Rev." 1531 (1973); Keeton, "Product Liability and the Meaning of Defect," 5 "St. Mary's L. J." 30 (1973); Wade, "On the Nature of Strict Tort Liability for Products," 44 "Miss L. J." 825 (1973); Walkowiak, "Product Liability Litigation and the Concept of Defective Goods: 'Reasonableness' Revisited," 44 "J. Air Law & Commerce" 705 (1978).

Much of the controversy appears to have sprung from the fact that the authors of Section 402A of the "Restatement (Second) of Torts" were focusing on problems relating to product mismanufacture or defective construction, and not on problems relating to defective design or the duty to warn. *See* "Restatement (Second) of Torts" Section 402A, Appendix (1965) (most cases cited deal with defects in construction cases); Wade, *supra,* 44 "Miss. L. J." at 830–32. In the 15 years following the publication of the "Restatement," courts have struggled to define standards of responsibility with respect to design and the duty to warn. *See, e.g.,* "Barker v. Lull Eng'r. Co.," 20 Cal. 3d 413, 573 P.2d 443, 143 Cal. Rptr. 225 (1978); "Cepeda v. Cumberland Eng'r. Co.," 76 N.J. 152, 386 A.2d 816 (1978); "Phillips v. Kimwood Mach. Co.," 269 Or. 485, 525 P.2d 1033 (1974).

In the course of this struggle, courts appear to have drifted away from rationales for imposing liability and toward verbal formulae that attempt to distinguish between negligence and strict liability.

The drafters of this Act have focused on the basic rationale of product liability and made decisions that should make it easier for courts to decide these cases. It was determined that "strict liability" is justified in two product liability areas—defects in construction and breach of express warranty.

The "Task Force Report" concluded that strict liability for defective construction can be absorbed within the existing liability insurance system. There is a degree of predictability with regard to these defective products that is not found with respect to products that are defective in design or to failure to warn. Strict liability for defective construction has also been predicated on Section 402A of the "Restatement" and implied warranty claims under Commercial law. These sources support the position that consumers have the right to expect that products are free from construction defects.

Strict liability cases involving breach of an express warranty can also be justified. If a manufacturer makes a specific representation about its product, it is fair to hold the manufacturer to that promise. Moreover, the consumer has the right to expect that a product will live up to the manufacturer's representations.

While some courts have indicated that strict liability should also be applied in design and duty-to-warn cases, it is difficult to find an adequate rationale to support that result. A few courts have sought to justify the result under a theory of "risk distribution" wherein the product seller distributes the costs of all product-related risks through liability insurance; however, this rationale breaks down in practice. The application of uncertain strict liability principles in the areas of design and duty to warn places a whole product line at risk; therefore, a firmer liability foundation is needed. In terms of creating incentives for loss prevention, the approach of applying strict liability principles to design and duty-to-warn cases represents an "overkill;" a fault system will provide the needed incentive.

If the costs of product-related injuries are always to be distributed through the price of the product, the mechanism to bring about this result should be an appropriate compensation system with limited damages, not the tort-litigation system. The former is the approach taken in Worker Compensation and automobile no-fault reparations systems. While courts that have applied strict liability in design and duty-to-warn cases have often stated that they are not imposing "absolute" insurer liability, they have not been able to articulate why they draw a line short of that particular point. The reason for this is that the risk distribution rationale provides no stopping point short of absolute liability. Thus, a number of courts have plunged into a foggy area that is neither true strict liability nor negligence. The result has been the creation of a wide variety of legal "formulae," unpredictability for consumers, and instability in the insurance market.

In light of these facts, this Act places both design and duty-to-warn cases on a fault basis.

The Act utilizes the word "defective" as a generic term covering all four types of unreasonably unsafe products. A product cannot be proven defective unless the claimant show that it is unreasonably unsafe under one or more Subsections under Section 104.[10]

---

[10] Liability can be imposed on non-manufacturer product sellers under Section 105 when they have been negligent.

This approach should not lead to problems of characterization. The claimant's pleading should indicate the theory on which it is based within the framework of Subsections (A), (B), (C), or (D). Of course, a product may be unreasonably unsafe in more than one way.

The manufacturer of a component part or parts is subject to liability under this Section for harms caused because that component part was defective. The manufacturer of a whole product is subject to liability under this Section for harms caused because the product, or any of its components, was defective.

The following commentary discusses each Subsection in turn.

(A) *The Product Was Unreasonably Unsafe in Construction.* The history of imposing strict liability for products which are unreasonably unsafe in construction goes back as far as 1913 when sellers of food were first held liable for their failure to produce a product reasonably fit for its intended use. *See* "Mazetti v. Armour & Co.," 75 Wash. 622, 135 P. 633 (1913); Prosser, "The Assault Upon the Citadel (Strict Liability to the Consumer)," 69 "Yale L.J." 1099 (1960).

Subsection (A) imposes pure strict liability on the manufacturer in accordance with Section 402A of the "Restatement (Second) of Torts." *Cf.* "Pabon v. Hackensack Auto Sales, Inc.," 63 N.J. Super. 476, 164 A.2d 773, 783 (1960) (implied warranty for defective ball bearing). The approach is also in accord with the overwhelming trend in case law in the United States. *See* Phillips, "A Synopsis of the Developing Law of Products Liability," 28 "Drake L. Rev." 317 344–45 (1979).

In the course of its study, the Task Force found that most product sellers can absorb the financial impact of strict liability for products which are defective in construction. *See* "Task Force Report" at VII–17.

The approach taken here is subject to theoretical criticism because

> (A) standard which judges a manufacturer by his own rather than industry standards could penalize the manufacturer who goes out of his way to build into his product a high safety level not mandated or followed by the industry.

Twerski & Weinstein, "A Critique of the Uniform Product Liability Law—A Rush to Judgment," 28 "Drake L. Rev." 221, 225 (1979).

Nevertheless, this criticism overlooks the fact that the manufacturer's self-imposition of a higher standard will function as a shield against claims alleging liability in the more costly area of defective design. By adopting a higher standard, a manufacturer may occasionally be subject to liability under Subsection (A), while another manufacturer may not be, but the first manufacturer does not place its whole product line at risk of being found unreasonably unsafe in design.

Not every minor variation from a standard will result in liability; rather, the variation must be a material one causing the claimant's harm.

In point of fact, there is no practical way to define defective construction except by the manufacturer's own standards. It is an optimal area for strict liability "because societal expectations are fairly well established with regard to such defects, and a ready gauge of acceptability exists by reference to like products that are non-defective." Phillips, "The Standard for Determining Defectiveness in Products Liability," 46 "U. Cin. L. Rev." 101, 104–05 (1977). Moreover, the imposition of strict liability with regard to defective construction is fair to the product user. Under a negligence system, the claimant would have the very difficult burden of showing that a manufacturer knew or should have known about a latent defect in one of thousands of mass-produced products.

(B) *The Product Was Unreasonably Unsafe in Design.* No court, in spite of some loose language that has been used, has imposed true strict or absolute liability on manufacturers for products which are unreasonably unsafe in design. *See* Henderson, "Manufacturers' Liability for Defective Design: A Proposed Statutory Reform," 56 "N.C. L. Rev." 625, 634–35 (1978). This is true because courts have appreciated the liability potential inherent in such cases—it is almost always possible to design a product more safely. Nevertheless, some courts in their instructions to the trier of fact have left juries "at sea." The jury is told to decide design cases by "considering" a number of factors; it is not given a guideline or formula for making the evaluation.

The approach taken here provides such a guideline. The trier of fact is instructed to impose liability if it finds that the product was unreasonably unsafe in design. The trier of fact is also given a formula to assist it in making this determination. The approach has its roots in the law of negligence[11] and has been put into modern and appropriate product liability terminology by some courts in their attempt to resolve the defective design dilemma. *See* "Hagans v. Oliver Mach. Co.," 576 F.2d 97, 99–100 (5th Cir. 1978); "Dreisonstok v. Volkswagenwerk, A.G.," 489 F.2d 1066, 1071 (4th Cir. 1974); "Jeng v. Witters," 452 F. Supp. 1349, 1356 (M.D. Pa. 1978).

Section 104 requires the court to make an initial determination as to whether the claimant has introduced enough evidence for the case to be considered by the jury. This requirement is especially important with respect to conscious design cases under Subsection (B). The dangers of the trier of fact introducing hindsight into the risk-utility analysis make it imperative for the court to apply its screening function carefully. *See* "Owens v. Allis-Chalmers Corp.," 83 Mich. App. 74, 268 N.W.2d 291 (1978); Henderson, *supra,* 73 "Colum. L. Rev." at 1531. *Cf.* Wade, *supra,* 44 "Miss. L. J." at 837–38 (suggesting that such formulae can *only* be applied by the court).

The formula set forth in Subsection (B) requires the trier of fact to balance two pairs of factors existing at the time of manufacture: (1) the likelihood that the product would cause the claimant's harm or similar harms, and the seriousness of those harms; against (2) the manufacturer's burden of designing a product that would have prevented those harms, and the adverse effect that alternative design would have on the usefulness of the product. *See* "Kerns v. Engelke," 390 N.E.2d 859, 865 (1979).

If the case is sent to the jury, the balancing formula should be placed in a jury instruction indicating that the claimant has the burden of showing, in light of the formula, that the product was unreasonably unsafe in design.

The Subsection also sets forth examples of important evidence that may be considered with respect to applying the formula.

First, warnings and instructions are important because, in an appropriate case, a product may be found not to be defective in design if the product seller has given an

[11] *See* "United States v. Carroll Towing Co.," 159 F.2d 169, 173 (2d Cir. 1947) (the "Learned Hand formula").

adequate warning about the product risk. *See, e.g.,* "Wagner v. Larson," 257 Iowa 1202, 136 N.W.2d 312 (1965); "Penn v. Inferno Mfg. Corp.," 199 So.2d 210 (La. App.) *aff'd,* 251 La. 27, 202 So. 2d 649 (1967). There are limits to this possibility, however, since a product seller will not be shielded from liability for an unreasonably unsafe product simply by indicating that the product "may be hazardous." Only a warning or instruction which, at the time of manufacture, substantially reduces the likelihood that the product would cause harm in the manner in which the claimant's harm was caused will affect the question of whether the product was defective in design.

Second, evidence relating to the technological and practical feasibility of designing and manufacturing a product which would have substantially served the expected user's needs, and would have also prevented the claimant's harm, addresses the side of the formula dealing with the manufacturer's burden. If an alternatively designed product which would have prevented the harm while preserving its usefulness could have been produced with a slight increase in cost, it is likely that the product is unreasonably unsafe. On the other hand, the manufacturer need not incorporate safety features that render a product incapable of performing some or all of the very functions that create its public demand. *See* "Hagans v. Oliver Mach., Inc.," 576 F.2d 97 (5th Cir. 1978); "Dreisonstok v. Volkswagenwerk, A.G.," 489 F.2d 1066 (4th Cir. 1974).

Third, it is important to consider evidence relating to the effect of the alternative design on the usefulness of the product. As learned scholars have observed, "it is virtually impossible to (evaluate a design defect case) without balancing risk and utility factors." *See* Twerski & Weinstein, *supra.* 28 "Drake L. Rev." at 229. *See also* "Phillips v. Kimwood Mach. Co.," 269 Or. 485, 525 P.2d 1033, 1038 (1974). It is important to note that this evidence is not directed to the general usefulness of the product in society, *i.e.,* the overall social worth of pharmaceuticals, lawnmowers, or other products.

Fourth, it is essential to consider evidence relating to the comparative costs of producing, distributing, selling, using, and maintaining the product as designed and as alternatively designed. This places the court and the trier of fact in the "real world" of design options.

Finally, if new or additional harms might have resulted if the product had been alternatively designed, the trier of fact should consider this factor in making its evaluation. Since this evidence will probably be introduced by the defendant manufacturer, it may be placed before the court and jury *after* the claimant's case has been presented.

In sum, Subsection (B) places the burden of proof on the claimant to show that in light of a balance of practical, objective factors, the product seller should bear the full cost of the injury and have the responsibility for attempting to distribute that cost through the price of its product. In light of the fact that the judgment is the equivalent of holding that the whole product line is defective, it is important that traditional tort law principles be followed and that the claimant retain the burden of proof. *See* Kalven, "Torts: The Quest for Appropriate Standards," 53 "Cal. L. Rev." 189

(1965). *But see* "Barker v. Lull Engineering, Inc.," 20 Cal. 3d 413, 573 P.2d 443, 143 Cal. Rptr. 225 (1978).

Neither the formula nor the detailed list of the more important evidentiary items includes what has been called the "consumer expectation test." The reasons for not including it are rooted in both economics and practicality. As Professor Wade, Reporter for "The Restatement (Second) of Torts," has stated:

> In many situations, particularly involving design matters, the consumer would not know what to expect, because he would have no idea how safe the product could be made.

Wade, *supra,* "Miss. L. J.," at 829.

The consumer expectation test takes subjectivity to its most extreme end. Each trier of fact is likely to have a different understanding of abstract consumer expectations. Moreover, most consumers are not familiar with the details of the manufacturing process and cannot abstractly evaluate conscious design alternatives. This has been recently recognized by the Supreme Court of Texas. "Turner v. General Motors Corp.,",——S.W.2d——, No. B–7747 (Tex. June 13, 1979); *see also* Green, "Strict Liability Under Sections 402A and 402B: A Decade of Litigation," 54 "Tex. L. Rev." 1185 (1976).

(C) *The Product Was Unreasonably Unsafe Because Adequate Warnings or Instructions Were Not Provided.* A manufacturer may be held liable under Subsection (C) regardless of whether the product was found to be unreasonably unsafe in construction or design. Even where the lack of scientific knowledge or cost factors preclude the use of an alternative design, the manufacturer may still be required to provide a warning about the product's hazard or to provide adequate instructions about the product's use. *See* "Jacobson v. Colorado Fuel & Iron Corp.," 409 F.2d 1263, 1271 (9th Cir. 1969).

It is important to note that Subsection (C) covers two arguably separate problems. First, was there a duty to warn or instruct about a particular matter? Second, assuming that a warning or instruction was given, was it adequate? While these two problems are theoretically separate, the underlying factors that must be taken into consideration in evaluating a manufacturer's duty with respect to them overlap; therefore, the two issues have been combined in Subsection (C). As will be indicated below, there may be a different evidentiary emphasis in the two types of cases.

The basic standard of responsibility for Subsection (C) is predicated on a fault basis. A "strict liability" base in this area creates unacceptable uncertainty within the tort-litigation system. This has recently been recognized by the Supreme Court of Michigan. "Smith v. E. R. Squibb & Sons," 405 Mich. 79, 273 N.W. 2d 476 (1979).

Under Subsection (C), the trier of fact is to place itself in the manufacturer's position *at the time the product was manufactured.* In order to impose liability on the manufacturer, the claimant must prove that the probability that the product would cause the claimant's harm and similar harms and the seriousness of those harms rendered the manufacturer's instructions inadequate, and that the manufacturer should and could have provided the warnings or instructions which claimant alleges would have been adequate. Obviously, where harms were likely to occur and unlikely to be recognized by the product user, the necessity of adequate warnings and instructions is correspondingly acute. On the other hand, the duty to provide adequate warnings and instructions cannot go beyond the technological and other information that was reasonably available at the time of manufacture. This concept is in accord with the overwhelming majority of court decisions. *See* Robbins v. Farmers Union Grain Terminal Ass'n.," 552 F.2d 788 (8th Cir. 1977) (collecting cases).

Unlike the basic formula for design cases, the utility of the product is not a consideration in deciding whether a warning is necessary. The focus is on the likelihood that the product would cause the claimant's harm, and the seriousness of that harm, the adequacy of the warnings that were provided, and the practical need for providing the warnings or instructions which claimant alleges would have been adequate.

Subsection (C)(2) lists examples of some of the more probative evidence that can assist the court and the jury in applying this formula.

Factor (a) focuses on the manufacturer's ability, at the time of manufacture, to be aware of the product's danger and the nature of the potential harm. This factor should not operate through hindsight.

Factor (b) involves evidence relating to the manufacturer's ability to anticipate that the likely product user would be aware of the product risk and the nature of the potential harm. The more serious the anticipated harm, the greater the duty to warn. *See* "Braniff Airways, Inc. v. Curtiss-Wright Corp.," 411 F.2d 451 (2d Cir. 1969), *on rehearing,* 424 F.2d 427 (2d Cir. 1970); "Davis v. Wyeth Laboratories, Inc.," 399 F.2d 121 (9th Cir. 1968).

Factor (c), the technological and practical feasibility of providing effective warnings and instructions, may not be significant in many cases because warnings are often relatively inexpensive to provide. However, in some situations, it may not be feasible as a practical technological matter to provide a warning or the type of warning that the claimant suggests should have been provided.

Factor (d), the clarity and conspicuousness of the warnings or instructions, is material in cases where claimant alleges that the warnings given were not adequate. As Professor Phillips has noted:

> To be adequate, warnings must be reasonably conspicuous, strong and clear. They must describe the danger and, where pertinent, the means of avoiding it.

Phillips, *supra,* 28 "Drake L. Rev." at 351.

Also highly relevant to this issue is Factor (e), evidence relating to the adequacy of the warnings or instructions that were provided. Again, as Professor Phillips has noted:

> The effectiveness of a warning may be diluted by other supplier representations of safety that lull the user into a false sense of security. While little or no warning may have to be given to the expert user, a clear and strong warning is required for dangerous products which the supplier can reasonably expect to be used by inexperienced persons.

Id. at 351–52.

Subsection (C)(3) sets forth a basic causation link for the Subsection. The claimant must show that if adequate warnings or instructions had been provided, the harm would have been avoided either because a reasonably prudent product user would have declined to use the product (a situation which may be most pertinent with respect to a pharmaceutical with a known risk), or because the product would have been used in a manner so as to have avoided the harm. *See* "Technical Chem. Co. v. Jacobs," 480 S.W. 2d 602 (Tex. 1972); *cf.* "Potthoff v. Alms," ——Colo. App.——, 583 P.2d 309 (Colo. Ct. App. 1978). While it has been suggested that no causation requirement should be required with respect to unavoidable pharmaceutical risks (*see* Twerski & Weinstein, *supra,* 28 "Drake L. Rev." at 236–37), the Act addresses itself to tort law, not the general public regulation of products. It is a basic requirement of tort law for the claimant to show that if the defendant had acted in a manner in which the claimant alleges was appropriate, then he or she would not have suffered harm. *See* W. Prosser, "Torts" at 236 (4th ed. 1971).

Subsection (C)(4) recognizes that a manufacturer should be able to assume that the ordinary product user is familiar with obvious hazards—that knives cut, that alcohol burns, that it is dangerous to drive automobiles at high speeds. Thus, the Act states that the manufacturer does not have to warn about dangers that are obvious. *See* "Kimble v. Waste Systems International, Inc.,"——Wash. App.——, 595 P.2d 569 (1979). While it has been suggested that this approach may encourage the manufacture of "obviously dangerous" products, this is unlikely to occur under this Act, since the manufacturer of an unreasonably unsafe product may be subject to liability under Subsection (B).

Requiring a manufacturer to warn about matters that are obvious would tend to reduce the effectiveness of warnings. As experts in the field have observed, "Warnings, in order to be effective, must be selective." Twerski, Weinstein, Donaher, & Piehler, "The Use and Abuse of Warnings in Products Liability—Design Defect Litigation Comes of Age," 61 "Cornell L. Rev." 495, 514 (1976). It is recognized that, in some jurisdictions, there is an open-ended duty to warn about obvious dangers when they are highly likely to cause very serious injuries. *See* Marschall, "An Obvious Wrong Does Not Make a Right: Manufacturers' Liability for Patently Dangerous Products," 48 "N.Y.U. L. Rev." 1065 (1973) (collecting cases). Again, the Act approaches this problem by potentially subjecting a manufacturer of a patently dangerous product to liability for an unreasonably unsafe design.

Similarly, the product manufacturer is not under an obligation to warn about misuses or alterations of products that would not be expected by an ordinary reasonably prudent person who is likely to use the product in the same or similar circumstances. *See also* Section 112(C).

Subsection (C)(5) indicates that in the normal course of events, a manufacturer should place its warning or instruction in a place or in a form where it can be communicated to the actual product user. On the other hand, there are some situations in which this is impossible or impracticable. *See* "Bryant v. Hercules, Inc.," 325 F. Supp. 241 (W.D. Ky. 1970). Therefore, the Subsection indicates that a warning or instruction may be given to a person who may be reasonably expected to assure that action is taken to avoid the harm, or that the risk of the harm is explained to the actual product user. By way of example, the Act sets forth situations where such a process is appropriate. Thus, communication to a using or supervising expert is explicitly stated to be adequate when the product—such as a prescription drug or a radioactive material—is one which may be legally used only by, or under, the supervision of such an expert. *See* "Carmichael v. Reitz," 17 Cal. App. 3d 958, 95 Cal. Rptr. 381 (Dist. Ct. App. 1971); "Terhune v. A.H. Robbins Co.," 90 Wash. 2d 9, 577 P.2d 975 (1978).

The manufacturer of tangible goods sold or handled only in bulk or of other workplace products may communicate warnings or instructions to the employer of the claimant when that is the only practical and feasible avenue for making a warning. *See* "Reed v. Pennwalt Corp.," 22 Wash. App. 718, 591 P.2d 478 (1979).

Other situations not specifically pointed out in the Act may arise where it is permissible for the manufacturer to convey warnings to persons other than a product user, *e.g.*, warnings to the parent of a young child with respect to a food product. *Cf.* "Spruill v. Boyle-Midway Inc.," 308 F.2d 79 (4th Cir. 1962).

Post-Manufacture Duty to Warn. Subsection (C)(6) recognizes a manufacturer's duty to warn after its product has been produced. The Subsection places an obligation on a manufacturer to act with reasonable prudence to learn about serious risks connected with products after they are manufactured. When it learns of such a risk, it is to act as a reasonably prudent manufacturer in the same or similar situation. This obligation is satisfied if the manufacturer makes reasonable efforts to inform product users or appropriate persons about the risk. The Subsection is in accord with basic negligence case law. *See* "Comstock v. General Motors Corp.," 358 Mich. 163, 99 N.W.2d 627 (1959); "Schenebeck v. Sterling Drug, Inc.," 423 F.2d 919 (8th Cir. 1970). The Subsection recognizes that in some situations, a general warning through an advertising medium may be all a manufacturer can provide. The standard is reasonableness, not absolute or strict liability.

(D) *The Product Was Unreasonably Unsafe Because It Did Not Conform to an Express Warranty.* When there has been an express warranty concerning the product, strict liability can readily be justified. The product seller has used specific words to induce the purchase of the product, and the Act indicates that it must be accountable for its representations. The term "express warranty" is separately defined in the Act in Subsection 102(K).

Since the case of "Baxter v. Ford Motor Co.," 179 Wash. 123, 35 P.2d 1090 (1934), courts have been virtually unanimous in imposing strict liability on product sellers when their statements about their products prove to be untrue. *See* W. Prosser, "Torts" at 652 (4th ed. 1971) ("decisions to the contrary have been amazingly few").

Thus, where a product seller advertised that its pharmaceutical was "free and safe from all dangers of addiction" and claimant, because of a rare and totally unforeseeable susceptibility, became physicially dependent on the drug, strict liability was imposed. "Crocker v. Winthrop Lab., Div. of Sterling Drug, Inc.," 514 S.W.2d 429 (Tex. 1974); "Spiegel v. Saks 34th Street," 43 Misc. 2d 1065, 252 N.Y.S. 2d 852 (App. Term 1964), *aff'd,* 272 N.Y.S.2d 972 (App. Div. 1966) (perfume advertised as "non-allergenic").

While many courts use the term "express warranty" to describe the cause of action set forth in Subsection (D), "warranty" is a term of commercial law which is appropriate in the ordinary sale of goods from an immediate buyer to an immediate seller. Here, the focus is solely on tort claims for personal injury and damage to property. In order to convey the tort basis of this cause of action, Section 402B of the "Restatement (Second) of Torts" (1965), utilized the term "misrepresentation" in place of the term "express warranty." Nevertheless, this parlance has not been generally accepted by courts, although they do appreciate the distinction between the tort action and commercial law. *See* "Drayton v. Jiffee Chem. Corp.," 591 F.2d 352, 359 (6th Cir. 1978) ("sounds distinctly in tort"). In deference to this common usage, the term "express warranty," as defined in Subsection 102(K), has been utilized.

Subsection (D) applies only to representations or warranties made by the manufacturer or by a person for whom it is legally responsible. In general, the representation must hve been made to the claimant, who must have relied on the warranty, and the harm must have resulted because of that reliance and because of the fact which was misrepresented. However, Subsection (D) does permit reliance by "one acting on behalf" of the claimant. Thus, if a wife purchases an automobile in reliance on a statement concerning its brakes and permits her husband to drive the car, this supplies the element of reliance although the husband, in fact, never learned of the statement. Otherwise, the Section is limited to consumers of products. *See* "Restatement (Second) of Torts" Section 402B, Comment j (1965).

The statement made by the product seller must be about a material fact or facts concerning the product. This does not include mere "puffing" or sales talk. Thus, the manufacturer of a grinding disk that broke was not deemed liable for a breach of express warranty after stating that the product was "stronger, sharper, and longer lived than ever before available anywhere." "Jakubowski v. Minnesota Mining & Mfg.," 80 N.J. Super. 184, 193 A.2d 275 (1963), *rev'd on other grounds,* 42 N.J. 177, 199 A.2d 826 (1964); *cf.* "Berkebile v. Brantly Helicopter Corp.," 462 Pa. 83, 337 A.2d 893 (1975) (helicopter "easy to operate"). In contrast, a manufacturer was deemed strictly liable when it advertised that a golf training device could be operated and the "ball will not hit player." A player of limited golfing ability was indeed hit by the ball, and the defendant was held liable. "Hauter v. Zogarts," 14 Cal. 3d 104, 120 Cal. Rptr. 681, 534 P.2d 377 (1975).

* * * * *

Code

Sec. 105. Basic Standards of Responsibility for Product Sellers Other Than Manufacturers

(A) A product seller, other than a manufacturer, is subject to liability to a claimant who proves by a preponderance of the evidence that claimant's harm was proximately caused by such product seller's failure to use reasonable care with respect to the product.

Before submitting the case to the trier of fact, the court shall determine that the claimant has introduced sufficient evidence to allow a reasonable person to find by a preponderance of the evidence that such product seller has failed to exercise reasonable care and that this failure was a proximate cause of the claimant's harm.

In determining whether a product seller, other than a manufacturer, is subject to liability under Subsection (A), the trier of fact shall consider the effect of such product seller's own conduct with respect to the design, construction, inspection, or condition of the product, and any failure of such product seller to transmit adequate warnings or instructions about the dangers and proper use of the product.

Unless Subsection (B) or (C) is applicable, product sellers shall not be subject to liability in circumstances in which they did not have a reasonable opportunity to inspect the product in a manner which would or should, in the exercise of reasonable care, reveal the existence of the defective condition.

(B) A product seller, other than a manufacturer, who makes an express warranty about a material fact or facts concerning a product is subject to the standards of liability set forth in Subsection 104(D).

(C) A product seller, other than a manufacturer, is also subject to the liability of manufacturer under Section 104 if:

(1) The manufacturer is not subject to service of process under the laws of the claimant's domicile; or

(2) The manufacturer has been judicially declared insolvent in that the manufacturer is unable to pay its debts as they become due in the ordinary course of business; or

(3) The court determines that it is highly probable that the claimant would be unable to enforce a judgment against the product manufacturer.

(D) Except as provided in Subsections (A), (B), and (C), a product seller, other than a manufacturer, shall not otherwise be subject to liability under this Act.

Analysis

Sec. 105. Basic Standards of Responsibility for Product Sellers Other Than Manufacturers

Section 105 is derived in part from Tennessee law. "Tenn. Code Ann." Section 23–3706 (Supp. 1978). The Section addresses the problem of excessive product liability costs for parties other than manufacturers in the distribution chain in a way that does not compromise incentives for loss prevention. It also leaves the claimant with a viable defendant whenever a defective product has caused harm.

The "ISO Closed Claims Survey" shows that manufacturers account for 87 percent of the total amount of product liability payments, while distributors, wholesalers, and retailers account for 4.6 percent. "ISO Closed Claims Survey," Report 3, at 35 (1977). Case law suggests that these non-manufacturer product sellers can usually shift their costs to the manufacturer through an indemnity suit. *See, e.g.,* "Hales v. Monroe," 544 F. 2d 331, 332 (8th Cir. 1976); "Anderson v. Somberg," 158 N.J. Super. 384, 386 A. 2d 413, 419–20 (1978); "Litton Systems, Inc. v. Shaw's Sales & Serv., Ltd.," 119 Ariz. 10, 579 P. 2d 48, 50 (1978).

Despite their relatively small role vis-a-vis manufacturers as product liability defendants, wholesalers, retailers, and distributors are frequently brought into a product liability suit. *See, e.g.,* "Tucson Indus., Inc. v. Schwartz," 108 Ariz. 464, 501 P. 2d 936 (1972); "Vergott v. Deseret Pharmaceutical Co., 463 F. 2d 12 (5th Cir. 1972); "Duckworth v. Ford Motor Co.," 320 F. 2d 130 (3d Cir. 1963). In light of ISO data showing that for every dollar of claims paid, at least 35 cents is spent in defense costs,[12] the net result is that wholesalers, retailers, and distributors are subject to substantial product liability costs in terms of both premiums and defense costs. These costs are added to the price of products and waste legal resources. *See* "Pender v. Skillcraft Indus., Inc.," 358 So. 2d 45 (Fla. Dist. Ct. App. 1978).

Under Section 105, product sellers other than manufacturers must exercise reasonable care in their handling of products. This obligation includes inspecting for hazards which a reasonably prudent product seller would have reason to discover. The focus of judicial inquiry will be on the opportunity the non-manufacturer product seller had to discover the hazard and on whether circumstances would permit a reasonable product seller to take corrective action. *See* "Edwards v. E. I. DuPont de Nemours & Co.," 183 F. 2d 165, 167 (5th Cir. 1950).

On the other hand, product sellers other than manufacturers are not liable for harms caused by products which are defective in construction or design, if those products were defective when they were received and the product seller had no reasonable opportunity to discover the defective condition. In addition, such product sellers are generally not liable for harms caused by breaches of the duty to warn or an express warranty unless the product seller's own conduct gave rise to the claim.

Subsection (A) provides that non-manufacturer product sellers are not subject to liability when they had no reasonable opportunity for product inspection which, in the exercise of reasonable care, would or should have revealed the existence of the defective condition. For example, if a retailer receives a defective product in a sealed container and there is no way for the retailer to be aware of the condition, the retailer will not be held liable. In general, Section 105 does not impose liability on non-manufacturer product sellers where there are defects in construction or defects in design that a reasonably prudent product seller would have had no opportunity to discover. The manufacturer can avoid many of these defects; the distributor or retailer cannot. However, a non-manufacturer product seller can waive the benefits of Subsection (A) through an express warranty that it makes or transmits to the product user. *Cf.* "Ky. Rev. Stat. Ann." Section 411.340 (Supp. 1978). The term "manufacturer" is defined in Subsection 102(B).

Under Subsection (A), non-manufacturer product sellers are required to exercise reasonable care in their handling and storage of products and to pass along warnings from the manufacturer. Non-manufacturer product sellers are also responsible for defects introduced into the product by virtue of their own negligent conduct (*e.g.*, faulty product preparation or storage). Failure to fulfill their responsibilities will subject non-manufacturer product sellers to liability for their contribution to the harm which results.

Under Subsection (B), the non-manufacturer product seller is subject to the same liability as a manufacturer if the non-manufacturer product seller makes an express warranty. In these situations, such product seller has induced the purchase of the product by these specific words, and courts have been virtually unanimous in holding

[12] *See* "ISO Closed Claims Survey," Report 14, at 118.

them responsible if the words prove to be untrue. *See* W. Prosser, "Torts" at 652 (4th ed. 1971).

Subsection (C) addresses the justifiable concern of Justice Traynor in "Vandermark v. Ford Motor Co.," 61 Cal. 2d 256, 391 P. 2d 168, 171, 37 Cal. Rptr. 896, 899 (1964), that:

> In some cases the retailer may be the only member of that enterprise reasonably available to the injured plaintiff. In other cases the retailer himself may play a substantial part in ensuring that the product is safe or may be in a position to exert pressure on the manufacturer to that end.

A majority of courts have followed the "Vandermark" case and have extended strict liability to retailers. *See, e.g.*, "McKisson v. Sales Affiliates, Inc.," 416 S.W. 2d 787 (Tex. 1967); "Housman v. C. A. Dawson & Co.," 106 Ill. App. 2d 225, 245 N.E. 2d 886 (1969). *See also* "U.C.C." Section 2-314.

Section 105 responds to Justice Traynor's concern in cases in which it is necessary to do so. If the manufacturer is not subject to service of process or has been judicially declared insolvent, or if a court determines that it would be highly likely that the claimant would be unable to enforce a judgment against the product manufacturer, the retailer, wholesaler, or distributor has the same strict liability obligations as a manufacturer. Thus, the limited liability shield set forth in Subsection (D) only operates when the product manufacturer is reasonably available for suit by the injured claimant.

Some economists may criticize the exception to the general rule set forth in Section 105. Another approach is that of a recently enacted Nebraska statute which flatly exempts non-manufacturer product sellers from liability unless they have been negligent. *See* "Neb. Rev. Stat." Section 25-21, 181 (Supp. 1978). *See also* "Shainberg v. Barlow," 258 So.2d 242, 244 (Miss. 1972) (same result under case law). However, the Nebraska approach can leave a person injured by a *defective* product (as defined in Section 104) without compensation. The Act makes clear that in these situations, the party who actually sold or commercially leased the defective product should bear the loss.

Procedurally, if the claimant commences an action against the retailer, wholesaler, or distributor, and the action is based upon a theory other than the retailer's, wholesaler's, or distributor's own negligence—such as Subsection 104(A)—the defendant would make a motion for dismissal. At that time, the claimant must show that the manufacturer is unavailable under the provisions of Subsection (C). The court would then consider and make a determination regarding thc three conditions listed in Subsection (C) concerning the manufacturer. If the claimant commences an action against the retailer, wholesaler, or distributor, and one of the claimant's theories is the negligent conduct of the defendant, the defendant may move to dismiss on the other theory, but the negligence theory will be litigated. If the action is dismissed against the retailer, wholesaler, or distributor under Section 105, the claimant retains the option to proceed against the manufacturer.

Subsection (D) makes clear that the Section sets forth the entire scope of liability of non-manufacturer product sellers.

However, it should be noted that retailers, wholesalers, distributors, or others can become manufacturers for the purposes of this Act to the extent that they design, produce, make, fabricate, construct, or remanufacture a product or component part of a product prior to sale. Such parties can also become manufacturers for the purposes of this Act if they hold themselves out as a manufacturer. *See* Section 102(B) ("manufacturer") and accompanying analysis.

In order for Section 105 to operate fairly toward claimants as well as non-manufacturer product sellers, it is suggested that:

(1) The non-manufacturer product seller be treated as a party for the purposes of discovery under the applicable procedural code. If this step is not taken, the Act may place an undue burden on the claimant in his or her attempt to prove the case; and

(2) The statute of limitations vis-a-vis the non-manufacturer product seller be deemed to have tolled in case the claimant is unable to enforce his or her product liability judgment against the manufacturer.

*   *   *   *   *

Code

Sec. 106. Unavoidably Dangerous Aspects of Products

(A) An unavoidably dangerous aspect of a product is that aspect incapable, in light of the state of scientific and technological knowledge at the time of manufacture, of being made safe without seriously impairing the product's usefulness.

(B) A product seller shall not be subject to liability for harm caused by an unavoidably dangerous aspect of a product unless:

(1) The product seller knew or had reason to know of the aspect and with that knowledge acted unreasonably in selling the product at all;

(2) The aspect was a defect in construction under Subsection 104(A);

(3) The product seller knew or had reason to know of the aspect and failed to meet a duty to instruct or warn under Subsection 104(C), or to transmit warnings or instructions under Subsection 105(A); or

(4) The product seller expressly warranted that the product was free of the unavoidably dangerous aspect under Subsection 104(D) or 105(B).

*   *   *   *   *

Analysis

Sec. 106. Unavoidably Dangerous Aspects of Products

Section 106 provides that, in general, a product seller will not be subject to liability for a product which is defective in design when a harm stems from an aspect of the product that is incapable of being made safe in light of the state of scientific and technical knowledge at the time of manufacture. The term "incapable" is meaningless unless it is placed in context. Therefore, Subsection (A) indicates that it applies when the danger cannot be avoided without seriously impairing the product's usefulness.

The approach taken in Section (A) recognizes that there may be circumstances in which a seriously injured person is left without compensation for an injury caused by an unavoidably dangerous aspect of a product; however, for reasons of policy that consumers can appreciate, Section 106 proposes that a product seller not be held responsible for harms that are simply unavoidable. *See* Johnson, "Products Liability 'Reform': A Hazard to Consumers," 56 "N.C. L. Rev." 676, 690 (1978). If the costs of unavoidable harms are to be shifted from the individual, they should be borne by society at large. The policy predicate underlying Section 106 is that it should help encourage research and development without unleashing unreasonably unsafe products on the public. It also makes clear to policymakers that the tort-litigation system is not the means for addressing injuries caused by all product hazards.

Section 106 is based on the "Restatement (Second) of Torts" Section 402A, Comment k (1965). *See also* "N.H. Rev. Stat. Ann." Section 507-D:4 (Supp. 1978).

With the exception of one Illinois decision, "Cunningham v. MacNeal Memorial Hosp.," 47 Ill. 2d 443, 266 N.E.2d 897 (1970), *subsequently overruled by* "Ill. Ann. Stat." ch. 91. Sections 181–84 (Supp. 1979), this approach has been followed by the common law courts throughout the United States. *See, e.g.,* "Moore v. Underwood Memorial Hosp.," 147 N.J. Super. 252, 371 A.2d 105 (1977) (serum hepatitis contracted from blood supplied); "Dalke v. Upjohn Co.," 555 F.2d 245 (9th Cir. 1977) (tooth discoloration from tetracycline); "Chambers v. G.D. Searle & Co.," 441 F. Sup. 377 (D. Md. 1975) (stroke allegedly from birth control pills); "Coffer v. Standard Brands, Inc.," 30 N.C. App. 134, 226 S.E.2d 534 (1976) (shell in nuts); "Hines v. St. Joseph's Hospital," 86 N.M. 763, 527 P.2d 1075 (1974) (blood transfusion).

Subsection (A) indicates that the time from which to judge the state of scientific and technological knowledge is the time of manufacture. *See* "Cochran v. Brooke," 243 Or. 89, 409 P.2d 904 (1966).

Subsection (B) indicates that the product seller shall not be subject to liability for harms caused by unavoidably dangerous aspects of products unless the claimant proves that one of four circumstances occurred.

The first circumstance involves the unusual situation in which the product seller knew or had reason to know of the unavoidably dangerous aspect and, with that knowledge, acted unreasonably in selling the product at all. An example is a product seller who markets a toy that is highly dangerous to children. This example can be contrasted with a pharmaceutical approved by the Food and Drug Administration, when both the government and the manufacturer know of the dangers connected with that product. In that situation, it is clear that this exception should not apply because it would not be unreasonable to sell the product.

The second circumstance deals with defects in construction. It is arguable that, even with the finest quality control, a product that is defective in construction can slip by inspection. Nevertheless, a judgment has been made by a majority of courts to impose strict liability on manufacturers for defects in construction. That judgment is preserved in this Act.

The third circumstance deals with the situation in which the product seller has failed to provide an adequate warning about an unavoidably dangerous aspect of a product. Section 106 is in accord with Subsections 104(C) and 105(A) and is predicated on a fault base—it is only to apply with respect to dangers which were known or could be discovered through the exercise of reasonable care. *See* "Dalke v. Upjohn," *supra;*

"Chambers v. G.D. Searle & Co.," *supra;* "Toole v. Richardson-Merrell, Inc.," 251 Cal. App. 2d 689, 60 Cal. Rptr. 398 (1967). As these cases reflect, the factual question underlying the legal issue of whether warnings or instructions were adequate is whether a product seller has met its duty to promulgate warnings and instructions commensurate with its actual knowledge gained from research and adverse reaction reports, and its constructive knowledge as measured by scientific literature and other available means of communication. *See* "Dalke v. Upjohn Co.," *supra,* 555 F.2d, at 248; "McEwen v. Ortho Pharmaceutical Corp.," 270 Or. 375, 528 P.2d 522, 528–29 (1974). *Contra,* "Bruce v. Martin-Marietta Corp.," 544 F.2d 442 (10th Cir. 1976).

The Section's cross-reference to Subsections 104(C) and 105(A) makes clear that the product seller must meet its obligation to warn, instruct, or transmit warnings or instructions based on new information about an unavoidably dangerous aspect of a product that is discovered *after* the product has been manufactured. *See* "Love v. Wolf," 226 Cal. App. 2d 378, 38 Cal. Rptr. 183 (1964); "Sterling Drug, Inc. v. Yarrow," 408 F. 2d 1978 (8th Cir. 1969). Only those harmed after the duty to warn arose would be entitled to a claim.

Finally, Section 106 makes clear that a product seller can be liable for an unavoidably dangerous aspect of a product if the product seller expressly warranted that the product was free from such aspect. *See* Subsections 104(D) and 105(B).

* * * * *

Code

Sec. 107. Relevance of Industry Custom, Safety or Performance Standards, and Practical Technological Feasibility

(A) Evidence of changes in (1) a product's design, (2) warnings or instructions concerning the product, (3) technological feasibility, (4) "state of the art", or (5) the custom of the product seller's industry or business, occurring after the product was manufactured, is not admissible for the purpose of proving that the product was defective in design under Subsection 104(B) or that a warning or instruction should have accompanied the product at the time of manufacture under Subsection 104(C).

If the court finds that the probative value of such evidence substantially outweighs its prejudicial effect and that there is no other proof available, this evidence may be admitted for other relevant purposes if confined to those purposes in a specific court instruction. Examples of "other relevant purposes" include proving ownership or control, or impeachment.

(B) For the purposes of Section 107, "custom" refers to the practices followed by an ordinary product seller in the product seller's industry or business.

(C) Evidence of custom in the product seller's industry or business or of the product seller's compliance or non-compliance with a non-governmental safety or performance standard, existing at the time of manufacture, may be considered by the trier of fact in determining whether a product was defective in design under Subsection 104(B), or whether there was a failure to warn or instruct under Subsection 104(C) or to transmit warnings or instructions under Subsection 105(A).

(D) For the purposes of Section 107, "practical technological feasibility" means the technological, mechanical, and scientific knowledge relating to product safety that was reasonably feasible for use, in light of economic practicality, at the time of manufacture.

(E) If the product seller proves, by a preponderance of the evidence, that it was not within practical technological feasibility for it to make the product safer with respect to design and warnings or instructions at the time of manufacture so as to have prevented claimant's harm, the product seller shall not be subject to liability for harm caused by the product unless the trier of fact determines that:

(1) The product seller knew or had reason to know of the danger and, with that knowledge, acted unreasonably in selling the product at all;

(2) The product was defective in construction under Subsection 104(A);

(3) The product seller failed to meet the post-manufacture duty to warn or instruct under Subsection 104(C)(6); or

(4) The product seller was subject to liability for express warranty under Subsection 104(D) or 105(B).

Analysis

Sec. 107—Relevance of Industry Custom, Safety or Performance Standards and Practical Technological Feasibility

Subsection (A) adopts a fundamental principle of evidence law for the purposes of product liability cases. It excludes the showing of post-manufacture changes in the design of or warnings about a product, technological feasibility, "state of the art," or industry custom when evidence of those changes is offered to show that the product was defective at the time of manufacture. *See* Fed. R. Evid. 407 and Advisory Committee Commentary. The term "state of the art," as used in the listing of evidentiary items in Subsection 107(A), is a general, commonly used phrase whose meaning may include industry custom or the most scientifically advanced developments in the field. As will be indicated in the discussion of Subsections (B) through (E), the Act has generally eschewed the phrase because of its ambiguity. Nevertheless, it has been utilized in Subsection (A) in order to assure that all post-manufacture change is excluded from evidence.

The reasons underlying the rule on which Subsection 107(A) is based are twofold: first, subsequent changes are deemed irrelevant (all they show is that "as one gets older, one may get wiser"); and second, admission of such evidence may discourage the making of improvements or repairs. While the latter rationale has been challenged (*see* "Ault v. International Harvester Co.," 13 Cal. 3d 113, 528 P.2d 1148, 117 Cal. Rptr. 812 (1975); Schwartz, "The Exclusionary Rule on Evidence of Repair—A Rule in Need of Repair," 7 "The Forum" 1 (1971)), the relevance of such evidence on the issue of defectiveness is of very limited value. On the other hand, the prejudicial effect of showing the subsequent change or repair—particularly one undertaken by the product seller itself—is quite substantial. *See* "LaMonica v. Outboard Marine Corp.," 48 Ohio App. 2d 43, 355 N.E.2d 533 (1976); "Haysom v. Coleman Lantern Co.," 89 Wash. 2d 474, 573 P.2d 785 (1978).

Subsection (A) permits the introduction of evidence which would otherwise be excluded under the Subsection, if that evidence is highly probative and necessary to prove a relevant matter other than the fact that the product was defective at the time of manufacture. Thus, evidence of such changes may be admissible to show that the product seller knew of the defect at a certain point in time after manufacture. In appropriate circumstances, this evidence may suggest that the product seller had a duty to take reasonable steps to warn product users about a newly discovered hazard. It may also be admissible when the product seller claims the product hazard was impossible to avoid. In cases of this kind, the court should make a finding that the probative value of the evidence substantially outweighs its prejudicial nature and that there is no other equally probative proof available. Allowing the introduction of evidence in these cases should *not* become a vehicle for avoiding the basic purpose of the rule.

Subsections (B), (C), (D), and (E) address one of the major issues that has divided product sellers and consumer groups concerned about product liability. Product sellers have vigorously argued that when their products comply with the ''state of the art,'' it is unfair to deem them defective. Further, they contend that industry custom is likely to incorporate all cost-justified product safety features. They have received some support for this contention from members of the academic community, at least in regard to purchasers, as contrasted with nonpurchaser product users, of the product. *See* R. Posner, ''Economic Analysis of Law'' 71 (1972).

Consumer groups respond that it is inappropriate to allow product sellers to fix indirectly their own standard of liability. *See* Johnson, ''Products Liability 'Reform': A Hazard to Consumers,'' 56 ''N.C. L. Rev.'' 677, 680–81 (1978).

When the issue is carefully analyzed, there is less dispute between product sellers and consumer groups than appears on the surface. Part of the sound and fury is a debate over the ambiguous term ''state of the art.'' The approach taken in Subsections (B), (C), (D), and (E) of not using the term ''state of the art'' eliminates that ambiguity and focuses on what is fair to each party.

Subsection (B) defines ''custom'' as the ''practices followed by the ordinary product seller in the defendant product seller's industry or business.'' *See* W. Prosser, ''Torts'' at 166 (4th ed. 1971).

Subsection (C) indicates that compliance with industry custom is merely evidence that the trier of fact may consider in determining whether a product was defective under Subsections 104 (B) and (C). There is strong support in the case law for this approach. *See, e.g.,* ''Bruce v. Martin-Marietta Corp.,'' 544 F.2d 442 (10th Cir. 1976); ''Barker v. Chrysler Corp.,'' 55 Cal. App. 3d 710, 127 Cal. Rptr. 745 (1978); ''Maxted v. Pacific Car & Foundry Co., 527 P.2d 832 (Wyo. 1974); ''Roach v. Kononen,'' 269 Or. 457, 525, P.2d 125 (1974); ''Olson v. Arctic Enterprises, Inc.'' 349 F. Supp. 761 (D. N.D. 1972).

Subsection (C) also permits introduction of evidence of non-compliance with custom—evidence likely to be introduced by a product liability claimant. While it might be argued that non-compliance with custom should indicate that the product was defective, situations may arise where a product seller followed an alternative procedure that was no less safe (perhaps even safer) than the custom in the industry. For that reason, non-compliance with custom does not create a situation where the trier of fact should consider the product defective *per se*.

Subsection (C) treats compliance or non-compliance with non-governmental product standards in the same manner as custom. Compliance or non-compliance with such standards is admissible in evidence when relevant to the issue before the court. Privately developed standards—for both design and performance—vary widely in their nature and quality. While almost all privately developed standards are labeled "minimum" (suggesting a standard below that which a product seller could reasonably achieve), some standards reach the best level that can be obtained as a practical technological matter. *See* "Task Force Report" at IV–13–17. On the other hand, some are clearly below the level of safety appropriate as a defense in a product liability case. *See* "Report of the National Commission on Product Safety" at 48 (1978) ("chronically inadequate both in scope and permissible level of risk").

Compliance with standards that are rigorous and objective (in that they were developed through careful, thorough product testing and a formal product safety evaluation, and up-to-date in light of the technological and scientific knowledge reasonably available at the time the product was manufactured) suggests that a product was not defective. Failure to comply with such standards, especially performance standards, suggests that it was defective. Nevertheless, because of the variance in the nature and quality of privately developed safety standards, the Act has eschewed *per se* rules in this area. *See* "Poches v. J. J. Newberry Co.," 549 F.2d 1168 (8th Cir. 1977).

Subsection (D), defining "practical technological feasibility," should be contrasted with Subsection (B)'s definition of "custom." The Subsection (D) definition contemplates a level of safety that was feasible, as a practical matter, at the time of manufacture. "Feasibility" includes economic considerations such as the ability of a product seller to price a product so that it is competitive, but excludes financial considerations peculiar to a particular product seller, such as its cash flow at the relevant time.

The definition's emphasis on *feasibility* addresses consumer concerns with "state-of-the-art" or "custom" defenses that could allow an industry or business to be shielded from liability when it has "negligently" lagged behind in both developing and utilizing safety technology.

Subsection (E) indicates that when a product seller proves by a preponderance of the evidence that it was not within practical technological feasibility to make the product safer, the product seller shall not be subject to liability. This is in accord with the great majority of case law. *See, e.g.,* "Olson v. Arctic Enterprises, Inc.," *supra;* "Wilson v. Piper Aircraft Corp.," 282 Or. 61, 577 P.2d 1322, 1326 (1978) (". . . plaintiff's *prima facie* case of a defect must show more than the technical possibility of a safe design"); "Bruce v. Martin-Marietta Corp.," *supra;* "Maxted v. Pacific Car & Foundry Co.," *supra;* "Roach v. Kononen," *supra. Cf.* "Ky. Rev. Stat. Ann." Section 411.310(2) (Supp. 1978) (includes custom). *But cf.* "Colo. Rev. Stat." Section 13–21–403 (Supp. 1978) ("state of the art" presumption only).

Significantly, only a few intermediate appellate court decisions, primarily from one state, impose liability if the product was in accord with the technological, mechanical, and scientific knowledge reasonably feasible for use at the time of manufacture. *See, e.g.,* "Gelsumino v. E.W. Bliss Co.," 10 Ill. App. 3d 604, 295 N.E. 2d 110 (1973), and its progeny. *But see* "McClellan v. Chicago Transit Authority," 34 Ill. App. 3d 151, 340 N.E.2d 61 (1975). *Compare* "Olson v. A. W. Chesterton Co.," 256 N.W. 2d 530 (N.D. 1977).

In order to meet appropriate consumer group concerns, Subsection (E) provides four exceptions to the defense. First, the defense will not apply if the product seller knew or had reason to know of the danger and, with that knowledge, acted unreasonably in selling the product at all. *See also* Subsection 106(B)(1) and analysis. This exception would only apply in very unusual situations. For example, a child's toy might comply with what was technologically feasible but, because of its danger, it would be unreasonable behavior to market the product for young children. Similarly, it would be unreasonable to manufacture a home heating unit with a radium core unless technology had reached a point at which the inhabitants of the home (and others) would be protected from radiation.

Second, although the product was in accord with the "practical technological feasibility," it may be defective in construction. It is a basic principle of this Act to apply strict liability against the manufacturer in that case. *See* Subsection 104(A) and analysis.

Third, although the product complied with the "practical technological feasibility" at the time of manufacture, the product may have failed to meet its post-manufacture duty to warn or instruct under Subsection 104(C)(6).

Finally, although its product was in accord with "practical technological feasibility," a product seller cannot escape strict liability for express warranty under Subsection 104(D) or 105(B).

* * * * *

Code

Sec. 108. Relevance of Legislative or Administrative Regulatory Standards and Mandatory Government Contract Specifications

(A) When the injury-causing aspect of the product was, at the time of manufacture, in compliance with legislative regulatory standards or administrative regulatory safety standards relating to design or performance, the product shall be deemed not defective under Subsection 104(B), or, if the standard addressed warnings or instructions, under Subsection 104(C) or 105(A), unless the claimant proves by a preponderance of the evidence that a reasonably prudent product seller could and would have taken additional precautions.

(B) When the injury-causing aspect of the product was not, at the time of manufacture, in compliance with legislative regulatory standards or administrative regulatory safety standards relating to design or performance, the product shall be deemed defective under Subsection 104(B), or, if the standard addressed warnings or instructions, under Subsection 104(C) or 105(A), unless the product seller proves by a preponderance of the evidence that its failure to comply was a reasonably prudent course of conduct under the circumstances.

(C) When the injury-causing aspect of the product was, at the time of manufacture, in compliance with a mandatory government contract specification relating to design, this shall be an absolute defense and the product shall be deemed not defective under Subsection 104(B), or, if the specification related to warnings or instructions, under Subsection 104(C) or 105(A).

(D) When the injury-causing aspect of the product was not, at the time of manufacture, in compliance with a mandatory government contract specification relating to design, the product shall be deemed defective under Subsection 104(B), or, if the specification related to warnings or instructions, under Subsection 104(C) or 105(A).

Analysis

Sec. 108. Relevance of Legislative or Administrative Regulatory Standards and Mandatory Government Contract Specifications

Product sellers have contended that it is unfair to deem a product defective when the challenged aspect of that product conformed to an applicable administrative or legislative regulatory standard. They note that considerable time and thought are spent in the development of such standards and that the standards are frequently subject to intense public scrutiny prior to the time of their official adoption. Product sellers point to legislative and administrative standards as a resource to provide some predictability within the scope of product liability law. They content that it is unfair to allow lay jurors to reevaluate a standard that has presumably been drafted by government experts. Furthermore, some product liability loss prevention experts suggest that a defense based on compliance with standards will create incentives for manufacturers to comply with such standards. *See* Task Force "Selected Papers" at 266 (Remarks of Professor Alvin. S. Weinstein).

On the other hand, some consumer groups maintain that government standards are often the result of compromise decisions—decisions that are sometimes unduly influenced by industry. These consumer groups point out that some government regulatory bodies may have insufficient personnel or expertise to make independent judgments. The general approach of courts, as well as that embodied in the "Consumer Product Safety Act," 15 "U.S.C." Section 2074(A) (1976) and the "National Traffic and Motor Vehicle Safety Act," 15 "U.S.C." Section 1391 (2) (1976), is that government standards are only minimum standards, and that compliance should not be deemed an absolute defense in product liability actions. *See* "Roberts v. May," ——Colo. App.——, 583 P. 2d 305, 308 (1978). In spite of this, some states have enacted statutes that grant this effect to such compliance. *See* "N.D. Cent. Code" Section 28-01.1-05(3) (Supp. 1979); "Utah Code Ann." Section 78-15-6 (1977); "Colo. Rev. Stat." Section 13-21-403 (Supp. 1978).

Nevertheless, case law also suggests that government safety standards are often deemed sound and appropriate for application to tort law claims. *See* "Jones v. Hittle Serv., Inc.," 219 Kan. 627, 549 P. 2d 1383 (1976) (universally accepted standards for odorizing LP gas outweigh expert opinion); "McDaniel v. McNeil Laboratories, Inc.," 196 Neb. 190, 241 N.W. 2d 822 (1976) (determination of the FDA prevails in absence of proof that the manufacturer furnished incomplete, misleading, or fraudulent information); "Simien v. S.S. Kresge Co.," 566 F. 2d 551 (5th Cir. 1978) (compliance with flammability standard); "Bruce v. Martin-Marietta Corp.," 544 F.

2d 442, 446 (10th Cir. 1976) (claimants did "not present any more stringent standards which might have been applicable at the time of manufacture").

The approach taken in Subsection (A) is based on these cases and on the "Restatement (Second) Torts" Section 288C (1965). When the specific injury-causing aspect of the product conformed to or was in compliance with the legislative or administrative regulatory standard, the product is deemed not defective under Subsection 104(B) when design is relevant, or under Subsection 104(C) or 105(A) when the duty to warn or instruct is relevant, unless the claimant proves by a preponderance of the evidence that a reasonably prudent product seller could and would have taken additional precautions.

This approach has enabled claimants to prevail when legislative or administrative standards did not meet an appropriate level of safety. For example, in "Raymond v. Riegel Textile Corp.," 484 F. 2d 1025 (1st Cir. 1973), the claimant was able to show that a standard promulgated under the "Flammable Fabrics Act" was outdated. *See also* "Burch v. Amsterdam Corp.," 366 A. 2d 1079 (D.C. 1976) (when manufacturer knows of greater dangers not included in a statutorily mandated warning, it should bring those precautions to the attention of product users). On the other hand, it recognizes that government safety standards *may* provide an adequate basis for evaluating safety in tort law.

Subsection (B) makes it clear that when the injury-causing aspect of the product did not conform or was not in compliance with a legislative or administrative regulatory standard, the product shall be deemed defective under Subsection 104(B), when design is relevant, or Subsection 104(C), when duty to warn is relevant, unless the product seller shows by a preponderance of the evidence that its failure to comply amounted to reasonably prudent conduct under the circumstances. *See* "Restatement (Second) of Torts" Section 286 (1965). A product seller may be able to prevail under Subsection (B) by showing that compliance would have created greater dangers than non-compliance would have. *Cf.* "Davison v. Williams," 251 Ind. 448, 242 N.E. 2d 101 (1968) (violation of safety regulation may be justified in circumstances).

Subsection (C) addresses a highly specialized problem with respect to a product that had been manufactured strictly in accordance with mandatory specifications set forth in a government contract. When compliance with such a standard leads to an injury, the government, not the product seller, is the appropriate defendant. As the court in "Hunt v. Balsius," 55 Ill. App. 3d 14, 370 N.E. 2d 617, 621–22 (1977), indicated, "public policy dictates that bidders who comply strictly with governmental specifications should be shielded from liability in any respect in which the product complies." When enacting this provision, a legislature should ensure that its own state government bears financial responsibility (either through tort law or through a compensation system) for the harm it has caused by directing that the product conform to contract specifications.

Subsection (D) provides a counterweight to Subsection (C). If the bidder fails to comply with a mandatory government contract specification, and this failure to comply caused the claimant's injury, the product seller will deemed liable under Subsection 104(B) if the specification related to design, or under Subsection 104(C) or 105(A) of the specification related to instruction or warnings. If the manufacturer's compliance exceeded the government regulation and the product failed, liability should not be imposed under this Section—in that case, the technical "failure to comply" would not be the proximate cause of the injury that befell claimant.

* * * * *

Code

Sec. 109. Notice of Possible Claim Required

(A) An attorney who anticipates filing a claim shall notify all product sellers against whom the claim is likely to be made. The notice of claim shall:

(1) Identify the product as specifically as possible;

(2) State the time, place, circumstances, and events giving rise to the claim;

(3) Give an estimate of compensation or other relief to be sought.

(B) The attorney shall give notice of claim within six (6) months of the date of entering into an attorney-client relationship with the claimant in regard to the claim. For the purposes of Section 109, such a relationship arises when the attorney, or any member or associate of the attorney's firm, agrees to serve the claimant's interests in regard to the anticipated claim.

(C) If the claimant's attorney requests the information at the time the notice of claim is given, the product seller receiving the notice of claim shall promptly furnish the claimant's attorney with the names and addresses of each person whom the product seller knows to be in the chain of manufacture and distribution of the product, and who is likely to be subject to liability under Sections 104 or 105. Any product seller who fails to furnish such information may be subject to liability as provided in Subsection (E).

(D) A claimant who delays entering into an attorney-client relationship so as to delay unreasonably the notice of claim required by Subsection (A) may be subject to liability as provided in Subsection (E).

(E) Any party to the product liability claim or any attorney representing such a party who suffers a monetary loss associated with the litigation of the claim caused by the failure of a claimant or a claimant's attorney, or of a product seller or its attorney, to comply with the requirements of this Section may recover pecuniary damages, costs, and reasonable attorneys' fees from that party. Failure to comply with the requirements of Section 109 does not affect the validity of any claim or defense under this Act.

Analysis

Sec. 109. Notice of Possible Claim Required

The purpose of Section 109 is to inform product sellers at an early date that the products they produce may be defective. Under present law, a claimant can delay informing a product seller of a claim until the statute of limitations has nearly expired. In most jurisdictions, this period is two or three years. Although 77.8 percent of all bodily injury claims are reported within six months, the 22.2 percent that are not reported during this period are of concern because they represent about 68 percent of the claim payments. "ISO Closed Claims Survey" at 100 (1977).

A reasonable notice of claim requirement in product liability law promotes the interests of consumers and product users because it is a low-cost means of helping to assure product safety. Presumably, if informed about defective conditions at an early stage, a product seller is likely to take action to correct such conditions and thus prevent future injuries. This is why notice-of-claim provisions have been utilized in other contexts. *See, e.g.,* "U.C.C." Section 2-607 (warranty breaches); 18 E. McQuillan, "Municipal Corporations" Section 53.154 (3d ed. 1977) (suits against municipalities for injuries); 3 A. Larson "Workmen's Compensation Law" Section 78.00 *et seq.* (1976) (notice of injury to employer). *See also* Comment, "Notice Requirement in Warranty Actions Involving Personal Injury," 51 "Calif. L. Rev." 586 (1963); Phillips, "Notice of Breach in Sales and Strict Tort Liability Law: Should There Be a Difference?," 47 "Ind. L. J." 457, 468–69 (1972) (observing that requiring notice of claim may encourage defendants to make reasonable settlements).

This Section is adapted from the recently enacted "Minn. Stat. Ann." Section 604.04 (Supp. 1978). It differs from analogous notice-of-claim provisions in that it does not provide that a claim or defense will be barred by the failure of the injured party to meet its conditions. As the court noted in "Greenman v. Yuba Power Prods., Inc.," 59 Cal. 2d 57, 377 P.2d 897, 27 Cal. Rptr. 697, 700 (1963), such a provision may

> become a booby trap for the unwary. The injured consumer is seldom 'steeped in the business practice which justifies the rule,' [James, "Products Liability" (pt. 2), 34 "Tex. L. Rev. 192, 197 (1955)] and at least until he has had legal advice it will not occur to him to give notice. . . .

Instead, Section 109 places a duty on the attorney to give the notice of claim. It imposes on the attorney the costs of investigation and other litigation expenses which stem from the failure to give notice.

Section 109 also places a burden on the product seller who is notified of an anticipated claim to provide the claimant's attorney with the names and addresses of others whom the product seller knows to be in the chain of manufacture and distribution of the product, and who are likely to be subject to liability under Sections 104 or 105. The product seller is not obligated, however, to supply long lists of every supplier of a component part of its product or every possible wholesale and retain purchaser of it. Product sellers may also be held liable under this Section for litigation costs that stem from the failure to provide the required names.

Subsection 109(E) is limited to losses associated directly with the litigation of the claim in issue and does not apply to possible losses suffered by persons other than a party to the product liability claim or any attorney representing such a party.

Claims arising under Section 109 can be consolidated with the principal product liability claim brought under this Act.

*   *   *   *   *

Code

Sec. 110. Length of Time Product Sellers are Subject to Liability

(A) *Useful Safe Life.*

(1) Except as provided in Subsection (A)(2), a product seller shall not be subject to liability to a claimant for harm under this Act if the product seller proves by a

preponderance of the evidence that the harm was caused after the product's ''useful safe life'' had expired.

''Useful safe life'' begins at the time of delivery of the product and extends for the time during which the product would normally be likely to perform or be stored in a safe manner. For the purposes of Section 110, ''time of delivery'' means the time of delivery of a product to its first purchaser or lessee who was not engaged in the business of either selling such products or using them as component parts of another product to be sold.

Examples of evidence that is especially probative in determining whether a product's useful safe life had expired include:

(a) The amount of wear and tear to which the product had been subject;

(b) The effect of deterioration from natural causes, and from climate and other conditions under which the product was used or stored;

(c) The normal practices of the user, similar users, and the product seller with respect to the circumstances, frequency, and purposes of the product's use, and with respect to repairs, renewals, and replacements;

(d) Any representations, instructions, or warnings made by the product seller concerning proper maintenance, storage, and use of the product or the expected useful sale life of the product; and

(e) Any modification or alteration of the product by a user or third party.

(2) A product seller may be subject to liability for harm caused by a product used beyond its useful safe life to the extent that the product seller has expressly warranted the product for a longer period.

(B) *Statute of Repose.*

(1) *Generally.* In claims that involve harm caused more than ten (10) years after time of delivery, a presumption arises that the harm was caused after the useful safe life had expired. This presumption may only be rebutted by clear and convincing evidence.

(2) *Limitations on Statute of Repose.* (a) If a product seller expressly warrants that its product can be utilized safely for a period longer than ten (10) years, the period of repose, after which the presumption created in Subsection (B)(1) arises, shall be extended according to that warranty or promise.

(b) The ten- (10-) year period of repose established in Subsection (B)(1) does not apply if thc product seller intentionally misrepresents facts about its product, or fraudulently conceals information about it, and that conduct was a substantial cause of the claimant's harm.

(c) Nothing contained in Subsection (B) shall affect the right of any person found liable under this Act to seek and obtain contribution or indemnity from any other person who is responsible for harm under this Act.

(d) The ten- (10-) year period of repose established in Subsection (B)(1) shall not apply if the harm was caused by prolonged exposure to a defective product, or if the injury-causing aspect of the product that existed at the time of delivery was not discoverable by an ordinary reasonably prudent person until more than ten (10) years after the time of delivery, or if the harm, caused within ten (10) years after the time of delivery, did not manifest itself until after that time.

(C) *Statute of Limitation.* No claim under this Act may be brought more than two (2) years from the time the claimant discovered, or in the exercise of due diligence should have discovered, the harm and the cause thereof.

* * * * *

Analysis

Sec. 110. Length of Time Product Sellers are Subject to Liability

Perhaps more significant than any other single factor alleged to be the cause of the nationwide product liability insurance problem are the rules governing the responsibility of product sellers for older products. Most product liabilty policies include claims based not only on products manufactured or sold during the given policy year, but also on products manufactured or sold in the past. In the case of sellers of durable goods, this creates an ''open-ended'' liability situation.

The Supreme Court of Oregon summarized the general common law rule for products with the statement: ''(P)rolonged use of a manufactured article is but one factor, albeit an important one, in the determination of whether a defect in the product made it unsafe. . . .'' ''Tucker v. Unit Crane & Shovel Corp.,'' 256 Or. 318, 473 P.2d 862 (1970) (boom crane manufactured in 1956, collapsed in 1965). *See also* ''Gates v. Ford Motor Company,'' 494 F. 2d 458 (10th Cir. 1974) (24-year-old tractor); ''Kaczmarek v. Mesta Machinery Co.,'' 463 F.2d 675 (3d Cir. 1972) (30-year-old pickling machine); ''Mondshour v. General Motors Corp.,'' 298 F. Supp. 111 (D. Md. 1969) (bus designed 17 years prior to accident).

Partly in response to this open-ended liability potential, a number of states have enacted statutes of repose that begin at the time a product is first sold and distributed. *See, e.g.,* ''1979 Ala. Acts'' No. 79-468 Section 3(b) (''10 years after the manufactured product is first put to use''); ''Ariz. Rev. Stat. Ann.'' Section 12-551 (Supp. 1978) (''12 years after the product was first sold for use or consumption. . .''); ''Fla. Stat. Ann.'' Section 95.031(2) (Supp. 1979) (''12 years after the date of delivery of the completed product''); ''Ill. Ann. Stat.'' ch. 83, Section 22.2(b) (Supp. 1979) (12 years from date of first sale or 10 years from sale to actual user-claimant—strict liability); ''Ind. Code Ann.'' Section 33-1-1.5-5 (Supp. 1978) (''10 years after the delivery . . . to the initial user''); ''Neb. Rev. Stat.'' Section 25-224 (Supp. 1978) (10 years after the first sale); ''Utah Code Ann.'' Section 78-15-3(1) (1977) (6 years after date of initial purchase; 10 years after date of manufacture).

The advantages of these statutes are that they: (1) establish an actuarially certain date after which no liability can be assessed; and (2) eliminate tenuous claims involving older products for which evidence of defective conditions may be difficult to produce. *See* ''Order of Railroad Telegraphers v. Railway Express Agency,'' 321 U.S. 342, 348-49 (1944).

On the other hand, a fundamental problem with these statutes is that they *may* deprive a person injured by a product of the right to bring a claim based on a defective product before the injury has actually occurred. *See* Johnson, ''Products Liability 'Reform': A Hazard to Consumers,'' 56 ''N.C. L. Rev.'' 677 689-90 (1978); ''Victorson v. Bock Laundry Mach. Co.,'' 37 N.Y.2d 395, 335 N.E.2d 275, 373 N.Y.S.2d 39 (1975).

The limited available data show that insurers' apprehension about older products may be exaggerated. *See* "ISO Closed Claims Survey" at 105–08 (indicating that over 97 percent of product-related accidents occur within six years of the time the product was purchased and, in the capital goods area, 83.5 percent of all bodily injury accidents occur within ten years of manufacture). Nevertheless, as the "Task Force Report" indicated, the underwriters' concern about *potential* losses associated with older products may be an important factor in the recent increase in liability insurance premiums for manufacturers of durable goods. *See* "Task Force Report" at VII–21.

Section 110 attempts to provide insurers and product sellers with some security against stale claims, while preserving the claimant's right to obtain damages for injuries caused by defective products. It accomplishes this result through provisions on useful safe life, a statute of repose, and a statute of limitation.

(A) *Useful Safe Life.* The common law in most states is that "(t)he age of an allegedly defective product must be considered in light of its expected useful life and the stress to which it has been subjected." "Kuisis v. Baldwin-Lima-Hamilton Corp.," 457 Pa. 321, 319 A.2d 914, 923 (1974) (brake-locking mechanism on a crane failed after more than 20 years of use). The "Kuisis" court noted further that "in certain situations the prolonged use factor may loom so large as to obscure all others in a case." *Id.*

The basic problem has been the vagueness of the concept. Thus, while the "Task Force Report" noted that "if a useful life limitation were identified in statutory form, it might be expected that it would be given more serious attention by both judge and jury" ("Task Force Report" at VII–27), it also observed that "the concept would still lack specificity." *Id.* Subsection (A) is designed to define the concept with as much specificity as possible.

The Subsection was derived from "Minn. Stat. Ann." Section 604.03 (Supp. 1978). It serves to remind the court and the trier of fact that a product seller may be held liable only for harms caused during the useful *safe* life of the product. It does not attempt to apply fixed useful safe life standards for all products. Such an approach is not possible as a practical matter. *See* Phillips, "An Analysis of Proposed Reform of Products Liability Statutes of Limitations," 56 "N.C.L. Rev." 663, 673 (1978). Rather, it identifies factors that will assist the court and the trier of fact in determining how long a product can reasonably be expected to perform or be stored in a safe manner.

Section 110 uses the term "useful safe life" (not "useful life," a term which has already acquired a meaning in the law of taxation), because the period in which the product can have some "utility" may be well beyond the period in which the product is "safe." For example, a driver may continue to "use" tires that lack sufficient treads for safety.

A product seller may raise the "useful safe life" of a product as an affirmative defense in a product liability claim. The period of time begins at the time of delivery of the product and extends through the time during which the product would normally be likely to perform in a safe manner.

"Time of delivery" is defined as the time of delivery of a product to its first purchaser or lessee not engaged in the business of either selling such products or using them as component parts of another product to be sold. "Time of delivery" is an important concept in the Act because it marks the last time a product seller has physical control of the product and the first time that the product is in the hands of someone other than a product seller. The useful safe life and repose periods of Section 110 begin to run from this point in time.

The Section then sets forth a series of factors that will be of assistance to the court and jury in determining whether the period of time has expired. The product seller need not introduce evidence with respect to each of the listed factors. Rather, each of the litigants in a product liability claim may introduce evidence on those factors listed which, they believe, will support their respective contentions. In some cases, evidence on one or a few of the factors may be regarded as dispositive of the "useful safe life" issue and, when this occurs, the lack of evidence on one or the other factors normally will not affect the outcome of the case. The product seller has the burden of proof upon the issue.

Factors (a) through (c) under Subsection (A) are basically self-explanatory. Factor (d) refers to the useful safe life stated *by the product seller.* A product seller can place some reliance on this provision when it has indicated that a product should not be used beyond a certain period of time. However, Subsection (A) does not give the product seller absolute power to limit a product's useful safe life. While this was suggested in "Velez v. Craine & Clark Lumber Corp.," 33 N.Y.2d 117, 305 N.E.2d 750, 350 N.Y.S.2d 617 (1973), almost all courts would insist on retaining judicial power to determine whether the product seller's limitation was a reasonable one. *Cf.* "Henningsen v. Bloomfield Motors, Inc.," 32 N.J. 358, 161 A.2d 69 (1960). Further, even the "Velez" court indicated that a product seller's limitation on useful life could not bind the rights of a non-purchaser claimant. Nevertheless, where the product seller imposes a reasonable limitation, made in good faith to protect the user, the trier of fact should give very serious consideration to this fact in determining whether the product was used beyond its useful safe life.

Factor (e), dealing with modifications of the product by users or third parties, relates to conduct that might shorten or lengthen the useful life of the product. While the Act treats product modifications in Section 112, they are also factors in determining whether a product has been used beyond its useful safe life.

(B) *Statute of Repose.*

(1) *Generally.* Statutes of repose differ from statutes of limitation in that they set a fixed limit after the time of the product's manufacture, sale, or delivery beyond which the product seller will not be held liable. The rationale of such statutes is threefold. First, the fact that a product has been used safely for a substantial period of time is some indication that it was not defective at the time of delivery. Second, if a product seller is not aware of a claim, the passing of time may make it extremely difficult to construct a good defense because of the obstacle of securing evidence. Although the burden of proof on the issue of defectiveness remains on the claimant under the Act, a jury, as a practical matter, may demand an explanation from a product seller when the claimant has suffered a severe injury. The third rationale is that persons ought to be allowed, as a matter of policy, to plan their affairs with a reasonable degree of certainty. This goes to the heart of the product liability insurance rate-setting problem.

Even though past data show that 83.5 percent of bodily injury claims arise within a ten-year period,[13] there is no safeguard in the existing law that the past will portend the future. There is always the possibility that the number of claims for older products will increase. *See* "ISO Closed Claims Survey" at 107.

On the other hand, consumers are justifiably concerned about overly broad absolute cut-offs of their right to sue. This provision recognizes consumer concerns in three basic ways:

(1) The term of the statute is ten years—beyond the term enacted or proposed in a number of states;

(2) The statute begins to run at the time of delivery, not the time of manufacture; and

(3) The statute does not contain an absolute cut-off, but rather a presumption that the product has been used beyond its useful safe life. Colorado law utilizes this approach. "Colo. Rev. Stat." Section 13-21-403(3) (Supp. 1978). Most other state product liability statutes do not.

Consumer concerns are also addressed by three of the four additional restrictions contained in Subsection (B)(2).

(2) *Limitations on Statute of Repose.* This Subsection contains four key limitations on its scope of operation.

First, Subsection (B) does not apply when a product seller has expressly warranted or promised that a product can be used safely for a period longer than ten years. *See* Subsection 102(K) (definition of "express warranty").

Second, the statute of repose provisions do not apply when a product seller intentionally misrepresented facts about its product and this misrepresentation was a substantial cause of claimant's harm.

Third, Subsection (B) does not affect contribution and indemnity claims. Thus, an intermediate product seller will not have to absorb a liability loss that was the true responsibility of the original manufacturer. *See* Defense Research Institute. "Products Liability Position Paper" at 22 (monograph 1976); *see also* Phillips, *supra,* 56 "N.C. L. Rev." at 670-71 (1978).

Fourth, there is an exception for products that cause perceptible harm only through prolonged exposure (*see e.g.,* "Michie v. Great Lakes Steel Div., National Steel Corp.," 495 F.2d 213 (6th Cir. 1974)), or that cause harms that take many years to manifest themselves. *See* "Sindell v. Abbott Laboratories," 85 Cal. App. 3d 1, 149 Cal. Rptr. 138 (1978). An exception is also made for the unusual situation in which a product contains, at the time of delivery, a hidden defect that is not discoverable by a reasonably prudent product user and does not manifest itself until after a ten-year period has expired. *See* "Mickel v. Blackmon," 252 S.C. 202, 166 S.E.2d 173 (1969) (plastic used on gearshift lost its resiliency when exposed to sunlight).

If the ten-year presumption does not apply, a product seller can still prove that the product has been utilized beyond its useful safe life under Subsection (A).

---

[13] Figure for capital goods.

(C) *Statute of Limitation.* Tort statutes of limitation traditionally begin at the time a person is injured. This Subsection follows that approach. Nevertheless, in accord with justified consumer concerns, Subsection (C) extends the limitation period beyond the time of harm in situations where the claimant would have no reason to know about the harm or the causal connection to a defective product (*e.g.*, the case of long-term pharmaceutical harms). This reflects a general trend in both statutory and case law. *See* Birnbaum, "'First Breath's' Last Gasp: The Discovery Rule in Products Liability Cases," 13 "Forum" 279 (1977); and Annot., 91 "A.L.R.3d" 991 (1979). The two-year period represents the length of the traditional state statute of limitation based on claims for negligence. In light of the Act's adoption of the discovery rule, this is the maximum period that seemed to be appropriate.

The underlying philosophy of this Section is congruent with Sections 105 and 106, which shield product sellers from liability for risks that they would have no reason to discover at the time of manufacture.

* * * * *

Code

Sec. 111. Comparative Responsibility and Apportionment of Damages

(A) *Comparative Responsibility.* All claims under this Act shall be governed by the principles of comparative responsibility. In any claim under this Act, the comparative responsibility of, or attributed to, the claimant shall not bar recovery but shall diminish the award of compensatory damages proportionately, according to the measure of responsibility attributed to the claimant.

(B) *Apportionment of Damages.*

(1) In all claims involving comparative responsibility, the court, unless otherwise agreed by all parties, shall instruct the jury to answer special interrogatories or, if there is no jury, the court shall make findings, indicating:

(a) The amount of damages each claimant would be entitled to recover if the comparative responsibility of each party were disregarded; and

(b) The percentage of the total responsibility of all parties to each claim that is to be allocated to each claimant; defendant; third-party defendant; person or entity who misused, modified, or altered a product under Subsection 112 (C) or (D), [or who voluntarily and unreasonably used or stored a product with a known defective condition under Subsection 112(B)]; and person released from liability under Subsection 113(E). Under this Subsection, the court may determine that two or more persons are to be treated as a single party.

(2) When the claimant's employer's or co-employee's fault is considered, damages shall be reduced in accordance with Subsection 114(A), if applicable, or by the percentage of responsibility apportioned to such employer or co-employee, if that amount is greater. When a person released from liability under Subsection 113(E) would otherwise be liable under this Act, damages shall be reduced by the percentage of responsibility apportioned to such person.

(3) In determining the percentages of responsibility, the trier of fact shall consider, on a comparative basis, both the nature of the conduct of each person or entity

responsible and the extent of the proximate causal relation between the conduct and the damages claimed.

(4) The court shall determine the award of damages to each claimant in accordance with the findings and enter judgment against each party liable. For purposes of contribution under Section 113, the court shall also determine and state in the judgment each party's equitable share of the obligation to each claimant in accordance with the respective percentages of responsibility.

(5) Damages are to be apportioned severally, and not jointly, when a party is responsible for a distinct harm, or when there is some other reasonable basis for apportioning that party's responsibility for the harm. Otherwise, judgment shall be entered against each party liable on the basis of the rules of joint and several liability.

(6) When one or more parties made a substantial contribution to an indivisible harm, or for other reasons under the common law of the state is a joint tortfeasor, upon motion made not later than one (1) year after judgment is entered, the court shall determine whether all or part of a joint tortfeasor's share of the obligation is uncollectible from that joint tortfeasor.

If the court's finding is in the affirmative, the court shall reallocate any uncollectible amount among a claimant found to be responsible and other parties who are joint tortfeasors with the party whose share is uncollectible. The reallocation shall be made according to the respective percentages of responsibility of each party.

* * * * *

Analysis

Sec. 111. Comparative Responsibility and Apportionment of Damages

(A) *Comparative Responsibility.* Subsection (A) attempts to resolve existing legal uncertainty about the relevance of a claimant's conduct and the comparative responsibility of others who contributed to the claimant's harm. It applies principles of comparative responsibility to situations where more than one person has some responsibility for the product-related incident. *Cf.* "Uniform Comparative Fault Act" ("UCFA") Section 1. The consumer-oriented fairness of pure comparative responsibility is adopted, as compared with the "non-discriminating rough justice of the modified type. "Prefatory Note," "UCFA".

Although there is no assurance that the use of comparative responsibility principles will lower the cost of product liability claims, the inherent fairness of such principles has led to their inclusion in the "UCFA" by the National Conference of Commissioners of Uniform State Laws. Section 111 borrows extensively from the "UCFA" and its accompanying commentary.

Some courts and commentators have voiced concern about the semantic and theoretical difficulties of mixing the "apples" of negligence with the "oranges" of strict liability. *See e.g.,* "Kirkland v. General Motors Corp.," 521 P.2d 1353 (Okla. 1974); Robinson, "Square Pegs (Products Liability) in Round Holes (Comparative Negligence)," 52 "Cal. St. B.J." 16 (1977). Nevertheless, these concerns appear to be more theoretical than real.

The utility of comparative responsibility for product liability cases has been appreciated both by state legislatures[14] and courts.[15] It has also been recommended by a congressional subcommittee. "LaFalce Subcommittee Report," *supra* at 76.

Section 111 places a strong incentive for loss prevention on the party who is best able to accomplish that goal. It also avoids burdening the careful product user with liability insurance costs assessed to persons who misuse or are otherwise at fault in their handling of products. While some economic analyses indicate that a comparative responsibility system creates a risk of economic inefficiency because of an overinvestment in safety, the drafters of the Act have made a value judgment that such an "overinvestment" is worth making.

(B) *Apportionment of Damages.* In order to apply comparative responsibility principles under this Act, it is necessary for the trier of fact to supply certain information in special interrogatories. Subsection (B)(1)(a), which is based on "UCFA" Subsection 2(A)(1), indicates that the trier of fact should set forth the amount of damages a claimant would receive if each party's comparative responsibility were disregarded. This helps assure that the trier fact does not inflate or deflate the amount of damages claimant would receive if the claimant were free from responsibility.

Subsection (B)(1)(b), which is based on "UCFA" Subsection 2(a)(2), requires the trier of fact to indicate the percentage of responsibility allocated to each claimant, defendant, third-party defendant, and person or entity who has misused, altered, or modified products under Subsections 112 (C) or (D). It also includes persons or entities who voluntarily and unreasonably used or stored a product with a known defective condition under Subsection 112(B)(2). As is noted in the analysis to that Subsection, this is an optional provision.

Although it is difficult to apportion the responsibility of an absent employer or co-employee who is immune from tort liability due to Worker Compensation laws, such an approach is necessary to ensure fairness to product sellers. It is also fair to employees because they have given up their right to sue in tort for harms caused by their employers' or co-employees' fault in exchange for their Worker Compensation benefits.

Subsection 111(B)(2) indicates that in cases of product misuse or alteration where an employer's or co-employee's fault is considered, damages should be reduced by the amount of Worker Compensation benefits the worker received or will receive in accordance with Subsection 114(A), or by the percentage of responsibility apportioned to such employer or co-employee, whichever is greater.

Thus, for example in a case in which a manufacturer is found to have been 40 percent responsible, the injured employee's employer was 60 percent responsible, and Worker Compensation benefits constituted 15 percent of the damages, then the

---

[14] *E.g.,* "Ark. Stat. Ann." Section 27-1763-1765 (Supp. 1977); "Me. Rev. Stat." tit. 14 Section 156 (Supp. 1978); "Mich. Comp. Laws Ann." Section 600.2949 (Supp. 1978), "Mich. Stat. Ann." Section 27 A.2949; Conn. (1979 Conn. Pub. Acts 79-483, Section 4).

[15] *E.g.,* "Thibault v. Sears, Roebuck & Co.," 395 A.2d 843 (N.H. 1978): "Daly v. General Motors Corp.," 20 Cal. 3d 725, 575 P.2d 1162, 144 Cal. Rptr. 380 (1978); "Busch v. Busch Constr., Inc.," 262 N.W.2d 377 (Minn. 1977); "Butaud v. Suburban Marine & Sport. Goods, Inc.," 555 P.2d 42 (Alaska 1976).

claimant's damages would be reduced by 60 percent, not 85 percent. On the other hand, if the manufacturer had been 80 percent responsible, the employer was 20 percent responsible, and Worker Compensation benefits constituted 30 percent of the damages, then the claimant's damages would be reduced by 30 percent, which was the amount of the Worker Compensation benefits and was greater than the employer's percentage (20 percent) of responsibility.

When a released party's fault is considered, the process is simpler. Damages are reduced according to the percentage of fault which the trier fact attributes to that person or entity.

Subsection (B)(1)(b) also indicates that persons who have been released under Subsection 113(E) shall be included in the apportionment of responsibility. This approach is in accord with the "UCFA" and the majority of cases that have addressed this issue. Again, while it is difficult to apportion an absent person's fault, the approach helps to ensure that all releases are executed in good faith. *See* "Frey v. Snelgrove," ——Minn.——, 269 N.W.2d 918 (1978); "Bartels v. City of Williston," 276 N.W.2d 113 (N.D. 1979); "Pierringer v. Hoger," 21 Wis. 2d 182, 124 N.W.2d 106 (1963).

Subsection (B)(3), which is based on "UCFA" Subsection 2(b), provides a general guideline to assist the trier of fact in comparing responsibility among the parties. The "UCFA" comments (Section 2) indicate that in appropriate cases, the trier of fact may also consider:

(1) Whether the conduct was mere inadvertence or engaged in with an awareness of the danger involved;

(2) The magnitude of the risk created by the conduct, including the number of persons endangered and the potential seriousness of the injury;

(3) The significance of what the actor was seeking to attain by his conduct;

(4) The actor's superior or inferior capacities; and

(5) The particular circumstances, such as the existence of an emergency requiring a hasty decision.

"UCFA Comment" Section 2 ("percentages of fault").

"The extent of the proximate causal relation between the conduct and the damages claimed" refers to proximate cause as opposed to cause-in-fact. While, at times, the distinction may be a difficult one to draw, this Act is premised on apportioning responsibility only—pure causation in terms of cause-in-fact is irrelevant to that concept. *See* Malone, "Ruminations on Cause-in-Fact." 9 "Stan. L. Rev." 60 (1956). Proximate cause, on the other hand, is an important concept in this Section. In order for the product user's conduct to bring about a reduction or apportionment of damages, it must be a proximate cause of the harm.

The importance of the distinction between cause-in-fact and proximate cause as applied to this Section may be illustrated by the so-called "second collision case" in which the claimant sues the manufacturer for enhanced injuries due to an alleged defect in the automobile, although the initial impact of the accident was caused by the claimant's or another person's negligent driving. When the enhanced injuries caused by the "second collision" within the automobile can be reasonably separated from those injuries caused by the initial collision, damages should be approximately divided. Nevertheless, the negligent driving should not be compared with the manufacturer's conduct because it is not the proximate cause of the enhanced injuries, even though it is clearly a cause-in-fact. *See* "Austin v. Ford Motor Co.," 86 Wis. 2d 628, 273 N.W. 2d 233, 239 (1979).

On the other hand, there may be "second collision cases" in which the enhanced injuries and the initial impact injuries cannot be reasonably separated. Such a case might arise when an allegedly defective automobile was hit at high speed. *See* "Fietzer v. Ford Motor Co.," 590 F. 2d 215 (7th Cir. 1978). In such a case, the driver's conduct is considered a proximate cause of the harm for purposes of comparative responsibility.

Subsection (B)(3), which is based on "UCFA" Subsection 2(c), helps to assure that the mathematics of comparative responsibility will be correctly determined. The court must determine the award for each claimant according to the findings made under this Subsection.

Subsections (B) (4) and (5) indicate that the common law rules of joint and several liability continue to apply under this Act. In this connection, it is important for the court to determine whether the defendant *is* a joint tortfeasor, *i.e.*, if its tortious conduct was a substantial cause of an indivisible injury, or it is otherwise deemed to have that status (*e.g.*, persons acting in concert, express or implied; persons vicariously liable for the torts of another). *See* W. Prosser, "Torts," at 297–99 (4th ed. 1971). A defendant who caused only a divisible part of the claimant's harm is only severally liable for that portion. *See* "UCFA Comment" Section 4, and "Restatement (Second) of Torts" Section 433A (1965).

As with "UCFA" Subsection 2(c), the judgment for each claimant will also show the share of each party's total obligation to the claimant. This should save litigation costs and avoid the need for a special motion or a separate action on the issue.

Subsection (B)(5) follows "UCFA" Subsection 2(d) in providing for the reallocation of damages among the parties responsible when one of the parties' share is uncollectible. The reallocation procedure applies to claimants who are contributorily at fault and joint tortfeasors who have made a substantial contribution to claimant's harm.

*   *   *   *   *

Code

Sec. 112. Conduct Affecting Comparative Responsibility

(A) *Failure to Discover a Defective Condition.*

(1) *Claimant's Failure to Inspect.* A claimant is not required to have inspected the product for a defective condition. Failure to have done so does not render the claimant responsible for the harm caused or reduce the claimant's damages.

(2) *Claimant's Failure to Observe an Apparent Defective Condition.* When the product seller proves by a preponderance of the evidence that the claimant, while using the product, was injured by a defective condition that would have been apparent, without inspection, to an ordinary reasonably prudent person, the claimant's damages shall be subject to reduction. The procedural principles governing reduction of damages are set forth in Section 111.

(3) *A Non-Claimant's Failure to Inspect for Defects or to Observe an Apparent Defective Condition.* A non-claimant's failure to inspect for a defective condition or to observe an apparent defective condition that would have been obvious, without inspection, to an ordinary reasonably prudent person, shall not reduce claimant's damages.

(B) *Use of a Product With a Known Defective Condition.*

(1) *By a Claimant.* When the product seller proves, by a preponderance of the evidence, that the claimant knew about the product's defective condition, and voluntarily used the product or voluntarily assumed the risk of harm from the product, the claimant's damages shall be subject to reduction to the extent that the claimant did not act as an ordinary reasonably prudent person under the circumstances. Under this Subsection, the trier of fact may determine that the claimant should bear sole responsibility for harm caused by a defective product. The procedural principles governing reduction of damages are set forth in Section 111.

*Optional Section

[(2) *By a Non-Claimant Product User.* If the product seller proves by a preponderance of the evidence that a product user, other than the claimant, knew about a product's defective condition, but voluntarily and unreasonably used or stored the product and thereby caused claimant's harm, the claimant's damages shall be subject to apportionment. The procedural principles governing apportionment of damages are set forth in Section 111.]

(C) *Misuse of a Product.*

(1) "Misuse" occurs when the product user does not act in a manner that would be expected of an ordinary reasonably prudent person who is likely to use the product in the same or similar circumstances.

(2) When the product seller proves, by a preponderance of the evidence, that product misuse by a claimant, or by a party other than the claimant or the product seller, has caused the claimant's harm, the claimant's damages shall be subject to reduction or apportionment to the extent that the misuse was a cause of the harm. Under this Subsection, the trier of fact may determine that the harm arose solely because of product misuse. The procedural principles governing reduction or apportionment of damages are set forth in Section 111.

(3) Under this Subsection, subject to state and federal law regarding immunity in tort, the trier of fact may determine that a party or parties who misused the product and thereby caused claimant's harm should bear partial or sole responsibility for harm caused by the product and are subject to liability to the claimant.

(D) *Alteration or Modification of a Product.*

(1) "Alteration or modification" occurs when a person or entity other than the product seller changes the design, construction, or formula of the product, or changes or removes warnings or instructions that accompanied or were displayed on the product. "Alteration or modification" of a product includes the failure to observe routine care and maintenance, but does not include ordinary wear and tear.

(2) When the product seller proves, by a preponderance of the evidence, that an alteration or modification of the product by the claimant, or by a party other than the

claimant or the product seller, has caused the claimant's harm, the claimant's damages shall be subject to reduction or apportionment to the extent that the alteration or modification was a cause of the harm. Under this Subsection, the trier of fact may determine that the harm arose solely because of the product alteration or modification.

This Subsection shall not be applicable if:

(a) The alteration or modification was in accord with the product seller's instructions or specifications;

(b) The alteration or modification was made with the express or implied consent of the product seller; or

(c) The alteration or modification was reasonably anticipated conduct under Subsection 102(G), and the product was defective under Subsection 104(C) because of the product seller's failure to provide adequate warnings or instructions with respect to the alteration or modification.

The procedural principles governing reduction or apportionment of damages are set forth in Section 111.

(3) Under this Subsection, subject to state and federal law regarding immunity in tort, the trier of fact may determine that a party or parties who altered or modified the product and thereby caused claimant's harm should bear partial or sole responsibility for harm caused by the product and are subject to liability to the claimant.

* * * * *

Analysis

Sec. 112. Conduct Affecting Comparative Responsibility

(A) *Failure to Discover a Defective Condition.*

(1) *Claimant's Failure to Inspect.* Under common law, the product user had an obligation to inspect for defects; failure to do so could bar a claim. *See* "Palmer v. Massey-Ferguson, Inc." 3 Wash. App. 508, 476 P. 2d 713 (1970). However, under modern tort law, the product user is entitled to assume that the product is reasonably safe for its ordinary use. *See* "Restatement (Second) of Torts" Section 402A (1965); "Cepeda v. Cumberland Eng'r. Co.," 76 N.J. 152, 386 A. 2d 816 (1978). Subsection (A) follows these cases and does not require the product user or consumer to inspect a product for a defect. *See* "Kassouf v. Lee Bros.," 209 Cal. App. 2d 568, 26 Cal. Rptr. 276 (1962) (plaintiff, without inspection, ate a chocolate bar containing worms and maggots).

(2) *Claimant's Failure to Observe an Apparent Defective Condition.* Cases can arise where a defect would be apparent, without inspection, to an ordinary reasonably prudent person. Subsection (A)(2) incorporates the Task Force's views in this area, permitting the trier of fact to consider this conduct and reduce claimant's damages. Under Comment n to the "Restatement (Second) of Torts" Section 402A, an individual who failed to discover an apparent defective condition would, theoretically, still be allowed a full claim. On the other hand, if that person knew about the defect and proceeded anyway, the claim would be totally barred. This approach has led to considerable litigation and expense over the issue of whether a claimant knew or did not know about a particular defect. *See* "Task Force Report" at VII-51-53; *see also*

"Karabatsos v. Spivey Co.," 49 Ill. App. 3d 317, 364 N.E. 2d 319 (1977); "Teagle v. Fischer & Porter Co.," 89 Wash. 2d 149, 570 P. 2d 438 (1977); "Poches v. J.J. Newberry Co.," 549 F. 2d 1166 (8th Cir. 1977). The Act eliminates this distinction and focuses on the true responsibility of the product user.

Thus, if a claimant with good eyesight ate a candy bar that had bright green worms crawling over it, Subsection (A)(2) permits the trier of fact to find that the claimant should bear some responsibility for any ill effects suffered. This example involves a defective condition that can be discovered without inspection. *Cf.* "Auburn Mach. Works Co. v. Jones," 366 So. 2d 1167 (Fla. 1979).

Subsection (A)(2) will not promote misconduct by product sellers. If they were aware of the defect in the goods at the time of sale, the punitive damages section of the Art (Section 120) would provide a strong incentive not to sell such a product.

(3) *A Non-Claimant's Failure to Inspect for Defects or to Observe an Apparent Defective Condition.* When a product seller has sold a defective product and an intervening product user negligently fails to discover the defect or to take precautions against the possible harm, case law is uniform that the product user's conduct does not relieve the product seller of liability. *See* "Ford Motor Co. v. Matthews," 291 So. 3d 169 (Miss. 1974); "Boeing Airplane Co. v. Brown," 291 F.2d 310 (9th Cir. 1961); "Comstock v. General Motors Corp.," 358 Mich. 163, 99 N.W.2d 627 (1959). In this instance, the product seller is required to bear responsibility for the defective product it placed on the market.

(B) *Use of a Product With a Known Defective Condition.*

(1) *By a Claimant.* When it is clear that a claimant voluntarily and unreasonably used a product with a known defective condition, the claimant's damages are subject to reduction. Care must be taken not to allow recovery of a claim in a situation where individuals, in effect, have created their own product liability claim. In that regard, it should be noted that consent is a defense even to intentional wrongs. *See* Prosser, "Torts" at 101 (4th ed. 1971).

However, there may be cases where an individual voluntarily uses a product with a known defective condition, but the reasonableness of this conduct becomes a matter of dispute. For example, if a person discovers a welt in a tire, should that person be required to stop immediately and call for assistance, or is it reasonable to proceed to a nearby gasoline station to have the tire repaired? The answer depends on the particular fact situation. Many cases arise in this shadowy zone. *See* "Henderson v. Ford Motor Co.," 519 S.W.2d 87 (Tex. 1974); "Ford Motor Co. v. Lee," 237 Ga. 554, 229 S.E.2d 379 (1976). Subsection (B)(1) allows the trier of fact to consider the claimant's conduct in the particular fact situation and to reduce damages to the extent that it is appropriate to do so. From both the claimant's and the product seller's perspective, this mitigates the "all-or-nothing" approach that has arisen as a result of some court interpretations of Comment to Section 402A of the "Restatement (Second) of Torts."

(2) *By a Non-Claimant Product User.* Subsection (B)(2) is placed in brackets as an optional section. It would apportion responsibility for injuries caused by a defective product between the product seller and a product user who voluntarily and unreasonably exposed the claimant to the product risk. Some case law and, perhaps,

proper placement of incentives for loss prevention support this result. *Cf.* "Aetna Ins. Co. v. Loveland Gas & Elec. Co." 369 F.2d 648 (6th Cir. 1966); "Drazen v. Otis Elevator Co.," 96 R.I. 114, 189 A.2d 693 (1963). On the other hand, case law will not shift responsibility where the product was entirely unfit for its intended use,[16] and Subsection (B)(2) may create a situation in which a claimant injured by a defective product cannot bring a successful suit against anyone. This could occur when the Subsection shields the seller of the defective product, and an immunity (*e.g.*, Worker Compensation) shields the negligent third-party actor. Moreover, as Professor Phillips has observed,

> The third party rarely intends to cause the plaintiff injury. Where there is no such intent, the third party's failure to prevent the injury is attributable to his inadvertence, regardless of whether he actually knew or merely should have known of the danger.

Phillips, supra, 28 "Drake L. Rev." at 372.

In light of the very close balance of equities with regard to this Section, it has been bracketed and should be regarded as optional.

(C) *Misuse of a Product.* Subsection (C) provides for a reduction or apportionment of the liability of the product seller when an injury occurs, in whole or in part, because the product user misused the product in some way that the product seller could not reasonably anticipate. *See* "Netzel v. State Sand & Gravel Co.," 51 Wis. 2d 1, 186 N.W.2d 258 (1971); "General Motors Corp. v. Hopkins," 548 S.W.2d 344 (Tex. 1977). The definition of "misuse" is based on the Act's concept of "reasonably anticipated conduct." *See* Subsection 102(G) and analysis.

Damages are reduced or apportioned "to the extent" that the misuse caused the harm and, under Subsection (C)(2), the trier of fact may determine that the harm arose *solely* because of product misuse. "Helene Curtis Indus. v. Pruitt," 385 F.2d 841 (5th Cir. 1967).

Subsection (C)(3) indicates that a third party who is not immune under state or federal law and who has misused a product may be subject to liability to the claimant.

(D) *Alteration or Modification of a Product.* Subsection (D) deals with the situation in which a person or entity other than the product seller has altered or modified the product and this has led to the claimant's harm. Alteration or modification (as contrasted with misuse) occurs when a claimant or third-party product user changes the product's design, construction, or formula, or modifies or removes instructions that accompanied or were displayed on the product.

Some courts have imposed liability on the product seller in this situation if the alteration or modification was in some manner "foreseeable." *See, e.g.*, "Blim v. Newbury Indus., Inc.," 443 F.2d 1126 (10th Cir. 1971) (machine safety guard removed by co-worker). Courts that have held the original product seller responsible in these instances have bordered on imposing absolute liability. Thus, insurers have a just concern about the broad-scale imposition of liability where intervention by

---

[16] *See, e.g.*, "Clement v. Crosby & Co.," 148 Mich. 111 N.W. 745 (1907); "Farley v. Edward E. Tower & Co.," 271 Mass. 230, 171 N.E. 839 (1930).

another party was the principal cause of the accident. As the American Insurance Association has noted:

> It is difficult enough to calculate the risk associated with a given product even where there is access to knowledge about its basic inherent characteristics. . . . The task becomes impossible if the premium calculations must take into account not only the inherent properties of the machine, but also its transformation in the hands of others, and their neglect of repair and maintenance.

AIA, "Product Liability Legislative Package" at 16 (monograph 1977).

Moreover, if the law ignores alterations and modifications or products, it fails to place an incentive for loss prevention on those who might engage in such conduct.

The authors of the "Restatement (Second) of Torts" Section 402A, Subsection 1(b), recognized this fact and subjected the product seller to liability only when the seller's product reached "the user or consumer without substantial change in the condition in which it was sold." Comment g to that Section stated the matter more firmly:

> The seller is not liable when he delivers the product in a safe condition, and subsequent mishandling or other causes make it harmful by the time it is consumed. The burden of proof that the product was in a defective condition at the time that it left the hands of the particular seller is upon the injured plaintiff; and unless evidence can be produced which will support the conclusion that it was then defective, the burden is not sustained.

Recently, a number of state legislatures have enacted the essence of this comment into law. "Ariz. Rev. Stat. Ann." Section 12-683(2) (Supp. 1978); "Ind. Code Ann." 33-1-1.5 Section 4(b)(3) (Supp. 1978); "Ky. Rev. Stat. Ann." Section 411-320 (1978); "N.H. Rev. Stat. Ann." Section 507-D:3 (Supp. 1978); "R.I. Gen. Laws" Section 9-1-32 (1978); "Tenn. Code Ann." Section 23-3708 (1978); "Utah Code Ann." Section 78-15-5 (1977).

According to the statistics of the Insurance Services Office, product modification only occurs in approximately 13 percent of product liability cases. Of these cases, the largest number of the product modifications (39 percent) result from the conduct of employers. *See* "ISO Closed Claims Survey" at 140-41. This raises the main problem with rules that limit a product seller's responsibility for subsequent product alterations or modifications—often the injured worker cannot sue the one who is really at fault because of the "exclusive remedy" provisions of Worker Compensation statutes. However, it is fair to state that the destruction of a tort remedy against the employer

> should not of itself create a third-party remedy against the manufacturer or distributor of the product in question. If Worker Compensation is regarded as a proper remedy in other cases of an exclusive employer's wrong, then so too should it be where that wrong involves the product acquired from third-party defendants.

AIA, "Product Liability Legislative Package," *supra* at 15-16.

Nevertheless, Subsection (D) takes account of the hardship that can result from an overly broad liability limitation in cases of product modification or alteration. Thus, the provision is very narrowly drawn.

Subsection (D)(2) ensures that the principles of comparative responsibility are correctly applied by reference to Section 111. If an alteration or modification was made by the claimant, damages are subject to reduction in accordance with the claimant's percentage of responsibility. If a party other than the claimant is responsible for the modification or alteration, damages are to be apportioned in accordance with the parties' percentages of responsibility.

In the case of an employer or co-employee immune from tort liability or a released party under Subsection 113(E), the rules set forth in Subsection 112(B)(2) would apply with regard to reduction of damages.

Under Subsection (D)(2), a product seller may avoid liability to the extent it proves that claimant's harm was proximately caused by the alteration or modification. If the harm arose solely because of the product alteration or modification, the product seller will not be liable at all. On the other hand, the rule adopted ensures that the product seller will remain liable to the extent that it is responsible for the harm. *See* "Fincher v. Surrette," 365 So. 2d 860, 863 (La. Ct. App. 1979). Subsection (D)(2) applies the comparative responsibility procedural principles set forth in Section 111.

As Subsections (D)(2) (a) and (b) indicate, the product seller cannot avoid responsibility for product alterations or modifications which the seller suggested (per instructions) or to which the seller expressly consented.

Subsection (D)(2)(c) indicates that the product seller may have a duty to warn against modifications or alterations of its product when it may reasonably anticipate that such conduct will occur on the part of persons who are likely to use the product. As Subsection 102(G) (definition of "reasonably anticipated conduct") indicates, this refers to conduct that would be engaged in by an ordinary reasonably prudent person.

Subsection (D)(2)(c) is not intended to encompass every type of act foreseeable by virtue of hindsight or otherwise. If alterations or modifications involve conduct which should have been reasonably anticipated by the product seller, such product seller will be responsible for harms that result if the failure to provide warnings against the type of alteration or modification at issue renders the product defective under Subsection 104(C). A general warning against any alterations or modifications will not suffice.

Subsection (D)(3) indicates that a third party who is not immune under state or federal law and who has negligently altered or modified a product may be subject to liability to the claimant.

* * * * *

Code

Sec. 113. Multiple Defendants: Contribution and Implied Indemnity

(A) A right of contribution exists under this Act between or among two or more persons who are jointly and severally liable, whether or not judgment has been recovered against all or any of them. It may be enforced either in the original action or by a separate action brought for that purpose. The basis for contribution is each person's equitable share of the obligation, including the equitable share of a claimant, as determined in accordance with the provisions of Section 111. For the purposes of this Act, contribution and implied indemnity are merged.

(B) If the proportionate responsibility of the parties to a claim for contribution has been established previously by the court, as provided in Section 111, a party paying more than its equitable share of the obligation may, upon motion, recover judgment for contribution.

(C) If the proportionate responsibility of the parties to the claim for contribution has not been established by the court, contribution may be enforced in a separate action, whether or not a judgment has been rendered against either the person seeking contribution or the person from whom contribution is being sought.

(D) Contribution is available to a person who enters into a settlement with a claimant only (1) if the liability of the person against whom contribution is sought has been extinguished by the settlement, and (2) to the extent that the amount paid in settlement was reasonable.

(E) A release, covenant not to sue, or similar agreement entered into by a claimant and a person liable discharges that person from all liability for contribution, but it does not discharge any other persons liable upon the same claim unless it so provides. However, the claim of the releasing claimant against the other parties is reduced by the amount of the released party's equitable share of the obligation, determined in accordance with the provisions of Section 111.

(F) If a judgment has been rendered, the action for contribution must be commenced within one year after the judgment becomes final. If no judgment has been rendered, the person bringing the action for contribution must have (1) discharged by payment the common liability within the period of the statute of limitation or repose applicable to the claimant's right of action against him and commenced the action for contribution within one year after payment, or (2) agreed while action was pending to discharge the common liability and, within one year after the agreement, have paid the liability and brought an action for contribution.

*　*　*　*　*

Analysis

Sec. 113. Multiple Defendants: Contribution and Implied Indemnity

Section 113 is based on Sections 4, 5, and 6 of the "Uniform Comparative Fault Act" ("UCFA"). Here, however, contribution and implied indemnity are merged in one section. Express indemnity—where one party has agreed to hold the other harmless for damages arising out of product liability actions—is left to commercial and common law. *See* "Task Force Report" at VII–99–103.

There is clear precedent for the merger of contribution and implied indemnity. *See* "Safeway Stores, Inc. v. Nest-Kart." 21 Cal. 3d 322, 579 P.2d 441, 146 Cal. Rptr. 550 (1978); "Skinner v. Reed-Prentice Division, Etc.," 70 Ill. 2d 1, 374 N.E.2d 437 (1977), *cert. denied,* 436 U.S. 946 (1978); "Busch v. Busch Constr. Inc.," ——Minn.——, 262 N.W.2d 377 (1977); "Dole v. Dow Chemical Co.," 30 N.Y.2d 143, 282 N.E.2d 288, 331 N.Y.S.2d 382 (1972); *see also* "N.Y. Civ. Prac. Law" Section 1402 (1976). This approach avoids the "all-or-nothing" aspect of implied indemnity law. In most situations, fault will be apportioned among product seller defendants. However, a situation could arise where the trier of fact could find that one product seller in the distribution chain was entirely responsible for a product harm. In that regard, this Section should be read in conjunction with Sections 111 and 112.

Subsection (A), which is based on "UCFA" Subsection 4(a), establishes a right of contribution which may be enforced in the original action or in a separate action and provides that contribution will be determined by the proportionate responsibility of the defendants. The Subsection outlines the procedure for the trier of fact to make the appropriate determination.

Subsection (B), which is based on "UCFA" Subsection 5(a), outlines a simplified procedure whereby a party is judged liable who has paid more than its proportionate share can recover from one who has paid less.

Subsection (C), which is based on "UCFA" Subsection 5(b), provides a mechanism for apportioning responsibility when all potential defendants were not parties to the original action. It indicates that if the court has not determined the proportionate responsibility of all parties in the original action, contribution may be obtained in a separate action.

Subsection (D), which is based on "UCFA" Subsection 4(b), makes if clear that a person who has settled a claim may seek contribution from another person. However, this Subsection limits the right of contribution in such a situation by requiring that the amount paid in settlement be reasonable and that the claimant's right to recover from the other person be extinguished by the settlement.

Subsection (E), which is based on "UCFA" Section 6, deals with the effect of the release of one or more, but not all tortfeasors. Under this Subsection, a released person is free from liability for contribution, and the liability of other persons to the claimant is reduced by the released person's equitable share of the responsibility as determined in accordance with the provisions of Section 111. Although this provision "may have some tendency to discourage a claimant from entering into a settlement, this solution is fairly based on the proportionate-fault principle." "UCFA Comment" Section 6. Furthermore, the provision that the liability of the non-settling persons is reduced by the settling person's percentage of the responsibility should discourage claimants from entering into collusive settlements with one defendant at the expense of the other parties.

The Act does not directly address the validity of "Mary Carter agreements." Such agreements are typically entered into between a claimant and one or more, but not all, of the product sellers. They are usually made in secret, and the agreeing product sellers remain as parties to the action. The agreeing product sellers' liability is decreased in direct proportion to the nonagreeing product sellers' increase in liability, and, in return, the agreeing product sellers guarantee the claimant a certain amount of money if the claimant does not obtain a judgment, or if it is less than a specified amount. While such an agreement appears collusive, some state courts currently regard "Mary Carter agreements" as valid. *See, e.g.,* Frier's, Inc. v. Seaboard Coastline Ry.," 355 So. 2d 208 (Fla. Dist. Ct. App. 1978). However, to the extent that a court chooses to regard a "Mary Carter agreement" as a *settlement,* Subsection (E) is intended to discourage such agreements.

Subsection (F) is based on "UCFA" Section 5 and sets forth the period of time in which an action for contribution may be brought.

*　　*　　*　　*　　*

Code

Sec. 114. Relationship Between Product Liability and Worker Compensation

(A) In the case of any product liability claim brought by or on behalf of an injured person entitled to compensation under a state Worker Compensation statute, damages shall be reduced by the amount paid as Worker Compensation benefits for the same injury plus the present value of all future Worker Compensation benefits payable for the same injury under the Worker Compensation statute.

(B) Unless the product seller has expressly agreed to indemnify or hold an employer harmless for harm caused to the employer's employee by a product, the employer shall have no right of subrogation, contribution, or indemnity against the product seller when the harm to the employee constitutes a product liability claim under this Act. Also, the employer's Worker Compensation insurance carrier shall have no right of subrogation against the product seller.

(C) When final judgment in an action brought under this Act has been entered prior to the determination of Worker Compensation benefits, the product seller may bring a subsequent action for reduction of the judgment by the amount of the Worker Compensation benefits, or for recoupment from the employee if the product seller has paid a judgement which includes the amount of such benefits.

* * * * *

Analysis

Sec. 114. Relationship Between Product Liability and Worker Compensation

The relationship between product liability and Worker Compensation is a major topic covered in depth in the "Task Force Report" at VII–85–113. Under current law in a number of states, the interaction of product liability and Worker Compensation law results in the manufacturer of a workplace product paying the entire out-of-pocket cost of a product-related workplace injury, plus damages for pain and suffering. This result occurs because the product manufacturer is unable to place a portion of the cost of that injury on an employer whose negligence may have helped bring about the claimant's injury. *See* "Seaboard Coast Line R.R. v. Smith," 359 So. 2d 427 (Fla. 1978); "Task Force Report" at VII–89–99.

After weighing many considerations, the Task Force and the United States Department of Commerce concluded that the development of Worker Compensation as a sole source of recovery in product-related workplace accidents would be the best solution to the problem, but only if the worker received additional benefits in the course of overall Worker Compensation reform. A model product liability law, however, is an inappropriate vehicle for making alterations of that dimension in Worker Compensation law.

The search for the next best solution is not an easy one. One approach is to permit a full contribution claim in all cases in which the employer is at fault. *See* "Dow v. Dole Chem. Co.," 30 N.Y. 2d 1, 282 N.E. 2d 288, 331 N.Y.S. 2d 382 (1972); "Skinner v. Reed-Prentice Division, Inc.," 70 Ill. 2d 1, 374 N.E.2d 437 (1977). This approach is in accordance with the principle of comparative responsibility, and it places strong incentives for loss prevention on the employer.

However, if full contribution or indemnity by the product manufacturer against the employer is permitted, the employer may be forced to pay an employee—through the conduit of the third-party tortfeasor—an amount in excess of the employer's statutory Worker Compensation liability. This thwarts a central concept behind Worker Compensation, *i.e.*, that the employer and employee receive the benefits of a guaranteed, fixed-schedule, no-fault recovery system, which constitutes the *exclusive* liability of the employer. The approach also increases transaction costs.

On the other hand, if contribution or indemnity is not allowed, the product seller might have to bear the burden of a full common law judgment, despite the possibly greater responsibility of the employer. As the Supreme Court of Minnesota recently noted, "[t]his obvious inequity is further exacerbated by the right of the employer to recover directly or indirectly from the third party the amount he has paid in compensation regardless of the employer's own negligence." "Lamberston v. Cincinnati Corp.,"——Minn.——, 257 N.W. 2d 679, 684 (1977).

Equally troublesome is the fact that the present system dulls employer incentives to keep workplace products safe. The "ISO Closed Claims Survey" suggests that employer negligence is involved in 56 percent of product liability workplace cases. "ISO Closed Claims Survey," Report 10 at 81 (1978).

The purpose of the solution adopted in Section 114 is to sharpen employer incentives to keep workplace products safe without undermining the limited-liability concept that is central to the Worker Compensation system. The approach is based, in substantial part, on a proposal developed by the American Insurance Association (AIA). *See* AIA, "Product Liability Legislative Package" at 75–76 (1977). This approach has also been incorporated in the "National Workers' Compensation Standards Act of 1979," S. 420, 96th Cong., 1st Sess. (1979) and "Standards for State Product Liability Tort Litigation Act," H.R. 1675, 96th Cong., 1st Sess. (1979), and recommended by the "LaFalce Subcommittee Report" at 74.

Subsection (A) reduces the liability of a product seller by the total amount that has been or will be awarded in a state Worker Compensation proceeding. This Subsection operates regardless of whether the employer was, in fact, at fault. *See also* Subsection 112(B)(4) and accompanying analysis.

Subsection (B) abolishes the subrogation lien of the Worker Compensation carrier, or the right of a self-insuring employer to contribution or indemnity, in all workplace harm cases which are covered by this Act, except where the product seller has expressly agreed to indemnify or hold the employer harmless for harm caused by the product. As with Subsection (A), Subsection (B) operates regardless of the employer's fault or lack thereof.

Subsection (C) provides a procedural mechanism for reducing the product seller's liability when final judgment has been entered before the amount of Worker Compensation benefits has been determined.

The principle benefit of the approach adopted in Subsections (A) and (B) is a reduction in litigation transaction costs. Subrogation actions are not allowed. Furthermore, proceedings under this Act will be streamlined because in cases of employer negligence, there will be no three-party litigation as to the relative percentages of fault of employers and manufacturers. *See* AIA, "Legislative Package" at 67–68.

An additional benefit of the approach in Subsections (A) and (B) is that an injured employee will recover the same benefits received under the present system. At the same time, Section 114 cuts off the ability of the Worker Compensation carrier or self-insuring employer to shift its liability to the manufacturer. The employer, therefore, will have a greater incentive to provide a safe workplace than it has under the present system.

A third benefit is that the approach will also, to some degree, eliminate the harshness of the present system as it applies to manufacturers, by allowing product sellers to reduce their liability for workplace injuries. It will do this in all cases, even where the employer was not at fault.

While cases may arise where a product seller may pay more that its fair share under a comparative fault system, they are likely to be few in number under this Act. This is because an employer's misuse, or improper alteration or modification of the product, will in turn reduce the employee's award under Section 112(C). As the analysis to that Subsection indicates, this is also fair to employees because they agreed, within the context of their Worker Compensation system, to forego their right to sue when it is based on their employers' or co-employees' fault.

A closely related alternative approach to Section 114 was advanced by the Supreme Court of Minnesota in "Lamberston v. Cincinnati Corp.," *supra.* The court in that case held that the product manufacturer would be allowed limited contribution up to the amount of the Worker Compensation lien. This reduces the inequity against the product manufacturer, but preserves the employer's interest in not paying more than its Worker Compensation liability. The principal disadvantage of the "Lamberston" approach, as compared with Section 114, is that "Lamberston" does not reduce transaction costs.

Finally, it should be noted that any modification of the present tort and Worker Compensation systems, short of a sole source remedy, retains the multiple transaction costs of having two separate proceedings—the Worker Compensation proceeding and then the product liability claim—address a single injury. However, considering all the equities involved, Section 114 appears to offer the soundest solution apart from modifying Worker Compensation law to create a sole source remedy.

* * * * *

Code

Sec. 115. Sanctions Against the Bringing of Frivolous Claims and Defenses

(A) After final judgment has been entered under this Act, any party may, by motion, seek reimbursement for reasonable attorneys' fees and other costs that would not have been expended but for the fact that the opposing party pursued a claim or defense that was frivolous. A claim or defense is considered frivolous if the court determines that it was without any reasonable legal or factual basis.

(B) If the court decides in favor of a party seeking redress under this Section, it shall do so on the basis of clear and convincing evidence. In all motions under this Section, the court shall make written findings of fact.

(C) The motion provided for in Subsection (A) may be filed and the claim assessed against a party or a party's attorney or both, depending on which person or persons were responsible for the assertion of the frivolous claim or defense.

(D) Claims for damages under this Section shall be limited to expenses incurred by parties to the action or persons under a legal or contractual duty to bear the expenses of the action.

* * * * *

Analysis

Sec. 115. Sanctions Against the Bringing of Frivolous Claims and Defenses

The ISO data indicate that substantial product liability costs are incurred in the defense of product liability claims and lawsuits. "ISO Closed Claims Survey," Report No. 14 (1977) (defense costs equal about 35 percent of claim payments). Some have placed the blame for unnecessary defense costs and needless litigation on the contingent fee system. Nevertheless, as the plaintiffs' bar properly observes, the contingent fee brings no return to a claimant's attorney when the claimant is unsuccessful. On the other hand, some have argued that the contingent fee system has a negative impact on certain product liability cases to the extent that it causes insurers to settle non-meritorious claims because the cost of defending such cases may be greater than the amount of settlement.

Analysis of the countervailing arguments suggests that the best solution to reducing unnecessary litigation costs is to address the heart of the problem by discouraging frivolous claims and defenses.

Section 115 is based, in part, on "Ill. Ann. Stat." ch. 110, Section 41 (Supp. 1979). It is also predicated on a proposal, of the California Citizens Commission on Tort Reform advocating sanctions against "frivolous" claims or defenses. Report of the California Citizens' Commission on Tort Reform, "Righting the Liability Balance" at 146–47, 153–54 (1977).

The underlying purpose of Section 115 has broad support in existing statutes and court rules. For example, Rule 11 of the Federal Rules of Civil Procedure subjects an attorney to disciplinary action if the attorney knowingly files a pleading or defense where no grounds support it. *See* "Barnett v. Laborers' Int'l Union of N. Am.," 75 F.R.D. 544 (W.D. Pa. 1977). Similarly, Federal Rule of Appellate Procedure 38 permits a court to award "just damages and single or double costs" to a party who has been subject to a "frivolous appeal.

Additionally, Federal Rule of Civil Procedure 37(c) provides sanctions for an unreasonable failure to admit averments of fact or the genuineness of documents. In the federal courts, the above rules are supplemented by 28 "U.S.C." Section 1927 (1976) (imposing costs on an attorney who "multiplies the proceedings . . . to increase costs . . .") *See* Annot. 68 "A.L.R.3d" 209 (1976).

The Section is not intended to affect the law relating to malicious prosecution.

Under Subsection (A), the statute may be invoked by either a product liability claimant or a product seller. Recovery is limited to reasonable attorneys' fees and other costs that would not have been expended but for the fact that the opposing party pursued a claim or defense that was frivolous.

In order to make a finding that the claim was frivolous, the court must conclude that the claim was without *any* reasonable legal or factual basis. Thus, this standard allows full room for bringing claims under novel legal theories.

Subsection (B) provides additional assurances that only those who bring frivolous claims will be penalized. First, the court may only impose damages under Section 115 on the basis of clear and convincing evidence, not merely a preponderance of the evidence. *See* "State of West Virginia v. Charles Pfizer & Co.," 440 F.2d 1079, 1092 (2d Cir. 1971) ("clear showing of bad faith"). Second, the court must set forth its findings of fact in writing.

Subsection (C) gives the court latitude to impose costs on either attorney or client. As the "Task Force Report" noted, it is unlikely that many claimants will be financially able to respond to such a claim. "Task Force Report" at VII–62. It must be remembered that the attorney is in the best position to make a judgment about the reasonableness of bringing a claim or raising a defense.

"ABA Code of Professional Responsibility," DR 7–102(A)(1)(2); *cf.* "Acevedo v. Immigration & Naturalization Serv.," 538 F.2d 918, 921 (2d Cir. 1976).

Subsection (D) makes clear that recovery under this Section is limited to expenses incurred by claimant or defendant or persons under a legal or contractual duty to bear the expenses of the action.

* * * * *

Code

Sec. 116. Arbitration

(A) *Applicability.*

(1) Any party may by a motion institute a pre-trial arbitration proceeding in any claim brought under this Act, if the court determines that:

(a) It is reasonably probable that the amount in dispute is less than $50,000, exclusive of interest and costs; and

(b) Any non-monetary claims are insubstantial.

(2) Arbitration may not be used if both the claimant and one or more defendants state that they do not want an arbitration proceeding.

(B) *Rules Governing.*

(1) *Substantive Rules.* The substantive rules of an arbitration proceeding under this Section are those contained in this Act as well as those in applicable state law.

(2) *Procedural Rules.* These are the procedural rules of an arbitration proceeding under this Section. If this Section does not provide a rule of procedure, reference may be made to the "Uniform Arbitration Act" or other sources of law. Any reference to other sources of law must conform to the intent and spirit of this Section.

*Optional Subsection

[(3) *Additional Rules and Administration.*

(i) The ——— (legislature to specify appropriate state agency or administrative body) is empowered to promulgate additional procedural rules for this Section.

(ii) The ——— (legislature to specify American Arbitration Association or similar organization) shall carry out the day-to-day administration of arbitration under this Section.]

(C) *Arbitrators.*

(1) Unless the parties agree otherwise, the arbitration shall be conducted by three persons: an active member of the state bar or a retired judge of a court of record in the state; an individual who possesses expertise in the subject matter area that is in dispute; and a layperson.

(2) Arbitrators shall be selected in accordance with applicable state law in a manner which will assure fairness and lack of bias.

(D) *Arbitrators' Powers.*

(1) Each arbitrator to whom a claim is referred has the power, within the territorial jurisdiction of the court, to conduct arbitration hearings and make awards consistent with the provisions of this Act.

(2) State laws applicable to subpoenas for attendance of witnesses and the production of documentary evidence apply in proceedings conducted under this Section. Arbitrators shall have the power to administer oaths and affirmations.

(E) *Commencement.* Arbitration hearings shall commence not later than thirty (30) days after the claim is referred to arbitration unless, for good cause shown, the court shall extend the period. Hearings shall be concluded promptly. The court may order the time and place of the arbitration.

(F) *Evidence.*

(1) The Federal Rules of Evidence (or designated state evidence code) may be used as a guide to the admissibility of evidence in an arbitration hearing.

(2) Strict adherence to the rules of evidence, apart from relevant state rules of privilege, is not required.

(G) *Transcript of Proceeding.* A party may have a transcript or recording made of the arbitration hearing at its own expense. A party who has had a transcript or recording made shall furnish a copy of the transcript or recording at cost to any other party upon request.

(H) *Arbitration Decision and Judgment.* The arbitration decision and award, if any, shall be filed with the court promptly after the hearing is concluded. Unless a party demands a trial pursuant to Subsection (I), the decision and award shall be entered as the judgment of the court. The judgment entered shall be subject to the same provisions of law, and shall have the same force and effect as a judgment of the court in a civil action, except that it shall not be subject to appeal.

(I) *Trial Following Arbitration.*

(1) Within twenty (20) days after the filing of an arbitration decision with the court, any party may demand a trial of fact or a hearing on an issue of law in that court.

(2) Upon such a demand, the action shall be placed on the calendar of the court. Except for the provisions of Subsection (3), any right of trial by jury that a party would otherwise have shall be preserved inviolate.

(3) At trial, the court shall admit evidence that there has been an arbitration proceeding, the decision of the arbitration panel, and the nature and amount of the

award, if any. The trier of fact shall give such evidence whatever weight it deems appropriate.

(4) A party who has demanded a trial but fails to obtain a judgment in the trial court which is more favorable than the arbitration award, exclusive of interest and costs, shall be assessed the cost of the arbitration proceeding, including the amount of the arbitration fees, and—

(i) If this party is a claimant and the arbitration award is in its favor, the party shall pay the court an amount equivalent to interest on the arbitration award from the time it was filed; or

(ii) If this party is a product seller, it shall pay interest to the claimant on the arbitration award from the time it was filed.

* * * * *

Analysis

Sec. 116. Arbitration

The "Task Force Report" suggested that mandatory non-binding arbitration may result in more accurate decisions, reduce overall litigation costs, and expedite the decision process in product liability cases. *See* "Task Force Report" at VII-229-39.

A synopsis of the basis for these conclusions is that: (1) cases will be decided more accurately because a small group, with a member who is an expert in the field, should be able to comprehend the esoteric details of product liability cases; (2) over time, the process will develop a resource bank of relatively neutral experts less easily misled in technical areas than a jury of laypersons; (3) arbitrators will be less affected by the emotional aspects of the case or by the artistry of counsel; and (4) the privacy of arbitration proceedings (as compared to judicial proceedings) will prompt more complete revelation of special manufacturing designs or processes. This, in turn, will permit more accurate judgments. *See* "Task Force Report" at VII-235.

The "ISO Closed Claims Survey" suggests further that arbitration will reduce accident reparation transaction costs. Even allowing for the fact that more substantial product liability claims are litigated to a verdict than are handled by arbitration, ISO data indicate that the average expense for attorneys and other allocated loss adjustment costs are considerably lower when the case is handled by arbitration as compared with a court verdict. *See* "ISO Closed Claims Survey," Report 14 at 120.

On the other hand, costs may increase under arbitration if there are numerous demands for trial following arbitration. This potential problem may not be as serious, however, as was once thought. Data collected by the Department of Justice show that appeal rates at the state level for a trial following arbitration have ranged from 5 to no more than 15 percent of all cases arbitrated. Hearings before the Subcommittee on Improvements in Judicial Machinery of the Senate Committee on the Judiciary, 95th Cong., 2d Sess. 22 (1978) (Statement of Former Attorney General Griffin B. Bell). *See also* report of the California Citizens' Commission on Tort Reform, "Righting the Liability Balance" at 143 (1977).

Broader use of arbitration should expedite the reparations process. The "Task Force Report" showed that in the medical malpractice area, for example, the arbitration process had achieved a more expeditious resolution of claims than the jury system. *See* "Task Force Report" at VII–238.

Indeed, the benefits of arbitration have prompted the Department of Justice to recommend that mandatory non-binding arbitration be used in federal courts in all tort and contract cases. The Department of Justice reached this conclusion after its Office of Judicial Improvements made a thorough analysis of the matter in a study conducted wholly independently of the "Task Force Report."

Section 116 draws on portions of the Department of Justice's proposed bill on mandatory non-binding arbitration. *See* S. 373, 96th Cong., 1st Sess. (1979); H.R. 2699, 96th Cong., 1st Sess. (1979); the Statement of Former Attorney General Griffin B. Bell, *supra;* as well as state legislation on the topic of arbitration.

(A) *Applicability*. The Act provides for arbitration when the amount in dispute is less than $50,000. This figure is to be determined by the court under a standard of reasonable probability. In this context, note that the sanctions imposed by Section 115 will apply to any party who delays the proceedings by making a frivolous assertion that the amount in dispute is above or below $50,000. Also, the proceeding is not mandatory if both the claimant and at least one defendant state that they do not want it.

The $50,000 figure is the same as that in the Department of Justice bill, and it should cover the bulk of product liability claims. In that regard, the ISO closed claims data, trended for severity, show that the average paid claim in bodily injury cases is $26,004. While some have suggested limiting arbitration to smaller claims, it is the larger claims that have been the greater transaction cost items in product liability cases. *See* "ISO Closed Claims Survey" at 113.

While there has been no state experience with cases at the $50,000 level, Former Attorney General Bell has noted that when Pennsylvania increased the jurisdictional amount for the state's arbitration program from $3,000 to $10,000, there was no increase in the appeal rate. Statement of Former Attorney General Griffin B. Bell, *supra* at 20.

It seems relatively certain that an arbitration procedure will help expedite and reduce costs connected with smaller claims. ISO closed claims data show that the large majority of product liability payments are relatively small (more than two-thirds are under $1,000—even when trended for severity). *See* "ISO Closed Claims Survey" at 113.

(B) *Rules Governing*. Subsection (B)(1) indicates that arbitrators shall apply the product liability substantive law rules of this Act. Where the Act does not provide a rule of decision, relevant state law should be applied.

Subsection (B)(2) indicates that where a procedure is not provided in Section 116—*e.g.,* when a court can vacate a judgment—the "Uniform Arbitration Act" (enacted in a number of states), or another appropriate source of law, is to be used as a resource.

Subsection (B)(3), an optional section, permits the state to designate a supplemental source of procedural rules and to empower the American Arbitration Association or similar organizations to carry out the day-to-day administration of arbitration.

This Subsection leaves a great deal of room for the states to develop their own arbitration systems. The drafters of the Act have chosen to include only the most important procedural points concerning arbitration. The goal of substantive uniformity in product liability law will not be compromised by allowing individual states the freedom to choose the arbitration procedures that they find are the most efficient and workable.

(C) *Arbitrators.* The rules under Subsection (C) provide latitude for the parties to select a single arbitrator. Otherwise, the arbitration is to be conducted by three persons, one who is an active member of the state bar or a retired judge, one who has expertise in the subject matter area that is in dispute, and one who is a layperson. This provision differs slightly from the Department of Justice proposal in light of the needs of product liability. Having an individual who is familiar with the scientific nature of the subject matter involved will help expedite the case and serve as a deterrent to the presentation of biased expert testimony.

In addition, Subsection (C) provides for a layperson to be included to help assure that the consumer perspective regarding product safety is represented. The process of selecting a layperson should not be complicated. It is suggested that either normal jury rolls be utilized or that a list of laypersons be compiled for this purpose.

Aside from general guidelines regarding fairness and lack of bias, the Act does not outline the method of choosing arbitrators, but leaves that matter to the individual states. A state can help implement the general guidelines by requiring each arbitration panel candidate to disclose any personal acquaintance with the parties or their counsel and allow a *voir dire* examination. *See* "Mich. Comp. Laws Ann." Section 600.5045(1)(2) (Supp. 1978). Some of the better procedures include:

(1) Having the American Arbitration Association select a pool of candidates according to its established selection procedures. Each party is allowed to reject certain candidates and rate the remainder in order of preference. Additional provisions take effect if this procedure fails to produce a panel. *See* "Mich. Comp. Laws Ann." Section 600.5044(4)(5) (Supp. 1978);

(2) Having the court appoint arbitrators. "Mass. Ann. Laws" ch. 231, Section 60(B) (Supp. 1978);

(3) Having an arbitration administrator appoint arbitrators. "Wis. Stat. Ann." Section 655.02 (Supp. 1979); and

(4) Having the parties and court combine to appoint arbitrators. "Neb. Rev. Stat." Sections 44-2840, 2841 (Supp. 1978); "Ohio Rev. Code Ann." Section 2711.21(A) (Supp. 1979).

(D) *Arbitrators' Powers.* These provisions are taken from the Department of Justice proposal on arbitration. They grant the arbitrators jurisdiction and also give them powers of subpoena.

(E) *Commencement.* This provision is also derived from the Department of Justice proposal. Its purpose is to help expedite the proceeding. The Act contains a slight modification of the Justice proposal in order to allow an extension for "good cause shown." This seems appropriate in light of the fact that some product liability cases are very complex. *Cf.* "Ariz. Rev. Stat. Ann." Section 12-567(C) (Supp. 1978) (medical malpractice).

(F) *Evidence.* One method of expediting the process is to use informal means of proof. Nevertheless, some guidelines are needed. The Act follows the Department of Justice proposal in referring to the Federal Rules of Evidence as general guidelines. Strict adherence to rules of evidence is not required. *See* ''Ariz. Rev. Stat. Ann.'' Section 12–567(D) (Supp. 1978).

(G) *Transcript of Proceeding.* With respect to the provision of a transcript of proceeding, the Act generally follows the Department of Justice draft.

(H) *Arbitration Decision and Judgment.* The Act follows the Department of Justice proposal's provisions on decisions and judgment. The parties may request a trial on issues of law or fact. If they do not so request in a timely manner, the action is at an end—there is no appeal.

(I) *Trial Following Arbitration.* The Act follows the approach taken by a number of state medical malpractice arbitration statutes. It admits the results of the arbitration proceeding into evidence before the jury. This should act as a deterrent against seeking unnecessary trials. *See, e.g.,* ''Ariz. Rev. Stat. Ann.'' Section 12–567(M) (Supp. 1978); ''Mass. Ann. Laws'' ch. 231. Section 60(B) (Supp. 1978). *Cf.* ''Wis. Stat. Ann.'' Section 655.19 (Supp. 1979) (excluding findings and order of arbitration panel).

The approach of Section 116 appears to be in accord with the Federal Constitution. *Cf.* ''*Ex parte* Peterson,'' 253 U.S. 300, 309 (1920). Moreover, with the exception of two Ohio lower court decisions, state courts have upheld the constitutionality of provisions that do admit panel findings before the jury. *See* ''Eastin v. Broomfield,'' 116 Ariz. 576, 570 P.2d 744, 750 (1977); ''Attorney General v. Johnson,'' 282 Md. 168, 385 A.2d 57, 67–68 (1978)'' ''Paro v. Longwood Hosp.,'' Mass. Adv. Sh. (1977) 2353, 369 N.E.2d 985 (1977); ''Prendergast v. Nelson,'' 199 Neb. 97, 256 N.W.2d 657 (1977); ''Strykowski v. Wilkie,'' 81 Wis. 2d 491, 261 N.W.2d 434 (1978), *contra* ''Simon v. St. Elizabeth Medical Center,'' 3 Ohio Op. 3d 164, 355 N.E.2d 903, 907–09 (C.P. 1976); ''Graley v. Satayatham,'' 74 Ohio Op. 2d 316, 343 N.E.2d 832 (C.P. 1976). *See generally* Reddish, ''Legislative Response to the Medical Malpractice Insurance Crisis: Constitutional Implications,'' 55 ''Tex. L. Rev.'' 759, 793 (1977); Lenore, ''Mandatory Medical Malpractice Mediation Panels—A Constitutional Examination,'' 44 ''Ins. Counsel J.'' 416, 422 (1977).

A possible drawback of this Section's approach is that a jury may have difficulty evaluating the conclusions of the panel where the jury is not privy to the prior factfinders qualifications and method of operation. Also, the jury may get sidetracked from the actual evidence in the case. *See* the observations of Judge Hinton in a classic comment, 27 ''Ill. L. Rev.'' 195 (1932); Annot., 18 ''A.L.R.2d'' 1287 (1951). *But see* Fed. R. Evid. 803 (22) (admitting felony convictions in a cognate civil case). Nevertheless, the benefits to be gained by a reduction in transaction costs outweigh these concerns and support the admission of the results of the arbitration proceeding into evidence at trial.

Subsection (I)(4) provides an additional deterrent against ill-considered appeals for trials following arbitration. If a party fails to obtain a judgment more favorable than the arbitration award, the court will assess the cost of the arbitration proceeding, including the amount of arbitration fees, plus interest, against that party.

In light of the fact that the present product liability system has created serious problems and the fact that mandatory non-binding arbitration has the potential for dealing with some of those problems, this slight incentive for retaining a sound arbitration award should not run afoul of constitutions in most states. *See* "Task Force Report" at VII–233. The Act does not enumerate grounds upon which a court may vacate an arbitration award. Guidance on this issue may be obtained from Section 12 of the "Uniform Arbitration Act."

* * * * *

Code

Sec. 117. Expert Testimony

(A) *Appointment of Experts.* The court may, on its own motion or on the motion of any party, enter an order to show cause why expert witnesses should not be appointed, and may request the parties to submit nominations. The court may appoint any expert witness agreed upon by the parties, and may appoint witnesses of its own selection. The court may consult with knowledgeable individuals or with professional, academic, consumer, or business organizations and institutions to assist with the selection process. An expert witness shall not be appointed by the court unless the expert consents to serve. An expert witness appointed by the court shall be informed of his or her duties in writing, a copy of which shall be filed with the clerk, or at a conference in which the parties shall have an opportunity to participate. An expert witness so appointed shall advise the parties of any findings; shall be available for deposition by any party; and may be called to testify by the court or any party. The court-appointed expert witness shall be subject to cross-examination by each party, including the party calling that expert as a witness.

(B) *Compensation.*

(1) Expert witnesses appointed by the court are entitled to reasonable compensation for their services in an amount to be determined by the court. The court, in its discretion, may tax the costs of such expert on one party or apportion them among parties in the same manner as other costs.

(2) In exercising this discretion, the court may consider:

(a) Which party, if any, requested the court appointment of the expert;

(b) Which party had judgment entered in its favor; and

(c) Whether the amount of damages recovered in the action bore a reasonable relationship to the amount sought by the claimant or conceded to be appropriate by the product seller or other defendant.

(C) *Disclosure of Appointment.* In the exercise of its discretion, the court may authorize disclosure to the jury of the fact that the court has appointed the expert witness.

(D) *Parties' Selection of Own Experts.* Nothing in this Section shall limit the parties in calling expert witnesses of their own selection.

(E) *Pre-Trial Evaluation of Experts.* The court in its discretion may conduct a hearing to determine the qualifications of all proposed expert witnesses. The court may order a hearing on its own motion or on the motion of any party.

(1) *Need for Pre-Trial Evaluation.* In determining whether to grant such a motion, the court shall consider:

(a) The complexity of the issues in the case; and

(b) Whether the hearing would deter the presentation of witnesses who are not qualified as experts on the specific issues.

(2) *Factors in Evaluation.* If the court decides to hold such a hearing, it shall consider;

(a) The background and skills of the proposed witness;

(b) The formal and self-education the proposed witness has undertaken relevant to the case or to similar cases; and

(c) The potential bias of the proposed witness.

(3) *Findings of Fact.* In making a determination as to whether a proposed expert witness is qualified, the court shall state its findings of fact to the parties.

(4) *Determination.* Based upon its findings of fact regarding the qualifications of any proposed expert witness, the court, in its discretion, may limit the scope of the witness' testimony, or may refuse to permit such witness to testify as an expert.

* * * * *

Analysis

Sec. 117. Expert Testimony

In General. The Task Force's "Legal Study" demonstrated that product liability cases are often compromised because of the lack of standards with regard to selecting and presenting expert testimony. *See* Volume IV, "Legal Study" at 153–155. One part of the problem is the biased expert; another is the unqualified expert.

Even if experts are properly qualified and objective, a jury of laypersons is often in a poor position to determine which expert is correct. For this reason, this Act gives the court power to make greater use of pre-trial arbitration where an unbiased, qualified expert will serve on the panel. *See* Section 116. Where arbitration is not used, however, this Section should promote the goal of presenting objective and sound expert testimony to the jury.

(A) *Appointment of Experts.* Subsection (A) is based on Rule 706 of the Federal Rules of Evidence and similar state rules. It indicates that courts have the power to appoint experts on their own authority. A number of courts have utilized this power even without the benefit of Fed. R. Evid. 706 or a similar state rule. *See* Annot., 95 "A.L.R.2d" 390 (1964). As the "Task Force Report" noted, the presence of a court-appointed expert "has a cautionary impact on the expert for hire whose theories at trial are subject to dispute not only by an adversary expert, but also by a neutral court-appointed one." "Task Force Report" at VII–43, *citing* Mitchell, "The Proposed Federal Rules of Evidence: How They Affect Product Liability Practice," 12 "Duquesne L. Rev." 551, 557–58 (1974). *See also* 2 J. Wigmore, "Evidence" Section 563, at 648 (3d ed. 1940) (". . . this expedient would remove most . . . abuses").

Subsection (A) also encourages the court to seek the assistance of various individuals, organizations, or institutions in making the selection of a court-appointed expert. The court may wish to utilize this opportunity to establish a panel of independent experts, recognized as such by their peers, from which selections for individual cases may be made. The court may also seek the assistance of these organizations to evaluate the credentials of expert witnesses nominated by the parties.

One problem with court-appointed experts is that the trier of fact may give them an aura of infallibility which they do not deserve. Under Subsection (A), this possibility is diminished because the experts are subject to cross-examination by *each* party. Also, Subsection (C) allows the court in its discretion to decline to disclose to the jury that the expert witness is, in fact, court-appointed.

(B) *Compensation.* Under Fed. R. Evid. 706 and similar state rules, compensation of experts is left to the judge's discretion. Subsection (B) goes a step farther and provides three guidelines for compensating experts. These guidelines should serve as an added inducement for attorneys to present objective expert testimony. The guidelines suggest that the court may impose the cost of the court-appointed expert on losing parties as well as on parties whom the court finds were substantially inaccurate in their estimation of damages.

(C) *Disclosure of Appointment.* Subsection (C) follows Fed. R. Evid. 706. In most instances, it is important for the trier of fact to appreciate that the witness is court-appointed. However, circumstances may arise in which the court believes disclosure of that fact will give the witness too much credence with the jury. Therefore, the court has the discretion to withhold the information when it is appropriate to do so.

(D) *Parties' Selection of Own Experts.* Subsection (D) also follows Fed. R. Evid. 706. Precluding the parties from introducing their own experts would vest too much power in court-appointed experts.

(E) *Pre-Trial Evaluation of Experts.* A rule authorizing a court-appointed expert does not, in and of itself, provide guidance about who is properly qualified to testify in product liability cases. There are many approaches to that issue. One approach, used in some medical malpractice statutes, would require that an expert witness spend a substantial portion of his or her professional time in the actual practice of his or her area of expertise. While this approach may be appropriate in the area of medical malpractice, it was not followed here because a person may be well-versed in technical product liability matters even if he or she does devote substantial time to research or other endeavors other than actual practice. *See* "Task Force Report" at VII–44. Unfortunately, it is impractical to utilize a "standard test" for all experts in product liability cases. *See* Donaher, Piehler, Twerski & Weinstein, "The Technological Expert in Products Liability Litigation," 52 "Tex. L. Rev." 1303, 1325 (1974).

(1) *Need for Pre-Trial Evaluation.* This rule gives some guidance to the trial court in deciding whether to conduct a pre-trial hearing on the qualifications of expert witnesses. It is not necessary or cost-efficient to utilize the procedure in *all* cases. It is appropriate to do so in more complex cases and also where the pre-trial hearings would serve as a deterrent to the presentation of witnesses who were not qualified. Such a deterrent should discourage parties from prolonging the litigation needlessly and, thus, encourage the expeditious resolution of claims under this Act. Either party may bring this matter before the court by motion.

(2) *Factors in Evaluation.* The factors in evaluation are drawn from Donaher *et al., supra,* 52 "Tex. L. Rev." 1303.

The court should examine the expert witness' background and skills and determine whether they are appropriate for the purposes of the case. The court should not only review the witness' formal education, but also whether the witness had undertaken specific preparation for the litigation before the court. Finally, the court should examine a witness for bias. A witness with marginal expert skills and a strong bias should be considered unqualified.

(3) *Findings of Fact.* If it seems clear to the court that the expert's background and experience do not qualify the expert to testify, it should state this conclusion in its findings of fact to the parties.

(4) *Determination.* This provision empowers the court to limit the scope of an expert's testimony to the witness' specific area of expertise. It also allows the court to refuse to permit the witness to testify as an expert when that individual is not qualified to do so.

* * * * *

Code

Sec. 118. Non-Pecuniary Damages

(A) For the purposes of this Section, ''non-pecuniary damages'' are those which have no market value and do not represent a monetary loss to claimant.

(B) When sufficient evidence has been introduced, the amount of non-pecuniary damages shall be determined by the trier of fact. However, the court shall have and shall exercise the power to review such damage awards for excessiveness.

*Optional Subsection

[(c) Non-pecuniary damages under this Act shall not exceed $25,000, or twice the amount of the pecuniary damages, whichever is less, unless the claimant proves by a preponderance of the evidence that the product caused claimant to suffer serious and permanent or prolonged (1) disfigurement, (2) impaired of bodily function, (3) pain and discomfort, or (4) mental illness.]

*Optional Subsection

[(D) Every third year following the effective date of this Act as stated in Section 122, the ——— Committee(s) of [each House of] the Legislature of this State shall review the monetary limitations contained in Subsection (C) to determine whether such limitations should be changed in view of the economic conditions existing at that time. Upon a finding that such change is warranted, said Committee(s) shall introduce legislation to amend the monetary limitations contained in Subsection (C).]

* * * * *

Analysis

Sec. 118. Non-Pecuniary Damages

Claimant's ''non-pecuniary damages'' include awards for pain and mental suffering. They have no market value and, thus, are to be contrasted with pecuniary damages which compensate victims for lost wages, medical and rehabilitation costs, and other actual expenditures brought about by an unreasonably unsafe product.

According to the "ISO Closed Claims Survey," 70 percent of claims closed with payment include amounts in addition to a claimant's pecuniary loss. *See* "ISO Closed Claims Survey" at 54. Moreover, the average amount of payment above pecuniary loss increases significantly in the higher payment range. *Id.* at 54–55. A most important reason for the difficulty in setting product liability rates is the "open-endedness" of damages for pain and suffering. *See* "Task Force Report," at VII–64–65. These escalating premiums have an inflationary impact on consumer prices as the product seller's insurance costs are passed on to the public. Damages that go beyond the amount necessary to ensure that the claimant receives reasonable compensation for the harm suffered represent an unwarranted cost.

The "Task Force Report" suggested that limits on awards for pain and suffering "would reduce uncertainty and thereby mitigate the 'apprehension factor' that has contributed to the rise in product liability insurance rates." *Id.* at VII–65. Nevertheless, such awards have deep historical roots and should not be limited in a manner that unreasonably curtails the rights of injured parties. Section 118 takes the position that a fixed limit on the amount of non-pecuniary damages is appropriate where claimant's harm is only temporary.

Section 118 is predicated on an examination of the weaknesses in the major rationales offered in support of awards for non-pecuniary damages. The award for non-pecuniary damages arose in early common law cases as a substitute for an injured claimant seeking personal "vengeful retaliation." *See* "Task Force Report," *id.* In those cases, the defendant usually committed an intentional wrong. This rationale has little application to cases arising under product liability. Under this Act, a product seller may be held liable for harm caused by products found to be defective in construction regardless of fault. The same result occurs when an express warranty is not true. In cases of harm caused by products found to be defective in design, or defective because of the absence of adequate warnings, the trier of fact must consider more sophisticated matters than would be applied under a general negligence standard.

A second rationale to support the award of damages for pain and suffering is that they have an important deterrent function. The "Task Force Report" found evidence that the general product liability problem caused manufacturers to devote more attention to product liability loss prevention techniques. *See* "Task Force Report" at VI–50. The approach taken in Section 118 retains this deterrent function while placing some reasonable limits on awards for pain and suffering.

A third rationale, supported by members of the plaintiffs' bar and some economic legal scholars, is that awards for pain and suffering are a reasonable attempt to reduce the serious discomfort endured by a claimant. *See* R. Posner, "Economic Analysis of Law" 82 (1972). On the other hand, studies have questioned whether monetary awards for pain and suffering do anything to alleviate the symptoms they are alleged to address. *See* J. O'Connell & R. Simon, "Payment for Pain and Suffering: Who Wants What, When & Why" (1972); Peck, "Compensation for Pain: A Reappraisal in Light of New Medical Evidence," 72 "Mich. L. Rev." 1355 (1974). This Section adheres to the former assumption to the extent that when a claimant suffers serious and permanent or prolonged (1) disfigurement, (2) impairment of bodily function, (3) pain and discomfort, or (4) serious mental illness, the amount of non-pecuniary damages is left to the sound discretion of the trier of fact with appropriate review by the court in cases of abuse of that discretion.

However, when the claimant has not suffered such serious and permanent or prolonged harms,[17] non-pecuniary damages are limited to $25,000 or twice the amount of pecuniary damages, whichever is less.

An ample body of case law in the area of Worker Compensation and, more recently, automobile injury reparation statutes, provides guidance for the court to determine whether a harm is permanent or prolonged. *See, e.g.,* "Falcone v. Branker," 135 N.J. Super. 137, 342 A.2d 875 (1975) (collecting cases); "Vitale v. Danylak," 74 Mich. App. 615, 254 N.W.2d 593 (1977) (summary judgment under automobile no-fault act); "*In re* Requests of Governor and Senate, Etc.," 389 Mich. 411, 208 N.W.2d 469, 480 (1973) (term "permanent" supplies basis for legal interpretation).

Courts also have defined and explained the term "mental illness" in a number of contexts. "Carroll v. Cobb," 139 N.J. Super. 439, 354 A.2d 355 (1976) (voter registration requirements); "Sachs v. Commercial Ins. Co.," 119 N.J. Super. 226, 290 A.2d 760 (1972) (insurance policy); "*In re* Humphrey," 236 N.C. 141. 71 S.E.2d 915 (1952) (incompetency proceedings); "Commonwealth v. Moon," 383 Pa. 18, 117 A.2d 96 (1955) (committal proceedings); "Interstate Life & Accident Ins. Co. v. Houston," 50 Tenn. App. 172, 360 S.W.2d 71 (1962) (insanity exclusion provision).

Objections to limits on awards for non-pecuniary damages take several forms. One is that such limits may violate due process or equal protection clauses of some state constitutions. *Cf.* "Wright v. Central Du Page Hosp. Ass'n.," 63 Ill. 2d 313, 347 N.E.2d 736, 743 (1976) (restriction on amount of general damages in medical malpractice); "Graley v. Satayatham," 74 Ohio Op.2d 316, 343 N.E.2d 832, 836 (C. P. 1976) (requiring list of collateral source benefits in medical malpractice). Another objection involves state constitutional prohibitions on damage limitations, *E.g.,* "Ariz. Rev. Stat. Ann.," Const. Art. 18, Section 6 (1956); "Ky. Rev. Stat. Ann.," Const. Section 54 (1891); Penn. Stat. Ann.," Const. Art. 3, Section 18 (1969). An argument that Section 118 does not violate such prohibitions is that a strict product liability cause of action did not exist at the time the state constitution was adopted and is therefore exempt from its interdictions. *See* "Rail N Ranch Corp. v. State," 7 Ariz. App. 558, 441 P.2d 786, 788 (1968).

These objections notwithstanding, Section 118 can be supported. First, the common law rule will continue to operate where injuries are serious. *Cf.* "Rybeck v. Rybeck," 141 N.J. Super. 481, 858 A.2d 828, 836 (1976), *appeal dismissed,* 150 N.J. Super. 151, 375 A.2d 269 (1977) (limited court access for pain and suffering in no-fault—"the law is permitted to treat large problems differently from small problems if there is a rational basis for the difference"). Second, some ceiling or limit on damages for pain and suffering will reduce uncertainty in one of the greatest liability insurance ratemaking problem areas. Third, the limit will help assure that there is ade-

[17]The Section does not address the question of whether non-pecuniary damages should be allowed or limited in wrongful death or survival actions.

quate insurance capacity to provide compensation for pecuniary losses caused by unsafe products.

Subsection (D) provides a mechanism for review and evaluation of $25,000 limitation contained in Subsection (C). It is anticipated that the legislature may wish periodically to modify this limitation in light of significant changes in economic conditions.

Because of the facts that (1) the topic of pain and suffering goes beyond product liability and is applicable to all of tort law, (2) the limitation as drafted may raise transaction costs in regard to the issue of whether a harm is "serious, permanent, or prolonged," and (3) constitutional problems that may arise in some states, Subsections (C) and (D) are placed in brackets as optional sections.

* * * * *

Code

Sec. 119. The Collateral Source Rule

In any claim brought under this Act, the claimant's recovery, or that of any party who may be subrogated to the claimant's rights under this Act, shall be reduced by any compensation from a public source which the claimant has received or will receive for the same damages. For the purposes of this Section, "public source" means a fund more than half of which is derived from general tax revenues.

* * * * *

Analysis

Sec. 119. The Collateral Source Rule

The collateral source rule is a principle of tort law under which the defendant is not permitted to take "credit" for any money that an injured claimant received from another (collateral) source. The rule embraces both payments for loss of wages and medical expenditures.

The rule may permit double recovery by the claimant and may increase transaction costs. This Section recognizes these possibilities and provides for a limited modification of the collateral source rule when the claimant has received compensation from a public source for the same damages. Its approach is similar to that followed in medical malpractice by the states of Tennessee and Pennsylvania. *See* Volume V, "Legal Study" at 146.

There are two significant arguments against proposals to modify the existing rule. The first is that the "wrongdoer" should not have the benefit of a windfall. Proponents contend that it is better that the claimant have the benefit of a windfall than the defendant.

This argument can be rebutted in the context of product liability. Under Section 104 of this Act, a manufacturer may be held liable for defects in construction or breach of an express warranty on a strict liability basis. In other cases, a product seller's liability is based on fault, but not on gross negligence or intentionally wrongful conduct. Therefore, a selective modification of the collateral source rule in the context of product liability may be justified. Indeed, some states have upheld such selective abolition or modification where liability was predicated solely on a fault basis. *See* "Eastin v. Broomfield," 116 Ariz. 576, 570 P.2d 744, 751–52 (1977); *But see* "Graley v. Satayatham," 74 Ohio Op. 2d 316, 343 N.E. 2d 832 (C.P. 1976) (holding unconstitutional selective abolition in medical malpractice context).

The second argument against modifying the collateral source rule is that a product seller should not be permitted to "externalize" the cost of an injury caused by its products. This argument is very strong when the injured claimant has purchased health and accident coverage. In that instance, the defendant product seller should not be able to benefit from the claimant's prior prudence. Nevertheless, some proposals have modified the rule in that situation. *See* "Neb. Rev. Stat." Section 44–2819 (Supp. 1978); "Prendergast v. Nelson," 199 Neb. 97, 256 N.W. 2d 657, 669 (1977); National Product Liability Council, "Proposed Uniform State Product Liability Act" Section 207 (undated). *See also* Comment, "An Analysis of State Legislative Responses to the Medical Malpractice Crisis," 1975 "Duke L.J." 1417, 1447–50. The argument is less persuasive when the claimant has not directly contributed to the insurance fund as is the case with Worker Compensation.

When the claimant has received damages from a public source, the argument loses all of its force. The benefits received were not through the claimant's pre-accidental financial planning or made a part of the claimant's remuneration as a condition of employment. Rather, they were derived from public tax funds that accumulated in part by contributions from the product seller. Since the product seller would be able to distribute the cost of a judgment that included this amount among consumers through product pricing, the public may be subjected to excessive, duplicative costs.

Section 119 defines a "public source" as a fund more than half of which is derived from general tax revenues. This would include welfare benefits and other forms of medical, hospitalization, and disability benefits which are funded by state or federal tax funds. It does not include Worker Compensation payments (which are specifically dealt with in Section 114), employee group insurance plans, or other similar sources. It also does not presently include payments received pursuant to the "United States Social Security Act." Although Social Security contributions are withheld from an employee's pay, they are not "general tax revenues." However, if the method of funding the Social Security system is changed, such payments might then come within the operation of this Section. *Compare* the approach taken in Section 119 *with* the various approaches taken in state medical malpractice statutes. *See, e.g.,* "Tenn. Code Ann." Section 23–3418 (Supp. 1978) (complete abrogation of collateral source rule expressly includes Social Security benefits); "Neb. Rev. Stat." Section 44–2819 (Supp. 1978) (partial abrogation of collateral source rule does not include Social Security benefits).

A probable effect of Section 119 will be to reduce double expenditures for medical costs. The "ISO Closed Claims Survey" suggests that medical costs represent approximately 19.7 percent of product liability claims. "ISO Closed Claims Survey" at 57. Nevertheless, the cost savings generated by this Section will probably be modest. The ISO closed claims data, which were quite limited on this point, show that approximately 6.4 percent of claimants have been reimbursed by public collateral sources.

See "ISO Closed Claims Survey" at 181. Collateral sources paid for 19.8 percent of the claims in those cases (this closely parallels the general percentage of medical benefits). Nonetheless, this Section should help reduce overall insurance costs. Liability insurers should take this matter into account when they formulate rates and premiums.

Section 119 also takes account of existing legislation that may authorize subrogation by public collateral sources. In order to reduce transaction costs and duplicative distribution costs, this Section prohibits such subrogation.

Finally, Section 119 does not alter existing law that prohibits the defendant from introducing into evidence the fact that the claimant has been indemnified by a collateral source. That alternative approach was rejected because it would leave the trier of fact in the role of balancing the delicate policy elements that surround proposals calling for abolition of the collateral source rule. This should be an issue of law for state legislatures or courts. Also, that approach would reduce the potential benefit of collateral source rule modifications in that it would increase transaction costs and lower predicatability and consistency in the allocation of collateral benefits. *See* "Task Force Report" at VII–74–75. *Cf.* Defense Research Institute, "Products Liability Position Paper" at 44–45 (1976) (advocating modification of evidentiary rules to allow trier of fact to consider all collateral benefits).

* * * * *

Code

Sec. 120. Punitive Damages

(A) Punitive damages may be awarded to the claimant if the claimant proves by clear and convincing evidence that the harm suffered was the result of the product seller's reckless disregard for the safety of product users, consumers, or others who might be harmed by the product.

(B) If the trier of fact determines that punitive damages should be awarded, the court shall determine the amount of those damages. In making this determination, the court shall consider:

(1) The likelihood at the relevant time that serious harm would arise from the product seller's misconduct;

(2) The degree of the product seller's awareness of that likelihood;

(3) The profitability of the misconduct to the product seller;

(4) The duration of the misconduct and any concealment of it by the product seller;

(5) The attitude and conduct of the product seller upon discovery of the misconduct and whether the conduct has been terminated;

(6) The financial condition of the product seller;

(7) The total effect of other punishment imposed or likely to be imposed upon the product seller as a result of the misconduct, including punitive damage awards to persons similarly situated to the claimant and the severity of criminal penalties to which the product seller has been or may be subjected; and

(8) Whether the harm suffered by the claimant was also the result of the claimant's own reckless disregard for personal safety.

* * * * *

Analysis

Sec. 120. Punitive Damages

Some product sellers and others have called for the abolition of punitive damages on the grounds that they serve no proper "tort law" purpose,[18] and at least one court has accepted these arguments in the area of product liability. *See* "Walbrun v. Berkel, Inc.," 433 F. Supp. 384-85 (E.D. Wis. 1976); "Roginsky v. Richardson-Merrell, Inc.," 378 F.2d 832 (2d Cir. 1967) (dictum).

Nevertheless, as Section 120 acknowledges, punitive damages serve an important function in deterring product sellers from reckless disregard for safety in the production, distribution, or sale of dangerous products. *See* "Toole v. Richardson-Merrell, Inc.," 251 Cal. App. 2d 689, 60 Cal. Rptr. 398 (1967); "Gillham v. Admiral Corp.," 523 F.2d 102 (6th Cir. 1975). At the same time, Section 120 recognizes and addresses punitive damages problems in the specific context of product liability.

While many product sellers have expressed great concern about the economic impact of punitive damages, the "ISO Closed Claims Survey" suggests that the number of cases in which such damages are imposed is insubstantial. "ISO Closed Claims Survey" at 183. Nevertheless, concern about punitive damages has caused some insurers to decline to provide insurance coverage for these damages. Also, a number of states and some insurers have declined to permit such coverage. They contend that a product seller should not be allowed to pass this cost on to an insurer. Transcending all of these concerns is the total lack of legal structure surrounding punitive damages. The approach taken in Section 120 is to provide such a structure, so as to reduce product sellers' reasonable concerns about punitive damages, while at the same time retaining the important deterrent function of punitive damages.

Subsection (A) addresses a basic argument against punitive damages—specifically that they apply a criminal law sanction to a civil law case, even though the defendant does not have the benefit of the constitutional protections that would be available under criminal law. Subsection (A) moves away from the ordinary "preponderance of evidence" test of civil cases and toward the criminal standard, but does not turn completely to a pure criminal standard of proof "beyond a reasonable doubt." Because the defendant is not subject to incarceration, and the "punishment" is more in the nature of a civil fine than a criminal sanction, the Act requires the claimant to prove by "clear and convincing" evidence that punitive damages are justified. *See* Subsections 102 (H) and (I) (definitions of "preponderance of evidence" and "clear and convincing evidence").

Subsection (A) also requires that the claimant prove that the product seller's conduct demonstrated reckless disregard for the safety of others. The phrase "reckless disregard"—the traditional barrier that the plaintiff must cross in order to obtain punitive damages—means a conscious indifference to the safety of persons who might be injured by the product. *See* Subsection 102(J) (definition of "reckless disregard");

[18] *See* "Proposed Uniform State Product Liability Act" Section 206 (National Product Liability Council) (undated); *see generally* Defense Research Institute, "The Case Against Punitive Damages" (monograph 1969) (marshalling arguments).

cf. Prosser, "Torts" at 9–10 (4th ed. 1971). The "reckless disregard" standard is identified in statutory form to avoid any possible misinterpretation of this basic area of law. Thus, it should be clear that a product seller does *not* have to pay punitive damages under ordinary strict liability or negligence standards which fall short of reckless disregard.

Subsection (B) follows the current common law system in allowing the trier of fact to determine at its discretion whether punitive damages should be awarded. *See* Prosser, *supra* at 9. On the other hand, this Subsection draws upon a newly enacted Minnesota statute in having the court, rather than the jury, determine the amount of those damages. "Minn. Stat. Ann." Section 549.21 (Supp. 1978). This approach is in accord with the general pattern of criminal law where the jury determines "guilt or innocence" and the court imposes the sentence. This is particularly appropriate in product liability cases where, under current law, product sellers are potentially subject to repeated imposition of punitive damages for harm caused by a particular product.

Subsection (B) provides guidelines for the court in determining the amount of punitive damages. The eight factors are derived from "Minn. Stat. Ann." Section 549.20(3) (Supp. 1978). The drafters of that statute relied on a very thorough analysis of product liability punitive damages. *See* Owen, "Punitive Damages in Products Liability Litigation," 74 "Mich. L. Rev." 1257, 1299–319 (1976).

Factors (1) and (2) are self-evident. If the facts show that the product seller was actually aware of the specific hazard *and* its seriousness, *and* marketed it anyway, a higher award is in order.

Factor (3), profitability, recognizes that punitive damages may be used to attack directly the profit incentive that generated the misconduct.

Factor (4) is important regardless of the basic requirement that the product seller must have reckless disregard for the safety of others. If the product seller consciously concealed its activities, this fact argues for a higher award.

Factor (5) acknowledges that the product seller who was reckless in producing the product, but who acted quickly to remove the product from the market upon discovery of the hazard, should not be subject to as harsh a sanction as one who failed to act. Some have suggested that punitive damages should be awarded only where corporate management has either authorized, participated in, or ratified conduct that shows a conscious or reckless disregard for public safety. *See* "Task Force Report" at VII–79. Section 120 rejects that approach because it could foster legal disputes as to whether an individual stood "high enough" in the corporate structure to bear responsibility for punitive damages. Nevertheless, in circumstances where a non-management employee caused the harm and management acted quickly to mitigate that harm once it was discovered, a lower award is appropriate.

Factor (6) permits the court to consider the impact of the award on the product seller in light of its financial condition. This consideration has deep roots in common law. It is one that has been subject to criticism from product sellers and economists. Nevertheless, in light of the fact that the deterrence of wrongful conduct is the principal rationale for punitive damages, it is appropriate to consider the impact an award will have on a particular product seller.

Factor (7) is more important in product liability cases than in other liability cases because it addresses the problem of multiple exposure to punitive damages. This factor directs the court to consider both criminal and civil liability to which the product seller has been or may be subjected.

Factor (8) recognizes that the injury may also be attributable in part to the claimant's reckless disregard for personal safety. In such instances where the defendant can show such reckless disregard on the part of the claimant, punitive damages may be diminished proportionately according to the comparative responsibility of that claimant. The comparison, therefore, is between the reckless disregard on the part of the product seller and that of the claimant, and *not* between the reckless disregard of the product seller and mere negligence of the claimant. *See also* Section 111.

The Act indicates that the award of punitive damages goes to the claimant and not to the state. While the argument that "since the damages are non-compensatory, they should go to the state" has some merit, the approach was rejected because of constitutional problems and the fact that it might place a claimant's attorney in a potential conflict of interest situation by forcing the attorney to represent both the claimant and the state. *See* "Task Force Report" at VII–79.

When the trier of fact determines that punitive damages should be awarded, one option available to the court is to limit the award to a multiple of the compensatory damages as is done in antitrust actions. While this approach has appeal, it is not appropriate in the case of product liability because this area of the law addresses a multiplicity of different kinds of wrongful acts. Antitrust law, on the other hand, addresses one basic kind of wrongful act: an antitrust violation. Under this Section, the defendant's wrongful conduct could range from that which merely could cause damage to property to conduct which could result in the deaths of many people. Antitrust law violations involve economic injury only, and rarely, if ever, result in serious physical injury or death. Thus, the punitive damages in product liability actions do not lend themselves to quantification in the same manner as do such damages in antitrust cases.

* * * * *

Code

Sec. 121. Severance Clause

If any part of this Act shall be adjudged by any court of competent jurisdiction to be invalid, such judgment shall not affect, impair, or invalidate the remainder thereof, but shall be confined to its effect to that part of this Act declared to be invalid.

* * * * *

Analysis

Sec. 121. Severance Clause

This Section makes clear that in the event any court of competent jurisdiction declares any part of this Act to be invalid, such action shall be confined to that part alone, and shall not affect the validity of the remainder of the Act. The source of this Section is "1976 N.Y. Laws," ch. 955 (12) (McKinney), which concerns medical malpractice.

* * * * *

Code

Sec. 122. Effective Date

This Act shall be effective with regard to all product liability claims filed on or after ———, 19——.

*Alternative Section

[This Act shall be effective with regard to all claims accruing on or after ———, 19——. It shall be prospective in operation, and shall only apply to a product-related harm occurring on or after this date. When the facts giving rise to a claim are discovered or should have been discovered after this date, this Act shall govern the claimant's action. When the facts giving rise to a product-related harm are discovered or should have been discovered prior to the effective date of this act, the law of this State which was applicable at the time of such discovery shall govern the claimant's action.]

* * * * *

Analysis

Sec. 122. Effective Date

The issue of the effective date of a tort-related statute has not been given intense analysis in legal periodicals—perhaps because there have been relatively few legislative initiative in the tort area. In an attempt to balance fairness to all parties against procedural convenience, the drafters of this Act have chosen to apply the statute to all claims *filed* after the effective date.

The shortcoming of this approach is that it may create a rush to the courthouse—or, conversely, a delay—by claimant's attorneys. Also, the new law will apply to some injuries that occurred *before* the effective date.

On the other hand, since the Act does not create new causes of action, but condenses, clarifies, and balances common law development, the approach taken is a fair one. Also, it allows claimants, product sellers, and insurers to know, with precision, what law will be applied to a claim. *See* "1979 Minn. Laws" ch. 81, Section 3; "Conn. Gen. Stat." Section 52-572 1 (rev. 1979); *cf.* "Peterson v. City of Minneapolis," 285 Minn. 282, 173 N.W.2d 353 (1969); "Godfrey v. State," 84 Wash. 2d 959, 530 P.2d 630 (1975); *see also* Annot., 37 "A.L.R.3d" 1438 (1971).

Because state legislatures are likely to differ about the issue of effective date, an alternative approach has been drafted. The alternative provision would have the Act apply only to a harm actually sustained or causes of action discovered, or which should have been discovered (*e.g.,* latent disease) on or after the effective date. This approach makes the Act fully prospective in nature and recognizes that certain illnesses, such as malignancies, only become discoverable some time after the actual contact with the product. In the case of disease or other illness with delayed effects, the Act would apply if the harm or the cause thereof were discovered on or after the effective date. *See* Section 109(C); *see also* 73 "Am. Jur. 2d" "Statutes" Sections 385 *et seq.* (1974).

A significant shortcoming of this alternative approach is that for many years it will leave claimants, product sellers, and insurance ratemakers with two potential sources of product liability law—existing common law and this Act. It should be noted that the phrase "the law of this State," as used in the alternative, includes a state's conflict of law rules as well as its substantive product liability law.

* * * * *

Appendix A—A Bibliography of Major Compendium Sources Reviewed in Connection With the Model Code

Final Report, Interagency Task Force on Product Liability (NTIS, 1977).

Product Liability Legal Study, Interagency Task Force on Product Liability (NTIS, 1977).

Product Liability Industry Study, Interagency Task Force on Product Liability (NTIS, 1977).

Product Liability Insurance Study. Interagency Task Force on Product Liability (NTIS, 1977).

Selected Papers, Interagency Task Force on Product Liability (NTIS, 1978).

Insurance Services Office, Product Liability Closed Claims Survey: A Technical Analysis of Survey Results (ISO, 1977).

Product Liability Insurance, A Report of the Subcommittee on Capital, Investment and Business Opportunities of the Committee on Small Business, H.R. Rep. No. 95-997, 95th Cong., 2d Sess. (1978).

"Impact on Product Liability": Hearings before the Senate Select Committee on Small Business, 94th Cong., 2d Sess., 95th Cong., 1st Sess. (1976-77).

"Product Liability Insurance": Hearings on S. 403 before the Consumer Subcommittee of the Senate Committee on Commerce, Science and Transportation, 95th Cong., 1st Sess. (1977).

Department of Commerce Task Force Report on Product Liability Insurance (State of Michigan, 1978).

Final Report of the Governor's Task Force on Product Liability (Maine, 1978).

Product Liability: An Overview, Wisconsin Legislative Council, Research Bulletin 78 (1978).

Illinois House of Representatives, Judiciary I Subcommittee on Product Liability, Report and Recommendations (1978).

Report of the Senate Product Liability Study Committee, State Capitol, Georgia (1978).

Report of the Senate Select Committee on Product Liability, Missouri Senate (1977).

American Law Institute, Restatement (Second) of Torts, Section 402A and Appendices (1965).

Defense Research Institute, Inc., Products Liability Position Paper (1976).

The Alliance of American Insurers, Product Liability Tort Reform Proposals (1976).

Proposed Uniform State Product Liability Act (National Product Liability Council).

American Insurance Association, Product Liability Legislative Package (1977).

The California Citizens' Commission on Tort Reform, Righting the Liability Balance (1977).

A review was also conducted of all enacted state product liability laws, all proposed federal product liability laws, and major proposed state product liability laws, as well as all law review and other related literature and major case law reported or published since the completion of the Interagency Task Force's seven-volume Legal Study in December 1976. That study reviewed case law and literature published prior to that date. Consideration was also given to pre-1976 sources that were not reviewed by the Legal Study.

[FR Doc. 79-33253 Filed 10-30-79; 8:45 am]

BILLING CODE 3510-17-M

Appendix 2
Doing A Pharmaceutical Business in a Product Liability Situation*

by Warren Freedman

PART I—INTRODUCTION

The pharmaceutical business, whether conducted by multinational corporations or by domestic companies, reflects today the universal concern of businessmen and their lawyers about the galloping "product liability situation". The issues in products liability are international in scope because products travel around the world, and the courts of the various countries have generally determined that consumers the world over must be protected, should they sustain property damage, personal injury or economic loss through the use or even misuse of a consumer product. For example, an Italian pharmaceutical manufacturer, selling its products in the United States, Japan, India, Brazil, or in the Common Market countries, simply cannot be indifferent to the "product liability situation" in each of these countries, if it intends to conduct business. Whether the corporation or entity is simply a distributor, parts or ingredient supplier, advertising agency, or sales agent, the product liability issues must be known and understood.

Foreign manufacturers, parts or ingredient suppliers, distributors, repackagers, as well as sellers of pharmaceutical products into the United States, for example, must understandably worry about their exposure to the "product liability situation" in the courts of the United States. On March 22, 1978, in *Hutson* v. *Acciaierie Wiessenfels,*[1] the 8th United States Court of Appeals held that an Italian repackager of a Yugoslav product, distributing the product through a New York-based distributor, may be subject to suit in a court in the State of Arkansas where the injured plaintiff resided. The federal court observed that the "long arm" statute in Arkansas permitted suit because the Italian repackager, through its American distributor in New York, had sold almost $75,000 worth of the product in the State of

*Madrid Conference on the Law of the World (Sept. 16–20, 1979.)

Arkansas over a period of four years, and this amount was sufficient to meet the "substantial revenue" requirement of the Arkansas statute. Furthermore, the four-year period of selling the product in Arkansas constituted sufficient "minimal contacts" with the State of Arkansas. On the other hand, a federal district court in Vermont, on October 1, 1977, in *W.T. Grant Company* v. *Unitikatsusho K.K.,*[2] found insufficient contacts with the State of Vermont by the Japanese manufacturer of childrens' sleepwear. The flammable Japanese product was distributed into Vermont through a New York-based retail chain. In declining jurisdiction the federal court pointed out that the sales contracts were negotiated in Japan and not in New York nor in Vermont; that the goods were shipped f.o.b. from Japan, and the Japanese product manufacturer did not ship the product into Vermont, nor own any property in Vermont. The point is therefore clear that, while the "long arm" statutes of each state may differ and therefore encompass within or exclude from its jurisdiction the non-resident product manufacturer, foreign corporations and foreign business entities will continue to be sued in American courts and be subject to the "product liability situation" in that state.

To achieve some degree of uniformity of law in the "product liability situation" the United States Department of Commerce in January 1979 released a draft of the Uniform Product Liability Act[3] for adoption by the several states. This proposed American legislation attempts to achieve uniformity of *substantive* law: it does *not* address the procedural problems of bringing suit or being sued in the several states. Most importantly, however, the draft Uniform Product Liability Act does achieve a *single* cause of action to supersede all existing theories of recovery, and therefore the Act should contribute some certainty to the "product liability situation". Indeed the Act "is intended to balance the interests of product users and sellers, and to provide uniformity in the major areas of tort law. . .".

In order to understand the *extreme* liberal position in which product liability law in the United States has been placed, one must appreciate that "caveat emptor" has been changed to "caveat vendor". It is the consumer who reigns supreme and whose interest is being protected against personal injury, property damage and economic loss that takes precedence over the reasonable profit motive of the product manufacturer. The American consumer movement truly began with the Congressional hearings of the late Senator Estes Kefauver, followed by the intrusive tactics of Ralph Nader and his "Nader's Raiders"; as the result, an injured consumer today is entitled to compensation from a product manufacturer as long as it can be shown that the product somehow caused the injury, damage or loss. The issue of "fault" has become irrelevant[4] because the product manufacturer should have realized that products will be misused, that product users are negligent and careless, and that injury, damage or loss is foreseeable. Therefore, the product manufacturer, who is charged with foreseeing the nature and the extent of the injury, damage or loss, has become a virtual insurer of the product. In the United States today an automobile is *not* a vehicle for transportation, but a vehicle that must protect the driver and occupants against every reasonably conceivable mishap occurring to that automobile, regardless of the negligence of the driver of the vehicle or the negligence of drivers of other vehicles.

The point is simply that the American consumer today is sitting in the cat bird's seat, protected against his or her foibles, because the American product manufacturer must respond to the needs of the consumer.

Some scholars explain this rule of absolute or pure Strict Liability in terms of the fact that products today are mass-produced and mass-distributed in callous disregard of the consumer's well-being, and therefore the impersonality of the product manufacturer (and distributor) requires that the personal user of the product be protected against every conceivable defect in that product.[5] Recently, the nations of the Common Market, in order to minimize severe dislocations brought about by the liberal extremes of American products liability law, promulgated at The Hague Conference of Private International Law, a Convention on the Law Applicable to Products Liability, dated October 2, 1973. (The Convention had been ratified only by Norway, Yugoslavia and France of the 28 member countries, as of early 1979). Unfortunately, that Convention dealt only with questions of choice of law,[6] not with substantive matter. Suppose plaintiff, a resident of "X" in response to an advertisement in an "X" newspaper purchases a product manufactured in "Y" State while he is traveling in "Z" State. In "Z" the product causes him a severe injury, so when he returns to "X" he institutes in "X" suit against the "Y" manufacturer. The applicable law under Article 4 of the Convention would be "Z" law, i.e., the State where the product was purchased and used. Furthermore, the law of "Z" would be applicable to all aspects of the litigation, procedural as well as substantive. (Common Market countries also rely on a Convention on the Jurisdiction of Courts and the Enforcement of Decisions in Civil and Commercial Matters, dated September 27, 1968). A Committee of the Council of Europe on January 27, 1977, however, drafted a Convention on Products Liability in Regard to Personal Injury and Death. The purpose of the Convention was to harmonize and make uniform the laws of products liability in these countries, but reserving, in a supplementary manner, the right of the consumer to an additional right of action against the producer of the product. The Commission of European Communities also approved on July 23, 1976 a draft dealing with the cost of indemnifying victims of product liability situations. But these legislative and administrative efforts in Europe have not yet left their imprint upon the "product liability situation".[7]

South America, being less industrialized than North America or Europe, has experienced few product liability situations. Argentina still distinguishes between contractual liability and extra-contractual liability: in the *former* situation the claimant must prove an obligation existed, that there was a default of that obligation, and that the default caused the damage; and in the *latter* situation the claimant must prove the damaging act, the existence of damages, that such damages were caused by the act, and the guilt of the defendant. The defendant, however, must prove he is not guilty if the damages were caused by "things", defective or inherently dangerous. Breach of warranty is also a viable route in Argentina for recovery of damages by an injured claimant.[8] These traditional views of civil liability in Argentina based upon privity of contract, represent the prevailing South American attitude.

South African law of products liability has little in common with American law of products liability. There are no juries in civil cases who can render emotional verdicts and astronomical damage awards; there are no "class actions", and the concept of Punitive Damages is not a feature of their LEX AQUILIA of Roman Law. Liability arises when the defendant fails to "foresee the reasonable possibility of his conduct injuring another in his personal property and causing him patrimonial loss"; and when the defendant fails to "take reasonable steps to guard against such occurrence".[9] South African remedies in the field of products liability appear inadequate to serve the interests of todays' consumers.[10]

Before proceeding with a delineation of the products liability situation in the United States and around the world we pause for a few important definitions—

PART II—DEFINITIONS

In 1932 in the English case, *Donoghue* v. *Stevenson* (A.C. 562), "products liability" was defined in these terms:—

> "A manufacturer of products which he sells in such a form as to show that he intends them to reach the ultimate consumer in the form in which they left him with no reasonable possibility of intermediate examination, and with the knowledge that the absence of reasonable care in the preparation of putting up the products will result in an injury to the consumer's life or property, owes a duty to the consumer to take that reasonable care".[11]

This 47-year-old English definition of products liability preceded by 28 years the landmark American decision in *Henningsen* v. *Bloomfield Motors,*[12] truly the progenitor of the Strict Liability doctrine in the United States. The English definition of "products liability" is not consonant with the doctrinal definition of Strict Liability in the United States. In the first place, the English definition is apparently limited to the product manufacturer provided that he sells the product, but does not delineate the liability of others in the chain of manufacture and distribution. Liability in England appears to be limited to the product "preparation" and does not include product advertising as well as countless other activities on the part of distributors, suppliers, selling agents, etc. Also the English definition does not clearly exclude liability where the product has been substantially changed, with or without regard to "form", or where the product has been misused in a manner not foreseeable. Furthermore, the English definition provides relief only for the *ultimate* consumer and with compensatory relief for injury to life or property only. The English duty of care does not go beyond the protection of the ultimate consumer; it does not encompass remote third-parties or bystanders who perchance are injured by the product in a foreseeable manner.

In the United States, a "product liability claim" may be defined as including all claims or actions brought for personal injury, death, property damage or economic loss, caused by the manufacture, construction, design formula, preparation, assembly, installation, testing, warnings, instructions, marketing, packaging, or labeling of any product.[13]

The definition of "manufacturer" varies country by country.[14] In some countries only the person or company which makes the *end* or finished product is held to be a "manufacturer"; in other countries the person or company making ingredients or parts can be held liable as the manufacturer, each according to the share of blame or fault. In some countries, there is an easier solution, i.e., national legislation requires a person or company to be registered as "producer" of the product in order to sell the product, and that "producer" is the person or company *totally* responsible for injury, damage or loss occasioned by that product. Under the 1973 European Convention on the Law Applicable to Products Liability it is the "producer" who is liable, i.e., "the manufacturer of finished product or of component parts and the producer of natural products". (Art. 2). Evidently it was not desirable to impose Strict Liability on a large number of persons, some of whom play only a secondary role in the production process. If the "producer" proves that the defect appeared *after* the product was put into circulation, the consumer will have to sue the immediate seller or the carrier, or any other intermediary who may be responsible under the applicable national legislation. The term "producer" in the European Convention is supplemented by Article 3(4) which establishes the liability of the "producer" of the component part when it is a defect in the component which caused the damage. According to this provision, when a component part of the product has been produced by another producer, both producers are jointly and severally liable. In the event that two or more persons are found liable for damage, neither the European Convention nor the proposed E.E.C. Directive[(15)] state how the liability is to be shared. (National law probably decides the question). Finally, under Article 3(2) "any person who has presented a product as his product by causing his name, trademark or other distinguishing feature to appear on the product, shall be deemed to be producer for the purpose of this Convention and shall be liable as such".[(16)]

Probably the most difficult definition is "defect" or "defectiveness of the product". American decisions have defined product "defect" in terms of (a) faulty production or construction, (b) improper design, and (c) failure to warn.[(17)] In Japan, according to Professor Kitagawa, "The Japanese Experience with Products Liability: A Parallel Development or Unique? in *Proceedings of the First World Congress on Product Liability,* p. 244(1977), Japanese product manufacturers have been held liable for *both* design and manufacturing defects, but Japanese case law provides little guidance as to the definition of product "defect". Articles 4 and 5 of the Japan Civil Code speak to the question of what weight should be given to evidence of defects in establishing a manufacturer's failure to fulfill its duty not to produce harmful products. Strict compliance with safety standards is not an absolute defense for a Japanese product manufacturer where the plaintiff proves a defect. But no liability attaches if the product could not have been considered "defective" in light of the technology available at the time of manufacture and/or sale.[(18)]

In England the 1977 Report of the Royal Commission on Civil Liability and Compensation for Personal Injury (under the chairmanship of Lord Pearson)[(19)] defined "defect" in terms of not providing the safety which a person is entitled to expect, having regard for all the circumstances, including the presentation of the product.[(20)] Obviously, this definition of "defect" is not objective nor definitive; it is purely a consumer expectations test, and therefore depends upon administrative and/or judicial interpretation. Indeed, a consumer expectations test has been rejected by the U.S.

Department of Commerce in its 1979 draft Uniform Product Liability Act. The European Convention in regard to Personal Injury and Death[21], which does away with the notion of Fault as a basis for products liability, defines "defect" in Article 2 identically with the definition of the Royal Commission in England. "Safety" and "legitimate expectation" are the basic elements of the definition, and therefore, the definition of defect is ambiguous and open-ended. The notion of "defect" may even be extremely restrictive because a product may cause damage without being defective, either because it is dangerous in fact, or for unknown reasons is dangerous. For that reason, the notion of "defect" has been refined and enlarged, and the courts in the twenty European countries have been instructed to consider all the circumstances of "legitimate expectation", including the presentation of the product and, more specifically, the absence of directions for use or warnings as to the dangerous character or a product, or the fact that these directions or warnings are incorrect or incomplete. The fact that the product producer observed statutory or administrative rules does not preclude liability.[22] "Defect" under this definition is thus not limited to *inherent* defects. The manner of use by the consumer must be taken into account as well as the legitimate expectations of the consumer. However, the State of Art or State of Technology defense is applicable to short-circuit a product producer's liability for product "defect".

The E.E.C. Directive decides *who* is the "claimant" and what damage is covered[23], i.e., any person who suffers injury or damage as a result of the defective product. Claims in respect of damage to property can be brought by the owner of the damaged property, provided the property is of a type ordinarily acquired for private use or consumption, and was not in fact acquired or used by the "claimant" for the purposes of his trade, business or profession. There are also three monetary limitations on recovery by a "claimant" provided by the E.E.C. Directive, which have been widely criticized *per se* for limiting recovery.[24] The avowed purpose of monetary limitations is simply to keep the potential liability of the producer within insurable limits.[25]

Pharmaceutical prescriptive products must be defined and distinguished from consumer products or over-the-counter products because prescriptive drug products are designed for professional use by the treating or prescribing physician. A prescriptive drug product is but a "tool" placed in the physician's hand, to be used by him or her within his or her sole, professional discretion. Furthermore, prescriptive products are delineated as UNAVOIDABLY UNSAFE products, i.e., in the present state of human knowledge are incapable of being made safe for their intended and ordinary use. Indeed, it is common to see such prescriptive products subject to testing by official bodies prior to distribution. Special licenses may be required not only to manufacture and distribute the prescriptive product but also to sell; in most countries, the sale of prescriptive drugs without a prescription from a licensed physician is prohibited. Pharmaceutical products do affect the chemistry of the human body, and generally side effects and contraindications must be anticipated; a failure to warn the physician will be construed as making the product "defective". The failure to warn, with few exceptions, is geared for the physician and not for the patient who is clearly distinguishable from the consumer of a consumer product.

PART V—SUBSTANTIVE LAW OF PRODUCTS LIABILITY IN THE UNITED STATES

In the United States the product liability action generally includes all actions brought for or on account of (1) personal injury, disease, disability, or death; (2) property damage; and (3) economic loss, i.e., lost wages or lost business opportunities. Such actions may be based upon NEGLIGENCE, BREACH OF EXPRESS OR IMPLIED WARRANTIES, FAILURE TO WARN OR INSTRUCT, MISREPRESENTATION, CONCEALMENT OR NON-DISCLOSURE, STRICT LIABILITY, or, in fact, any other substantive legal theory in tort or contract. It is unfortunate that there is such a diversity of actions because the diverse defenses may or may not be applicable to each cause of action. The U.S. Department of Commerce 1979 draft Uniform Product Liability Act reduces all these causes of action to a *single* action, entitled "product liability claim". (While an argument may be made that negligence theory is qualitatively different from strict liability and, therefore, should be preserved, product liability theory and practice has become an entity in and of itself and can only be stabilized if there is one, and not a multiplicity of causes of action).

At the outset, the prescriptive drug product, it is submitted, should not be subjected to the same substantive law applicable to *consumer* products because the former is *not* a consumer product. The prescriptive drug product is unique in that (a) proximate cause is exceptionally difficult to prove in face of the complexity of cause and effect upon the human body; (b) there is an inherent reasonable risk in *every* prescriptive pharmaceutical product simply by the nature of the product; unknown and unforeseeable side effects are always possible, as are the synergistic effects of some drug products; (c) the concept of product "defect" is not suitable in face of the utility of the product; (d) the injury, disease, disability or death is not truly compensable because it can never be substantiated that the prescriptive drug did cause the injury, disease, disability, or death; (e) there is no need to warn the patient-user of the product where the prescribing physician is adequately warned; and (f) prescription drug products are generally subject to governmental regulations.[26] There is indeed a BASIC EXCEPTION for prescriptive pharmaceutical products in the United States under the Strict Liability doctrine of Section 402A of the *Restatement of Torts Second:*

> "There are some products which, in the present state of human knowledge, are quite incapable of being made safe for their intended and ordinary use. These are especially common in the field of drugs. An outstanding example is the vaccine for the Pasteur treatment of rabies, which not uncommonly leads to very serious and damaging consequences when it is injected. Since the disease itself invariably leads to a dreadful death, both the marketing and the use of the vaccine are fully justified, notwithstanding the unavoidable high degree of risk which they involve. *Such a product, properly prepared, and accompanied by proper directions and warning, is not defective, nor is it unreasonably dangerous.* The same is true of many other drugs, vaccines, and the like, many of which for this very reason cannot legally be sold except to physicians, or under the prescription of a physician. It is

> also true in particular of many new or experimental drugs as to which, because of lack of time and opportunity for sufficient medical experience, there can be no assurance of safety, or perhaps even of purity of ingredients, but such experience as there is justifies the marketing and use of the drug notwithstanding a medically recognizable risk. *The seller of such products, again with the qualification that they are properly prepared and marketed, and proper warning is given, where the situation calls for it, is not to be held to strict liability for unfortunate consequences attending their use, merely because he has undertaken to supply the public with an apparently useful and desirable product, attended with a known but apparently reasonable risk.* (Comment 'k')''.

Indeed, prescriptive drugs are ''unavoidably unsafe'' and therefore constitute universally an exception to the American strict liability doctrine.

Products liability today in the United States may generally be delineated in terms of twelve (12) *basic* facets: (a) the applicable statute of limitations; (b) the issue of product modification or alteration and subsequent repairs or improvement to the product; (c) the State of the Art defense; (d) the defense of proximate cause; (e) exemptions or exculpations from or disclaimers of liability; (f) the duty to warn; (g) punitive or exemplary damages; (h) coordination with workman's compensation payments; (i) limitations on applicability of the Strict Liability doctrine; (j) settlement techniques generally; (k) countersuit by defendants; and (l) the arbitration alternative.

American products liability relates to personal injury, property damage and economic loss, but the European Convention does not—only to personal injury or death. While the European Convention delineates Strict Liability, there are interesting exceptions or exemptions from liability, i.e., (1) where the producer has not put the product into circulation; (2) when the product was not defective at the time it was put into circulation; and (3) where the product was not manufactured for sale or circulated in the course of business. However, a product causing injury or death is presumed to be defective until the product producer proves otherwise (Article 5[1]). Comparative Negligence is applicable under the European Convention, and Contributory Negligence may reduce liability on the part of the European producer.[27] The American product producer generally does not get such favorable relief, and furthermore, must look to the varying law and decisions of 50 jurisdictions to understand the ''products liability situation'' Comparative Negligence in the United States is a relatively new device.

The Statute of Limitations, for example, varies in every one of the 50 American jurisdictions.[28] The European Convention attempts to strike a balance between the interests of the consumers and those of the producers by subjecting proceedings to a limitation period of three (3) years from the time the claimant became aware or should reasonably have become aware of the injury, the defect, and the identity of the producer (Article 6). This period is, however, subject to another limitation, i.e., the right to compensation under the European Convention is extinguished if proceedings are not brought within ten (10) years[29] from the date on which the producer put into circulation the particular product which caused the damage (Article 7). In the United States, statutes of limitations and statutes of repose not only vary with the tort or the contract or the statutory basis of the cause of action, but with the nature of the loss, i.e., personal injury or property damage. The limitation of time for commencement of the American action runs the gamut from one(1) year to six(6) years for tort actions, and from two(2) years to ten(10) years for actions based upon warranty or contract.[30] Periods of time for Strict Liability vary with jurisdictions. In Japan[31] Articles 8 and 9 of the Civil Code set forth a three-year statute of limitations running from the time the injured party becomes aware of the injury and the identity of the party responsible for it. An outside limit of twenty (20) years begins to run from the date of injury (Article 724) in Japan!

Under Section 109 of the draft Uniform Product Liability Act of the United States Department of Commerce, pharmaceuticals are exempted from the three-year statute of limitations. The reasoning is that pharmaceuticals "cause harms that take many years to manifest themselves", and furthermore are "products that cause perceptible harm only through prolonged exposure". This reasoning is not necessarily true in all cases, but the exemption of pharmaceuticals means that the injured plaintiff can have extra time for bringing the product liability action. In general, such actions rely upon "failure to warn", and yet warnings for pharmaceuticals are designed not for the patient but for the prescribing physician![32]

Defenses based upon product alteration or subsequent repairs to the product should be self-evident, except that claimant's objection to the manufacturers' defense of the "state of the art" persists. Indeed, products marketed twenty years ago may cause injury today. Present day technology may attest to the need for a formula change, or a protective guard, or even a totally new product design. Shall the product producer be held to the state of the art as of today, or to the state of the art of the time of manufacture? Why should the product manufacturer be penalized today for what was scientifically acceptable yesterday? Under Section 106 of the draft Uniform Product Liability Act of the United States Department of Commerce, compliance with the state of the art as to time of manufacture raises a presumption that the product was *not* defective either as to design or failure to warn, but not as to construction or manufacture. This presumption may be rebutted only by *clear and convincing* evidence, as defined in Section 102(7) of the Act.

Proximate Cause as a defense should be crystal clear but American courts have sometimes distinguished "producing cause" and "contributing cause", stating that the latter was not "proximate cause".[33] In Sweden, it is conceded that it is often difficult to show, in the individual case, the casual connection between the injury and the use of medicines. Accordingly, the Swedish Product Liability Committee proposed a relaxation of the burden of proof on the part of the injured person, so that a *predominant probability* of a casual connection will be sufficient in claims involving medicines. (This relaxation, however, applied only to physical injuries).

Exemptions or exculpations from or disclaimers of liability are recognized in the United States only if they are conscionable and conspicuous.[34] But Japanese law, unlike American law, does not permit avoidance or limitation of tort liability by way of contract (Article 10 of the Civil Code). In Sweden, the Tort Liability Act has certain financial limitations on liability, to wit: in any one calendar year total payments for liability cannot exceed the equivalent of thiry four million dollars and not more than 50% of that amount can be spent for injuries derived from unknown and unexpected effects of medicine. The cost of these injuries is borne by the Swedish drug manufacturer and the Swedish importer of medicines, but the choice of the insurance company is made by the Swedish Government. It should be noted that the effective date of the Swedish Compensation System for injuries due to medicines was July 1, 1977.

Duty to warn in American law is both affirmative and negative, in the sense that courts impose an affirmative duty upon the product producer to disclose everything known about the product, and omission of a material representation is as evil as commission in the nature of a material misrepresentation. Inadequate warnings or unclear instructions are poor educational tools for the user or consumer, and therefore may constitute the basis upon which liability may be predicated. Such factors as likelihood and seriousness of harm, technological feasibility, cost, as well as the seller's ability to anticipate at the time of manufacture that the expected product user would be aware of the product risk, must be considered. Indeed, product warnings or instructions are not adequate unless designed to reach the person or persons best able to take precautions![35] Of course, the claimant must demonstrate that, had adequate information been provided, a *reasonably* prudent person would not have suffered harm.[36]

American courts generally frown upon punitive or exemplary damages in a civil suit.[37] A punitive remedy is simply not necessary to deter unsociable conduct, although there has been a *minority* of American decisions to the contrary.[38] The Second United States Court of Appeals in 1967 in *Roginsky* v. *Richardson-Merrill*[39] held that punitive damages were *not* appropriate because (1) such damages would punish innocent shareholders of the defendant drug company; and (2) multiple awards of punitive damages to multiple plaintiffs do excessively punish or might even bankrupt the defendant. In Argentina "indirect" damages may be awarded where the defendant has acted with malice; otherwise, only direct, compensatory damages can be recovered by the Argentina claimant.

In England the Consumer Safety Act of 1978, designed as far-reaching consumer legislation, is, unfortunately, a *criminal* statute rather than a *civil* statute. English product manufacturers as well as others in the chain of distribution, are made "potential criminals". The definition of "safe" in Clause 9, i.e., "prevent or adequately reduce the risk of death and in risk of personal injury from goods or from circumstances in which goods might be used or kept", does not provide clarity nor completeness. Safety can only be evaluated in terms of reasonableness. What is reasonable depends upon all the facts and circumstances of the given products liability situation. Furthermore, product standards promulgated by governments introduce undesirable rigidity, and the rule of reason is generally not applicable. The cost to the consumer who insists upon unnecessary and irrelevant product standards and specifications simply puts the cost of that product out of proportion to the material benefits of the product. The end result is the discontinuance of production of that product, followed by unemployment and dislocation in our economic system. Under the Consumer Safety Act of 1978, the English Government has power to take hazardous products off the market, but the responsibility is placed in the hands of *local* officials and therefore uniformity of enforcement simply cannot be achieved. Clause 6 spells out the fact that obligations imposed by safety regulations and by prohibition orders and notices constitute a legal duty, the breach of which is *civilly* actionable. Nevertheless, these obligations imposed upon the product manufacturer, distributors and even retailers, may be, in fact, weaker than those imposed by Strict Liability in the United States.

Workman's Compensation payments in the United States are made to the injured employee, and generally constitute the extent of payments collectible by the employee from the employer or its insurance carrier. Recent exceptions to this rule permit a third-party suit by the injured employee against the tortfeasor (most frequently a product manufacturer) who may, in turn, implead or cross-claim against the employer. Under these circumstances the employee sues indirectly his employer for *additional* compensation. California, however, bars the defendant third party tortfeasor (often the product manufacturer) from obtaining indemnification from the employer[(40)] so that the employer cannot be made to pay additional monies to either the employee or to the product manufacturer. In Japan employees are *not* statutorily barred from recovering *additional* payments from their employers, over and above the generally inadequate workman's compensation amounts. Section 113 of the draft Uniform Products Liability Act of the United States Department of Commerce delineates the relationship between product liability and "worker compensation" and concludes that "the development of worker compensation as a sole source for recovery in product-related accidents would be the best solution to the problem, *but only if the worker received additional benefits in the course of overall worker compensation reform*". Section 113 permits the product manufacturer to have LIMITED CONTRIBUTION up to the amount of the worker compensation lien, and thus, the employer cannot exceed his worker compensation payment.

The Strict Liability doctrine in the United States is not unequivocably applicable to all consumer products, and certainly not to the prescriptive pharmaceutical product. The proposed EEC Directive in Europe provides that the producer of an article shall be liable for damage caused by a defect in the article, whether or not he knew or could have known of the defect. It is no defense for the producer to argue that the product could not have been regarded as defective in the light of the scientific and technological development at the time when he put the article into circulation. Japan also restricts the strict liability doctrine under Article 717 of its Civil Code to defects in buildings and paved roads! Japanese courts generally adhere to negligence as the basic frame of reference (Article 709).[(41)] Argentina does not recognize Strict Liability, and the few Argentine cases of product liability are based upon traditional theories of civil liability (intentional acts or negligence). Finland has a Strict Liability proposal for drug products, which proposal was submitted in late February 1979 to the parliament; inherent in the Finnish legislation is a collective insurance fund to which all drug manufacturers and importers would contribute. Finland proposes an "enterprise liability" which does not require identification of the particular product of the particular manufacturer!

Settlement of claims in the United States is not necessarily the *summum bonum* because avid plaintiffs generally have such exaggerated ideas of what their claim is worth that defendant product producers or manufacturers deem time their greatest ally. In France it is reported that a large number of claims are settled on a negotiated basis, probably because many French court decisions continue to allow a reduction in the amount of indemnity to be carried by the manufacturer-seller by taking into account the fault of the victim or the fault of a third party, or even "force majeure" which can be considered as the sole and responsible cause of damage suffered by the victim.

To put a reasonable damper on the volume and frequency of products liability litigation[42] the device of a countersuit by the victim of the frivolous claim is commended. For example, where a product manufactuer is sued because the product was believed to have caused the injury but in reality that product was *not* used nor otherwise involved, that product manufacturer should have some recourse against the frivolous suit brought by a claimant. The physician who is frivolously sued by a patient who should have known that the named defendant physician had never treated the patient, should be entitled to compensatory and perhaps exemplary damages. There must be sanctions against bringing of frivolous claims and also against frivolous defenses. Section 115 of the draft Uniform Product Liability Act of the United States Department of Commerce recognizes that need, and provides the remedy of reasonable attorney's fees and other costs that would not have been expended but for the fact that the opposing party pursued a claim or defense that was frivolous.

Arbitration in the "product liability situation" has not yet come into its own in the United States, but the simplicity of the arbitration machinery is commendable for product liability situations. Arbitration can result in more accurate decisions, reduce overall litigation costs, and expedite the decisional process. The arbitrator can be an expert in the particular product field and capable of comprehending even the esoteric details of the product liability situation. Also, the privacy of arbitration proceedings should prompt more complete revelation of special manufacturing designs or processes, and therefore result in more accurate judgments. Hopefully, such arbitration could be compulsory and binding so as to avoid the expenses of a subsequent trial de novo.

PART VI—PRODUCTS LIABILITY INSURANCE

The cost of products liability insurance in the United States has skyrocketed during the past ten or more years, not only because verdicts and judgments have run into hundreds of thousands of dollars (and even millions of dollars), but because a huge volume of claims, estimated to be almost one million per year, has resulted.[43] The in surance premium, to be sure, is based upon many factors peculiar to the individual risk, such as the nature of the product or products sold, the more or less extensive role played by the insured in the design of the product, in the supply of raw materials, in the manufacture, in the packaging, in the instructions for use, in the post-sales service, in the destination of these products (particularly important is the export turnover figure, due to the additional costs envisaged for settlements in some foreign countries), in the limits of liability agreed on a case-by-case basis, in the possible application of a deductible agreed to in negotiation with the insured with respect of small claims, and, lastly, in the intrinsic quality of the insured undertaking which will be judged, in the light of good or bad past experience. Also of concern to the insurance carrier is how effective is state regulation and how successful is the insurance industry in addressing the rate-making problem, i.e., whether premiums more closely reflect actual product risk, and whether self-insurance groups will continue to complicate these insurance problems. The U.S. Department of Commerce draft Uniform Product Liability Act seeks "to provide uniformity in the major areas of tort law that may affect product liability insurance rate-making".

Products liability insurance in New Zealand is handled by a state fund—the Accident Compensation Act; and while costly, there is coverage for every conceivable injury and payments are promptly made in amounts determined by governmental administration.[(44)]

Argentina has no limit on the scope of civil liability which may be covered by insurance, and therefore Argentina insurers are prepared for all major coverages.

In Sweden the social insurance system authorized insurance benefits that frequently are so large that an insured employee with an average income could receive compensation for more than 90% of loss of income! This scheme is also costly because the Swedish insurer's right of recoupment has been abolished.[(45)]

Part VII—Reform of the Tort System

The doctrine of No Fault has not yet made its formal entry into the American products liability situation.[(46)] Basically, this is so because the American products manufacturer does not want to admit liability nor accept the stigma attached thereto. It took the American employer a long time to accept the No Fault concept in Workman's Compensation. But in recent years there have been numerous legislative efforts by the several states at reform of American tort law, but all fell short of invoking No Fault. For example, on December 12, 1978, the State of Michigan passed a products liability law calling for a three-year statute of limitations; but where the product has been in use for not less than ten (10) years, the injured claimant must prove his or her cause of action without the benefit of any presumption that the product might be outdated or even defective. Contributory negligence is not an absolute bar to recovery, and damages will be administered in proportion to the amount of negligence of the injured claimant. A product manufacturer in Michigan may introduce defense evidence that the cause of the injury was the alteration or modification of the product by the user. Similarly, the product manufacturer may introduce evidence of compliance with product standards or state or federal laws. Post-production product changes are not admissible in evidence. These and other statutory changes in Michigan simply reflect *minimal* reform, revolving about such issues as (1) statute of limitations; (2) state of the art as a defense; (3) modification of product as a defense; and (4) the collateral source rule.

In the State of Connecticut the Governor in 1978 vetoed a piece of legislation which had five major tort reform provisions: (1) an eight-year statute of repose; (2) an absolute defense for substantially modified products; (3) recognition of an express disclaimer of duty to warn for obvious risks in the use of the product; (4) reduction of employee's judgment against a third party by the amount of workman's compensation received; and (5) acceptance of defenses based upon claimant's failure to follow instructions.

The uniform or model law drafted in January 1979 by the United States Department of Commerce for adoption by the several states may truly reform the tort system. Among the major features of this proposed legislation for the states are the following: (1) the jury or trier of fact will decide whether punitive damages and/or damages for pain and suffering are appropriate, but the court will decide the amount; (2) there would be a ten-year statute of repose beginning with the date of first sale, except for certain products like chemicals or drugs which take longer to detect in the body; however, litigation must begin within three years from injury or when claimant should have known of the injury, and after ten years damages would be limited to medical costs and lost wages; (3) use of an obviously defective product would diminish the damage award or result in dismissal of the claim; (4) compulsory, but non-binding arbitration for claims under $30,000; (5) costs and attorney's fees would be paid by the frivolous plaintiff; (6) awards for pain and suffering would be limited to $25,000 unless injury is permanent; (7) notice of claim must be given within six months of plaintiff's lawyer's decision to take the case, or costs would be assessed against the party failing to do so; and (8) a *single* cause of action entitled "product liability claim" replaces all causes of action in the "product liability situation".

In summary, doing a pharmaceutical business in a "products liability situation" poses a myriad of complex problems which only a specialist in the field of products liability can unravel. Hopefully, uniform and simplified legislation will solve these problems. The extreme liberality of American products liability is but the forerunner of the consumer movement all over the world.

FOOTNOTES

* Contributions to this article are gratefully acknowledged from Reno A. Stradiotto (Canada); Klein and Mairal (Argentina); Professor Thomas Wilhelmsson (Finland); and Webber Wentzel & Co. (South Africa).

1. Unofficially reported.
2. Unofficially reported.
3. Federal Register, Vol. 44, No. 9, January 12, 1979, pp 2996–3019.
4. In Argentina, FAULT is relevant and material to the product liability situation. The Argentina defendant is NOT liable if the damage was caused by the claimant because the claimant used the product knowing of the defect, failed to take normal precautions, or did not follow instructions.
5. It is possible that 100,000 Dutch people can suffer an itching disease from a mistake in the formulation of margarine. It is possible that 100,000 Americans can die in automobile accidents because the vehicles did not withstand collisions with other vehicles. Hundreds of deformed children can result from their mother's ingestion of thalidomide. The hue and cry of peoples everywhere caused the machinery of the law to react to these changed scientific circumstances, but it was easier for a country with a common law background, such as the United States, to react more rapidly. Section 402A of the *Restatement of Torts Second,* establishing Strict Liability, is one example.

6. "Article 4

The applicable law shall be the internal law of the State of the place of injury, if that State is also—

a. the place of the habitual residence of the person directly suffering damage, or
b. the principal place of business of the person claimed to be liable, or
c. the place where the product was acquired by the person directly suffering damage.

Article 5

Notwithstanding the provisions of Article 4, the applicable law shall be the internal law of the State of the habitual residence of the person directly suffering damage, if that State is also—

a. the principal place of business of the person claimed to be liable, or
b. the place where the product was acquired by the person directly suffering damage.

Article 6

Where neither of the laws designated in Articles 4 and 5 applies, the applicable law shall be the internal law of the State of the principal place of business of the person claimed to be liable, unless the claimant bases his claim upon the internal law of the State of the place of injury"

A qualification of these articles is stated in Article 7 which provides that neither the law of the state of injury nor of the habitual residence of the person directly suffering damage shall be applied if the defendant established that "he could not reasonably have foreseen that the product or his own products of the same type would be made available in that State through commercial channels".

It should be noted that the American plaintiffs' bar bitterly opposed United States adherence or ratification to this Convention!

7. National legal barriers in Europe appear to be bending with respect to lawyers appearing in and practising law in any court in the Common Market. The German rechtsanwalt, the Italian avvocato, the French avocat, and the English solicitor should soon be working closer together in the field of products liability. We understand that since March 1979 all Common Market member countries are obliged to welcome into their courtrooms lawyers certified by other member states, according to directives issued by the Council of the EEC. (In practice most countries are requiring visiting lawyers to practice jointly with a member of the host state's bar!) Incidentally, French law, under modern construction, is closest to the American Strict Liability doctrine, contemplated by Article I of the draft directive. It should be observed that Scandinavian countries with their compulsory broad social insurance programs automatically cover personal injury and death. Whether these changes approach the utter liberality of American products liability law is open to question.

8. Argentina prefers to base product liability situations upon tort, not contract. In one case involving a restaurant owner who sold contaminated food, the Court of Appeals found for the plaintiffs based upon breach of the contractual obligation to provide healthy food. But the Supreme Court of the Province of Buenos Aires based its affirmance upon Tort liability in that defendants had not refuted the presumption of guilt (June 22, 1965, REV LA LEY t.119 p. 383, fallo 1541056). See also another case where the manufacturer of a medicinal product was found liable in *tort* for damages caused by its deficient preparation (C Mec [BA]), February 6, 1969, JA 1969-Resenas, 465-S-28).

"In Australia product liability is based upon (1) contract, (2) negligence or (3) obligations imposed by statute. The basis of liability on Negligence and Contract presents little variation from the traditional view, except the following:

(1) *Negligence*

(a) the product must be dangerous, not just inferior;
(b) no recovery for economic loss or purely pecuniary losses;
(c) disclaimers of liability are recognized.

(2) *Contract*
   (a) no recovery for economic loss;
   (b) privity of contract is preserved;
   (c) disclaimers of liability are recognized;
   (d) under Trade Practices Act of 1974 the consumer price of the product cannot exceed $15,000.

(3) The Obligations Imposed by Statute concern (1) false representations or deceptive conduct; (2) failure to comply with product safety and information standards under Section 52, 53, 63 and 64 of the Trade Practices Act, for example; and (3) manufacturer's warranties. But disclaimers of liability are not generally recognized.

9. Holmes JA in *Kruger* v. *Coetzee* 1966 (2) (SA) 430. In the case of *Herschel* v. *Mrupe* 1954 (3) (SA) (AD), Van den Heerver J A expressed the view that, by putting into circulation potentially harmful things, a manufacturer was doing more than simply exercising a legal right, and was encroaching upon the rights of others not to be exposed when going about their lawful occasions, and when accepting the implied general invitation to acquire and use such commodities.

10. In the recent case of A. Gibb and Son (Pty) Limited v. Taylor and Mitchell Timber Supply Company (Pty) Limited 1975 (2) S A 457 W. it was pointed out by Coetzee J. that there is no reason why a negligent merchant seller should not be delictually liable in appropriate circumstances for harm caused by defects, whether latent or patent, in the goods which he sells to the public, quite apart from the profession of special knowledge. If the particular market is studied, the kind of trade which is conducted, the methods employed and the expectations of those who customarily deal in it, the study may reveal a duty on the part of the seller to exercise reasonable care to inspect the goods to discover defects. If he fails to do so and foreseeable harm is caused he may be liable in delict to the buyer. This approach is, with respect, to be very much welcomed bearing in mind the extreme conservatism of South African courts in the specific fields of negligent ommissions and negligent misrepresentations and in the contraction of the concept of the profession of special knowledge.

11. Canada deems this English decision to be its landmark decision in the field of products liability. This "snail in the bottle" case is invariably quoted in every Canadian products liability decision. (Mrs. Donoghue drank some ginger beer bought for her by a friend at a cafe; the ginger beer was contaminated with the decomposed remains of a snail and she suffered severe food poisoning. She had no recourse against the cafe owner who sold the ginger beer because she was not the buyer. But she did successfully sue Stevenson, the manufacturer, because she was able to show that the contamination was his fault and that he owed a duty of care to purchasers and consumers). However, since 1932 Canadian jurisprudence has expanded and generously interpreted the principle of Lord Atkin in favor of the injured consumer.

On the other hand, The Sale of Goods Act in Ontario, Canada, for example, is retrogressive in that privity of contract is required for the breach of warranty cause of action.

South Africa delineates product liability OUTSIDE the realm of contract; see footnotes 9 and 10. For contractual examples of implied warranty against latent defects, see *Hall and Company* v. *Kearns,* (1893) 10 SC 152; and *S.A. Oil and Fat Industries, Ltd.* v. *Park Rynie Whaling Co., Ltd.,* (1916) AD 400. For contractual circumstances render which the seller is not responsible for latent defects, see *Knight* v. *Trollip* (1948) (3), SA 1009 (N), and *Fine and Gluckman* v. *Heyneke* (1915) GPD 211. As to contractual remedies of the buyer where the seller is in default, see *Labuschagne Broers* v. *Spring Farm* (Pty.) Ltd., (1976) (2) SA 824 (7).

12. 32 NJ 358, 161 A2d 69 (1960).

13. See Section 102(2) of the draft Uniform Product Liability Act of the United States Department of Commerce. The "product liability claim" includes but is not limited to, all actions based on the following theories: strict liability in tort; negligence; breach of warranty, express or

implied; breach or failure to discharge a duty to warn or instruct, whether negligent or innocent; misrepresentation, concealment, or nondisclosure, whether negligent or innocent; or under any other substantive legal theory in tort or contract.

14. See Section 102(5), *supra* note 11: "Manufacturer includes product sellers who design, assemble, fabricate, construct, process, package, or otherwise prepare a product or component part of a product prior to its sale to a user or consumer. It includes a product seller or entity not otherwise a manufacturer that holds itself out as a manufacturer".

15. The statutory authority for the EEC Directive is Article 100 of the Treaty of Rome which enables the Council of Europe to issue directives for harmonising the laws of the Member States in those fields which affect the functioning of the Common Market. Uniform laws on product liability are regarded as central to the functioning of the Common Market for three separate reasons: distortions of competition within the Common Market; free movement of goods; and consumer protection.

16. Also, (1) the producer of any material or component; (3) where the producer of the article as previously defined cannot be identified then each supplier of the article is treated as its producer unless he informs the injured person of the identity of the producer or of the person who supplied him with the article; this definition could embrace commodity agents or brokers although they would normally be able to identify the previous supplier; and (4) any person who imports into the European community an article for resale or similar purpose is treated as its producer.

17. The State of California issues jury instructions known as "BAJI" which remarkably state the law. For example, BAJI 9.00.3 defines "defect in manufacture";—

> "The manufacturer of a product is liable for injuries a proximate cause of which was a defect in its manufacture which existed when it left possession of defendant[s], provided that the injury resulted from a use of the product that was reasonably foreseeable by the defendant[s]."
>
> "A defect in the manufacture of a product exists if the product differs from the manufacturer's intended result or if the product differs from apparently identical products from the same manufacturer".

"Defect in design" under BAJI 9.00.5 reads as follows:

> "The manufacturer of a product is liable for injuries a proximate cause of which was a defect in its design which existed when it left possession of defendant [ ] provided that the injury resulted from a use of the pro product that was reasonably foreseeable by the defendant [ ]."
>
> "A product is defective in design [unless the benefits of the design of the product as a whole outweigh the risk of danger inherent in the design] [or] [if the product failed to perform as safely as an ordinary consumer of the product would expect when used in a manner reasonably foreseeable by the defendant[ ]]."
>
> "[In determining whether the benefits of the design outweigh such risks you may consider, among other things, the gravity of the danger posed by the design, the likelihood that such danger would cause damage, the mechanical feasibility of a safer alternate design at the time of manufacture, the financial cost of an improved design, and the adverse consequences to the product and the consumer that would result from an alternate design.]"

18. The problem with the Japanese concept of "defect" is illustrated by two automobile accident cases:

> *Recovery*—A rear seat passenger suffered injuries when the back of an automobile's front seat gave way in a sudden stop; plaintiff proved a defect and was allowed damages, *Kamesaki* v. *Mitsubishi Heavy Industries, Co., Ltd.,* Yokohama District Court, February 4, 1975. Hanta No. 324, at 268.

No Recovery—A rear seat passenger struck a metal fitting on the front seat's safety belt in a sudden stop; plaintiff sustained injuries but was unable to prove a defect so recovery was denied, *Yoshie* v. *Toyota Motor Co., Ltd.,* Kyoto District Court, November 30, 1973. *Hanrei Jiho* No. 738, at 89.

In France the claimant must prove hidden defect of "vice-cache", i.e., that the manufacturer must have known of such a defect.

19. In particular, it recommended that No-Fault compensation for injuries and diseases contracted at work should continue to be provided by the industrial injuries scheme, that a No-Fault compensation scheme (financed by a levy on gasoline) should be introduced for motor vehicle injuries, and that "producers" should be strictly liable in tort for death or personal injury caused by defective products.

20. Volume three is entitled "Overseas Systems of Compensation" and contains a comparison of the legal systems of compensation in many countries throughout the world, specifically covering product liability in each of those countries.

21. Adapted by the Council of Europe in January 1977.

22. In Canada, there are numerous federal and provincial acts which govern Canadian "producers", such as The Hazardous Products Act, The Explosives Act, The Motor Vehicle Safety Act, The Consumer Packaging and Labelling Act, and The Food and Drugs Act. These acts spell out certain prohibitions and there are penalty provisions contained within the acts. These acts are generally considered to set put a reasonable standard of conduct which ought to be complied with, and, thus, if there is a violation of a governing statute it can be argued that it is a clear indication of a failure to adhere to a reasonable standard of conduct. The more vexing question is whether or not a violation of a governing statute, per se, constitutes a cause of action. We know of cases wherein a judge has held that the violation of a provision of a governing statute in itself constituted the basis of a civil cause of action. The case that comes to mind is one in which a housewife found a dead mouse in a 100 lb. bag of flour. The producer of the flour was held to be in violation of Section 4 of the Federal Food and Drugs Act which provides that no person shall sell an article of food that consists in part of any filthy, disgusting, rotten, decomposed or diseased animal substance, etc. The trial judge concluded that the violation of this provision of the statute in itself constituted the basis for a cause of action against the producer for the injuries she sustained as a result of finding the dead, decomposed mouse in the bag of flour.

The question of whether or not violation of a statute in itself constitutes a cause of action is a complex question because in Canada it often involves jurisdictional problems. Matters of civil rights come within the jurisdiction of each province and case law has, therefore, held that violations of federal statutes cannot constitute civil causes of action.

23. In respect of death the EEC Directive does not specify the class of persons who could claim against the producer but it is presumed that normal national laws relating to claims in respect of death arising out of tort will apply.

24. (i) In the case of moveable property the injured consumer cannot recover more than 15,000 European Units of Account (approximately £9,000); (ii) In the case of immoveable property the limit is 50,000 Units of Account (approximately £30,000); (iii) The total liability of the producer for all personal injuries caused by identical articles having the same defect shall be limited to 25,000,000 Units of Account (approximately £15,000.000).

25. Note that monetary limitations are set in the Warsaw Convention relating to air travel, in the International Convention relating to the Liability of Owners of Sea-Going Ships (1975) and in the International Convention on Civil Liability for Oil Pollution Damage (1969), for example.

26. Interestingly there appears to be no American prescriptive drug cases involving liability on

the part of the governmental authority, except for the FDA's liability for (1) releasing polio vaccine exceeding the FDA virulence standards, and (2) permitting the distribution of the swine flu vaccine. Most countries preclude liability of a regulating or testing authority. On the other hand, in the European communities, the principle of liability of regulatory bodies for the consequences of their negligence was laid down by the English Court of Appeal in *Dutton* v. *Bognor Regis* Building Company (1972, 1 A.E.R. 462), in which a local borough council was found liable to a building owner for the negligent exercise of its powers of controlling building work within the borough, leading to consequent damage being suffered by such building owner. Japan has no sovereign immunity doctrine, and the National Compensation Act provides that the Government is obligated to compensate a party negligently or intentionally injured by a public employee who was exercising public authority in the performance of duty. Thus far, Japanese consumers have not been very successful under this statute in a products liability case, although in the thalidomide cases Japanese consumers were able to get settlement concessions from the Government.

27. In France, contributory negligence is no defense, and the court may apportion damages (Supreme Court of France, July 24, 1918; S 1920 I359). The Trial courts assess percentages of fault between parties, either 100%, 50–50, or whatever the court decides. Thus, if the court finds each side equally at fault, plaintiff gets one-half of what his award in money otherwise would be. This is referred to as "partage" or a part of what otherwise would be paid. This partage doctrine can also work another effect unknown in the United States:—where, in a two-car collision, each driver is suing the other and the court finds both equally at fault, then plaintiff's carrier pays defendant one-half of defendant's damages, whether large or small, and defendant's carrier pays plaintiff one-half of his damages, whether large or small,—which is to say, each side repairs the damages of the other side, whether for personal injuries or property damages.

28. In Canada, generally speaking, the time limit within which actions in negligence must be brought is six (6) years, and the time runs from the time when the damages were sustained and not necessarily when the negligent act was committed. There are specific time limitations that apply to certain entities, such as doctors (two years), public authorities (six months), etc. But apart from specific legislation providing for specific time limitations the Canadian period is six (6) years.

29. This overall limitation may well lead to difficulties for product manfacturers since it would require them to maintain full documentation of the manufacturing process for at least ten years from the date on which the particular defective product was first put into circulation. This leads to insurance problems since the producer will need to insure against the risk of claims being brought in respect of all products sold by him in the previous ten years.

30. *Schwartz* v. *Heyden Newport Chemical Co.* (12 NY2d 374 188 NE2d 142, amended 12 NY2d 1073, 190 NE2d 253, cert den 374 US 808, 1963); *Urie* v. *Thompson* (337 US 163, 1949); and *Raymond* v. *Eli Lilly Co.* (371 A2d 170, NH 1977).

31. Japan is a civil law (as opposed to common law) jurisdiction. Although based on the German Civil Code, the Japanese Civil Code has not undergone the same doctrinal evolution in product liability matters. Orban, "Product Liability: A Comparative Legal Restatement—Foreign National Law and the EEC Directive", 8 Ga. J. Int'l. & Comp. L. 342, 358 (1978).

In Argentina, the statute of limitations is generally ten (10) years for breach of warranty, but only two (2) years for tort liability.

32. *See Dunkin* v. *Syntex Laboratories, Inc.*, 443 F Supp 121 (1977) where Chief Judge Brown opined that "prescription drugs are sold on a prescription basis and not over the counter because of the special expertise a trained physician is necessary for their use. Thus, an effective warning could only be to the medical profession, and not to an untrained patient. Moreover, concern has

been expressed that attempts to give detailed warnings to patients could mislead patients and might also tend to interfere the physician/patient relationship. On the other hand, it has been recognized that an effective warning regarding a prescription drug must go to the medical profession generally and not to the prescribing physician alone, since the patient may not return to the original prescribing physician when problems occur. This is not to suggest that persons using prescription drugs should receive no warnings of the dangers involved in the use of those drugs. Rather, it is this court's determination that the duty to warn the patient, if one exists, lies with the physician and not with the drug manufacturers''.

33. However, proximate cause is decided on an individual case basis. In the case of *Vincent* v. *Thompson,* 50 AD2d 211, 377 NYS2d 118, the New York court considered the case of a child who had become ill following the administration of a vaccine known as Quadrigen. An earlier federal decision had established that the Quadrigen vaccine was in fact defective resulting in serious injuries to another plaintiff. Vincent here sought to invoke the doctrine of collateral estoppel to reduce the case to an issue of damages alone, but the Court rejected this theory noting that even assuming defective design the injuries to any one particular patient may have resulted from a variety of factors completely unrelated to the design defect and there may in fact have been factors in the plaintiff's background which changed the risk.

34. In 1972 Ontario, Canada, enacted legislation which renders null and void and disclaimer clause in a consumer sale.

35. Again, the pharmaceutical product is the exception. In *Reyes* v. *Wyeth Laboratories,* F. Supp., the court observed: ''Prescription drugs are likely to be complex medicines, esoteric in formula and varied in effect. As a medican expert, the prescribing physician can take into account the propensities of the drug, as well as the susceptibilities of his patient. His is the task of weighing the benefits of any medication against its potential dangers. The choice he makes is an informed one, and individualized medical judgment bottomed on the knowledge of both patient and palliative. Pharmaceutical companies then, must warn ultimate purchasers of the dangers inherent in patent drugs sold over the counter, and selling prescription drugs are required to warn only prescribing physician who acts as 'learned intermediary' between manufacturer and consumer''.

36. In Argentina, the defendant must refute guilt by showing that he gave proper instructions for the use of the product. He may also have to prove the fault of the claimant or of a third party for failure to warn.

It should be noted that in the United States the prescriptive drug product is generally deemed to be an *UNAVOIDABLY UNSAFE* product, and therefore is readily distinguishable from the consumer product. Under Section 105 of the draft Uniform Product Liability Act of the United States Department of Commerce, for example, sellers are NOT liable for unavoidably unsafe products unless inadequate warnings or instructions were provided, or unless the seller had *expressly* warranted that the prescriptive drug product was free of such unsafe aspects, either by words or by actions.

37. Canada also frowns upon punitive damages.

38. A 1914 Wisconsin court is *Luther* v. *Shaw* (157 Wis. 234 at p. 238) declared:

> ''The law giving exemplary damages is an outgrowth of the English love of liberty regulated by law. It tends to elevate the jury as a responsible instrument of government, discourages private reprisals, restrains the strong, influential, and unscrupulous, vindicates the right of the weak, and encourages recourse to, and confidence in, the courts of law by those wronged or oppressed by acts or practices not cognizable in, or not sufficiently punished by, the criminal law''.

Of course, these words are glaringly oblivious to the realities of *civil* litigation, which is not criminal in nature!

39. 378 F2d 832 (2d Circ. 1967).
40. *American Motorcycle* v. *Superior Court,* 146 Cal. Rptr. 182, 578 P2d 899, (1978).
41. Recovery for eye injury:—in circumstances of personal injury to the buyer of eye lotion, the plaintiff proved negligence and the Japanese court allowed recovery from the manufacturer, *Kato* v. *Nanso Pharmaceutical Co., Ltd.,* Tokyo District Court, July 14, 1955. Kaminsyu Vol. 6, at 1440.
42. One anomoly of American legal practice is the Contingency Fee System. Its rationale is that it provides a means by which an individual without adequate funds can secure legal representation by highly skilled and competent trial counsel. Counsel retained by the claimant advances all monies required to prosecute the action, and it is counsel, not the client, who, in the first instance, pays the cost of securing and reproducing hospital records, the retaining investigators, filing and court costs, the retention of experts and other professionals to do medical and pharmaceutical research, for example. Prosecution of the action is therefore independent of the ability of the client to pay. These costs absorbed by counsel in the average pharmaceutical products liability or medical malpractice case can be staggering, and may in many instances exceed $10,000. The attorney, in turn, if he prevails, receives out of the recovery, reimbursement of all costs and disbursements advanced, and then after deducting these sums from the amount recovered, receives a legal fee of generally one-third of the cause of action, this fee may vary from 20% to 50%.

In the United States, unlike Canada and England, the losing party does not pay counsel fees except where permitted in certain cases but the amount is restrictively small.
43. Admittedly there is another side to the American issue of high insurance premiums: the Subcommittee on Capital, Investment, and Business Opportunities of the Committee on Small Business, House of Representatives, concluded in Report No. 85-997, March 1978, that "several insurers have engaged in advertising practices using false and misleading information". Aetna Insurance and Crum and Foster Insurance Companies, for example, both published advertisements bemoaning the one million product liability claims filed in 1976, although they had good reason to know that figure was wrong. (The figure may be as low as 140,000). Also, reports of disastrous miscarriages of justice have been widely disseminated, including the notorious case of the consumer who used a lawnmower to trim a hedge and then recovered damages for his misuse of the product. That example was widely touted by proponents of tort law changes; however, when pressed, no one was able to substantiate its existence, so it seems.
44. The Swedish insurance systems apply in many special areas, for example; since July 1, 1976, Traffic Insurance provides full coverage for personal injuries in connection with an automobile accident. Union workers have a kind of insurance known as "Safety Insurance" which provides compensation for practically all injuries sustained at work. "Patient Insurance" has, since 1976, in Sweden, compensated for injuries from incorrect treatment or malpractice, as well as from accidents in the course of medical treatment. In March 1973 the Swedish Government established the Product Liability Committee to draft rules for personal injuries and property damage caused by industrial products. The Committee's investigation related to dangerous industrial products, and its first report dealt with Medicines. The result was a "Medicine Compensation System" whereunder the insurer's responsibility is not based on the existence of liability for damages on the part of the drug manufacturer or even on the part of other persons, but is a compulsory accident insurance for injuries caused by Medicines, payable by drug manufacturers and drug importers. Medicine insurance is available on a commercial basis, and compensation is paid even for injuries sustained from medicines which may have been sold illegally if the insured person was unaware of the illegal sale. The right of compensation is, therefore, based upon strict liability without negligence. However, there are some restrictions such as the kind

and degree of severity of the illness, the insured person's state of health, the known effects of the medicine, etc., etc. The Swedish compensation system covering Medicines is designed for the serious and unexpected injuries; for example, no payment is made where the injury is caused by the failure of the medicine to have any effect whatsoever.

45. See Warren Freedman, "Why Not an Accident Compensation Act? Your Company Should Elect a 'No-Fault' Modus Operandi", Insurance Law Journal 668, (Sept. 1978), pp. 511–529, Incl.

46. See Warren Freedman, "No-Fault and Products Liability: Can One Live Without The Other?", Vol. XII, the Forum (Fall 1976), pp. 100–129 Incl.

Appendix 3
Why Not an Accident Compensation Act? Your Company Should Elect a "No-Fault" Modus Operandi*

By Warren Freedman

Mr. Freedman suggests that an elective no-fault system of compensation for injured consumers, with built-in predictable limits, is a viable proposition for modern corporations. He believes that the New Zealand Accident Compensation Act, although government-administered, contains the essential elements of such a system, especially waiver of the right of accident victims to sue in tort, warranty or strict liability, and can serve as a model plan for corporations to follow.*

The inequitable rigors of today's products liability law, emphasizing the right of the injured consumer to compensation regardless of fault or misuse of the product, has prompted the modern corporation to think in terms of defining this expected loss with some degree of predictability. An elective system of compensation for injured consumers that has built-in, predictable limits is an economically viable proposition. It is submitted that the Accident Compensation Act of New Zealand, effective April 1, 1974, contains those essential elements[1] and is adaptable to the needs of the modern

---

*Reprinted from the September, 1978 Issue of THE INSURANCE LAW JOURNAL Published and Copyrighted 1978 by Commerce Clearing House, Inc., Chicago, Illinois 60646 All Rights Reserved

*The author delivered an address based upon this paper on September 8, 1978, before the New Zealand District Law Society in Auckland.

[1] However, according to Maxwell H. Vautier, Barrister and Solicitor of Auckland: "The scheme as now operating in New Zealand for providing compensation for persons suffering injury by accident cannot really be accurately described as an example of a scheme for 'No-Fault' insurance for accident victims. It would, as will be seen, be more accurately described as a State operated welfare scheme to provide compensation for the victims of accidents. Financed by taxation in the forms of levies imposed on various selected sections of the community, this scheme is provided as a complete substitution for all legal rights which such persons formerly had in New Zealand either at common law or under Statute to claim damages against any other person

corporation, especially the waiver of the right of accident victims to sue in tort, warranty or strict liability.[2]

Indeed, New Zealand has abolished the right to bring civil proceedings for damages arising out of personal injury sustained, directly or indirectly, in New Zealand and, in a limited number of cases, for personal injury sustained overseas. The Accident Compensation Act encompasses products liability, except (1) where a New Zealand consumer has a right of action against an overseas manufacturer, or (2) where an overseas consumer has a right of action against a New Zealand manufacturer, or (3) where the circumstances surrounding the products liability situation give rise to criminal proceedings.

The New Zealand Law— Objectives and Operation

The concept of corporate responsibility for the injured consumer and the concept of his/her comprehensive entitlement to care, treatment, rehabilitation and compen-

---

or legal entity whose negligence played a part in bringing about the injury." *International Bar Journal* (May 1975), pp. 41–47.

[2] The means by which the common law action is blocked is worthy of study. Section 5 of the Accident Compensation Act 1972 is as follows:

"5. Act to be a code—(1) Subject to the provisions of this section, where any person suffers personal injury by accident in New Zealand or dies as a result of personal injury so suffered, or where any person suffers outside New Zealand personal injury by accident in respect of which he has cover under this Act or dies as a result of personal injury so suffered, no proceedings for damages arising directly or indirectly out of the injury or death shall be brought in any Court in New Zealand independently of this Act, whether by that person or any other person, and whether under any rule of law or any enactment.

"(2) Without limiting the generality of subsection (1) of this section, the action for loss of services (known as the action *per quod servitium amisit*) and the cause of action for loss of consortium (known as the action *per quod consortium amisit*) are hereby abolished.

"(3) Nothing in this section shall affect—

"(a) Any action which lies in accordance with section 131 of this Act; or

"(b) Any action for damages by the injured person or his administrator or any other person for breach of a contract of insurance; or

"(c) Any proceedings for damages arising out of personal injury by accident or death resulting therefrom, if the accident occurred before the 1st day of April 1974.

"(4) No person shall have cover under this Act in respect of personal injury by accident if the accident occurred before the 1st day of April 1974.

"(5) Where in any proceedings before a Court a question arises as to whether any person has cover under this Act, the Court shall refer the question to the Accident Compensation Commission for decision, and the Commission shall have exclusive jurisdiction to determine the question.

"(6) The Commission may, on the application of any person who is a party to any proceedings or contemplated proceedings before a Court, determine any such question.

"(7) Subject to Part VII of this Act, a subsisting decision of the Commission under subsections (5) and (6) of this section shall be conclusive evidence as to whether or not the person to whom the decision relates had cover under this Act."

See generally Palmer, "Accident Compensation in New Zealand: The First Two Years." 25 *American Journal of Comparative Law* 1–45 (1977). Professor Palmer is a member of the law faculty at Victoria University of Wellington, New Zealand.

sation should no longer be seriously challenged.[3] That philosophy is already applied in the field of workmen's compensation and in the "no-fault" automobile liability statutes. Therefore, the New Zealand Accident Compensation Act, which has three objectives of equal importance, namely: (1) the promotion of product safety;[4] (2) the rehabilitation of the injured consumer,[5] and (3) prompt and realistic compensation for the injured consumer, should be adaptable to corporate needs. In New Zealand, the Act extends to all New Zealand residents who are injured by accidents in New Zealand—from the smallest children to the oldest citizen. Only personal injuries *by accident*[6] are covered, and payment of compensation is made regardless of who is to

---

[3] Professor Palmer, cited above at footnote 2, at 2, in evaluating the success of the New Zealand legislation, concluded: "The signal achievement of the first two years lies in the simple fact that the scheme is running fairly smoothly, and it has done so since its inception with few signs of public dissatisfaction." Furthermore, "public criticism of the scheme has been rare during the first two years. Compensation for those injured in the course of committing a crime has come under fire. Employers have been concerned at what they see as increased absentee rates caused by 100% of wages paid for the first week of incapacity. The self-employed, especially farmers, have been concerned about assessment of their earnings." *Id.*

[4] Professor Palmer, cited above at footnote 2, at 15, points out that the Accident Compensation Commission "has absorbed all the staff of the National Safety Association and now carries out all its functions. It has a substantial number of safety advisers working in the field. A great many seminars, forums and courses on safety have been organized. The 1975 Amendment Act provides for an Occupational Safety Trust Board to be established to administer an occupational safety trust fund. And the Commission has money to finance safety programs and research." But "many organizations, both governmental and private, have responsibilities in the area of safety. Some guard those responsibilities jealously. The statute gives the Commission 'an active and co-ordinating role' but no teeth exist by which that role can be exercised. The Commission is dependent upon enthusiasm, tact, and money." *Id.*

[5] According to Professor Palmer, cited above at footnote 2, at 15–16: "The problems faced by the Commission in rehabilitation are similar to those in safety. The Commission has important responsibilities in the field of rehabilitation but the co-ordination of rehabilitation policy is shared with a number of other agencies. The Department of Health assumes the major role in medical rehabilitation in conjunction with Hospital Boards and the medical profession. Other Government Departments also have important responsibilities: Social Welfare, Education, and Labour. And, of course, a multitude of specialized voluntary bodies exist. The policies of the Government agencies, including the Commission, are co-ordinated by the National Civilian Rehabilitation Committee which consists of representatives of each concerned department and of the Commission. Ministerial responsibility is similarly divided. Those with experience in government might be pardoned for wondering whether this is the classic prescription for a bureaucratic battleground in which the person requiring rehabilitation is the first casualty. There are many special interests in rehabilitation with special axes to grind. Medical rehabilitators think they should be in charge; para-medical people think the doctors should not be in control; those who work in occupational rehabilitation tend to discount the efforts of medical people in favor of more emphasis on re-training. Then there are the special interests classified by nature of disability, the paraplegics, the blind, crippled children, the deaf, and so on. The whole area requires some proper means of determining priorities and developing an overall rehabilition plan."

[6] Section 2 of the Accident Compensation Act of 1974 contains the following definition of "personal injury by accident":

"(a) Includes—

"(i) The physical and mental consequences of any such injury or of the accident

"(ii) Medical, surgical, dental or first aid misadventure

blame and regardless of the cause of the accident—without the old legal strictures. [Even a *visitor* to New Zealand has such protection while on New Zealand soil![7]] The Act, however, does not embrace sickness or disease[8] which is not the consequence of an injury or an accident, nor is compensation payable to a person for injury which has been willfully self-inflicted. Payment is automatic and is based upon the fact of injury. Wage-earners can recover loss of earnings up to 80 per cent of normal income up to $15,600. [It was not until the 1973 amending act that *non-earners* were allowed to claim under a supplementary scheme, which now pays lump sums up to $17,000 for loss of bodily function, pain and suffering, and loss of amenities as well as medical and rehabilitation expenses.[9] Non-earners do not receive *periodic* payments.] Generally, lump sums are payable for loss or impairment of bodily function, for pain

---

"(iii) Incapacity resulting from an occupational disease or industrial deafness to the extent that cover extends in respect of the disease or industrial deafness under sections 65 to 68 of this Act

"(iv) Actual bodily harm arising in the circumstances specified in section 105B of this Act, which section was inserted by section 6 of the Accident Compensation Amendment Act 1974

"(b) Except as provided in the last preceding paragraph, does not include—

"(i) Damage to the body or mind caused by a cardio-vascular or cerebro-vascular episode unless the episode is the result of effort, strain, or stress that is abnormal, excessive, or unusual for the person suffering it, and the effort, strain, or stress arises out of and in the course of employment of that person as an employee

"(ii) Damage to the body or mind caused exclusively by disease, infection, or the aging process."

Section 105B states that "actual bodily harm" includes pregnancy and mental or nervous shock. Also, "For the purposes of subsection (2) of this section, a person shall be deemed to have intended an act or omission within the description of any of the offences mentioned in that subsection, notwithstanding that reason of age, insanity, drunkenness, or otherwise he was legally incapable of forming a criminal intent." The crimes which are thus referred to are those of rape, sexual intercourse with a girl under the age of 12, and willfully and without lawful justification or excuse causing or producing in any other person any disease or sickness.

[7] "As now operating the scheme embraces every person who sustains injury by accident within the confines of New Zealand whatever the cause of the accident may be. There is no qualification as to domicile, citizenship, length of residence and, indeed, New Zealand residents who are temporarily absent from New Zealand may claim compensation under the Act in respect of accidents sustained by them outside New Zealand." Vautire, cited above at footnote 1, at 41.

[8] Occupational disease is covered. The Act requires that the disease be "due to the nature of any employment in which the earner was employed . . ." [Section 67(1)]. The problems which have arisen include: glandular fever and hepatitis contracted by nurses, dentists and doctors; brucellosis contracted by freezing workers; leptospirosis contracted by farmers and freezing workers; inhalation of dust causing silicosis; dermatitis conditions where a question arises whether the matter with which the person came into contact at work caused the condition. Most of the cases have concerned dermatitis and hepatitis. The Commission's policy is to follow decisions of the High Court of Australia interpreting workers' compensation legislation [for example, *Commonwealth* v. *Bourne*, 104 CLR 32 (1960)]. According to this view the work must have an inherent tendency to cause the particular disease. The tendency must exist because the work itself possesses or contains a particular property or characteristic which gives rise to that disease. Such tendency must be peculiar to the work and not found in employment generally. Because of the distinctive tendency the employee must face a special risk of contracting the disease, a risk not faced in other employment." Palmer, cited above at footnote 2, at 40.

[9] New Zealand Accident Compensation Amendment Act (No. 2) 1973.

and mental suffering, and for disfigurement. Medical, hospital and transportation expenses are covered, as are funeral expenses which may go directly to widows and orphans, together with lump sums and continuing compensation payments. The New Zealand "No-Fault" plan does *not* cover property damage. Unemployed persons do *not* receive payments for "loss of earnings" while injured. The enormous cost of the New Zealand plan is met through levies on employers and on the self-employed, through payments by vehicle owners, and through general taxation.[10]

Benefits under the New Zealand legislation, while subject to some limitations,[11] include (1) earnings-related compensation; (2) reasonable cost of medical and/or dental treatment; (3) reasonable cost of transportation to and from doctor and hospital for initial treatment; (4) reasonable cost of meals and accommodations to receive medical or rehabilitative treatment; (5) damages to or loss of clothing, spectacles, and so forth, worn or used as the time of the accident; (6) reasonable cost of necessary continuous personal attention following injury; and (7) actual and reasonable expenses directly suffered as the result of the accident.[12] A lump sum for permanent physical

---

[10] "The movement away from ordinary insurance concepts can be seen in the provisions made as regards the provision of the necessary funds for payment of the benefits claimable under the legislation. There are at present four sources of such funds—(1) a levy payable by all owners of motor vehicles fixed annually and paid at the time of the annual registration of the vehicle; (2) a levy payable by employers in the form of a percentage of the amount of all salaries and wages payable by the employer; (3) a levy on the earnings of all self-employed persons by way of a percentage of those earnings; and finally (4) the provision out of ordinary Government taxation revenue of funds necessary for the supplementary compensation fund referred to above out of which compensation is payable in respect of those accidents which are not motor accidents and not accidents occurring in the course of the person's employment." Vautier, cited above at footnote 1, at p. 45.

[11] Interestingly, the New Zealand Accident Compensation Act also uses $5,000, but as the "maximum lump sum" in a "very elaborate schedule whereunder fixed percentages of this sum may be paid in respect of various designated bodily injuries ranging from 100 per cent for the total loss of both legs by above-knee or below-knee amputation or the total loss of both arms, down to 2 and ½ per cent for the total loss of a toe other than a great toe. Percentages have been fixed for all sorts of other orthopaedic outcomes of injury such as arthrodesis of the various joints of the arms and legs, parellectomies, muscle spasms with degenerative lipping in the spine and a long list of others. There is also provision for a lump sum up to a maximum of $7,500 in respect of the loss of amenities or capacity for enjoying life including loss through disfigurement and also for pain and mental suffering including nervous shock and neurosis. The two maximum sums referred to above have from the 8th of November, 1974 been increased to $7,000 and $10,000. There was originally an overall limit as regards the position when claims were made under both sections of $12,500 and this has now been increased to $17,000." *Vautier,* cited above at footnote 1, at 45.

[12] Section 121 covers these issues:

"121. Compensation for pecuniary loss not related to earnings—

"(1) Where a person suffers personal injury by accident in respect of which he has cover under this Act, or where a person dies as a result of personal injury so suffered, the Commission, having regard to any other compensation payable and any rehabilitation assistance provided or to be provided, may, under this subsection, pay to him, or in the event of his death to his administrator, in addition to any other compensation and rehabilitation assistance to which he is entitled under this Act, compensation of such amount (if any) as it thinks fit for actual and reasonable expenses and proved losses necessarily and directly resulting from the injury or death, not being—

"(a) Any expense or loss in respect of damage to property; or

"(b) Any expense or loss incurred after the death of that person in respect of the administration of his estate; or

"(c) Any expense or loss arising from damage in respect of which, or to the extent to which, no payment is to be made under subsection (1) or subsection (1A) of section 110 of this Act, by reason of subsection (2) of that section; or

"(d) The loss of an opportunity to make a profit; or

"(e) Any loss arising from inability to perform a business contract; or

"(f) Any loss that has not for the time being actually occurred, whether or not the amount thereof is ascertainable before it occurs; or

"(g) Any expense or loss in respect of or towards payment of which compensation is otherwise payable under this Act.

"(1A) Notwithstanding anything in subsection (1) of this section, unless (in the opinion of the Commission) there are special circumstances that justify a payment being made under that subsection, no payment shall be so made in respect of any expense or loss if the Commission considers that the expense or loss is similar in nature to an expense or loss for which compensation is payable under any other provision of this Act.

"(2) Where a person suffers personal injury by accident in respect of which he has cover under this Act, or where a person dies as a result of personal injury so suffered, the Commission, having regard to any other compensation payable, may—

"(a) Pay to any member of the household of which the injured or deceased person was a member on the date of the accident such compensation as the Commission thinks fit for any quantifiable loss of service proved to have been suffered by the person to whom the payment is made as a result of the injury or death for such period as the Commission thinks fit, not being longer than the period for which that member could reasonably have expected to receive the service:

"(b) Pay to any person, or to the administrator of the person, such compensation as the Commission thinks fit for any identifiable actual and reasonable expenses [or losses] incurred by the person in giving help to the injured person while he is suffering from incapacity resulting from the injury or in taking any necessary action following and consequential upon the death of the injured person.

"(3) Where a person suffers personal injury by accident in respect of which he has cover under this Act and the injury is of such a nature that he must have constant personal attention, the Commission, having regard to any other compensation payable, may pay to that person, or if it thinks fit to the administrator of that person, in addition to all other compensation and rehabilitation assistance to which he may be entitled, such amounts as the Commission from time to time thinks fit in respect of the necessary care of the person in any place of abode or institution.

"(4) Where a person dies as a result of personal injury by accident in respect of which he has cover under this Act, and any superannuation, pension, or annuity terminates or is reduced upon his death, if in the opinion of the Commission any dependent of the person, being a dependent who was dependent through him on that superannuation, pension, or annuity immediately before the date of the death, suffers any loss of support by reason of the termination or reduction thereof, the Commission, having regard to any other compensation payable and to the circumstances of the dependent and to any other relevant circumstances, may pay to that dependent such compensation as it thinks fit in respect of the loss which in the opinion of the Commission is so suffered for such period as it thinks fit, not being a period extending beyond the shortest of the following periods:

"(a) A period equal to the expectation of life of a normal person of the same age and sex as the deceased person; or

"(b) The period for which earnings related compensation would be payable to the dependent under subsection (2) of section 128 of this Act if that subsection applied to the dependent; or

"(c) Any period other than the lifetime of the deceased person for which the superannuation, pension, or annuity would have continued if the deceased person had not died."

disability, a lump sum for pain and suffering, disfigurement, and loss of enjoyment of life are also recognized benefits. A dependent spouse[13] (including a de facto spouse) and one in loco parentis for children are entitled to a lump sum if death resulted from accident. Earnings-related compensation may also be paid the beneficiary. Compensation is payable to a member of the household for loss of services or for loss of support through injury or death by accident. Indeed, compensation may be paid to anyone[14] who can show actual and reasonable expenses in helping the accident victim, including reasonable funeral expenses.

The New Zealand concept of earnings-related compensation,[15] or ERC, is interesting because the injured consumer must establish that, at the time of the accident, he or she was an earner, that is, self-employed or employed. There are four periods of time covered: (1) the first week of incapacity during which no payment is made except for time actually lost from work; (2) the short-term, that is, from the seventh day to the thirty-fifth day *after* the accident, when payments are 80 per cent of "relevant earnings"[16] or the normal average weekly earnings of the injured person, but the

---

[13] Section 2 provides: "Dependent," in relation to any person, means any other person whom he had a legal duty to support in whole or in part at the time when the dependency has to be determined; and includes any other person whom he might then reasonably regard or have regarded himself as having a moral duty to support in whole or in part, and whom he was then supporting in whole or in part; and includes a child of his born after his death; and 'dependent,' 'totally dependent' and 'partially dependent' have corresponding meanings.'" Section 127 contains the rules for determining dependency and would appear to be based on a different view of what is involved in dependency. Palmer cited above at footnote 2, at 43. That provision erects a statutory presumption of dependency "in the absence of proof to the contrary," that is, where a husband and wife are living together, the wife is totally dependent on the husband; where they are living apart, she is dependent to the extent of any maintenance order or agreement including any amount he may be paying voluntarily in excess of the order of agreement [Section 127 (1)(b)]. A child under 16 is presumed to be "totally dependent upon each of its parents." [Section 127(1)(c)] Apart from those rules, the section makes dependency a question of fact, and so there are numerous problems of definition!

[14] Victims of a crime are *not* generally compensated. Vautier, cited above at footnote 1, at 44.

[15] According to Professor Palmer, at 4–5, the main problem areas, after the first two years of the Act, are: "1) Assessing earnings-related compensation for periods of incapacity suffered by the self-employed. Most agree that this has been the most important problem and the one least capable of easy solution; 2) Pain and suffering compensation, Section 120; 3) Section 114, Permanent partial incapacity; 4) The need to obtain authoritative medical assessments, especially for cases of permanent incapacity; 5) The proper limits of compensation available under Section 121 which allows payment for 'actual and reasonable expenses and proved losses necessarily and directly resulting from the injury or death . . .'; 6) Occupational diseases. There has been dissatisfaction from some claimants who believe the Commission has wrongly rejected claims based on the allegation that a particular disease was due to the nature of the employment; 7) The range of cover included by the words 'medical, surgical, dental or first aid misadventure' in Section 2; 8) How to obtain adequate accident statistics; 9) Classification of risks and variable levies for employers; 10) Increases in claim rates resulting from 100% compensation for first week of incapacity where the injury arises out of and in the course of the employment; 11) 'Dependency' in death cases."

[16] Should there be any difficulty in establishing "relevant earnings," the Commission is empowered to make an assessment "at such amount as it considers will provide fair and just compensation," without making assessments of relevant earnings if "undue delay would be involved in making such assessments" [Section 114(1)(d), referring to Section 113 (4B)]

amount of payment has regard for his or her work history and period of residence [a special formula is applicable for the self-employed];[17] (3) a further period of incapacity up to the date when a decision is made as to permanent incapacity, if any; and (4) the period of incapacity, following the decision as to permanent incapacity, and then compensation is paid up to $300 a week. Generally, ERC may be paid until the age of 65, or for five years after the date of the accident. Incidentally, all ERC is subject to personal income taxation, and the income tax is withheld in advance.

The operation of the accident compensation scheme[18] in New Zealand is handled by liaison offices throughout New Zealand.[19] A local decision is subject to the right of appeal, first by seeking a review of the decision before the Accident Compensation Commission,[20] then by appeal to an APPEAL AUTHORITY, which has full power

---

[17] Professor Palmer, cited above at 27, writes:

"In regard to the self-employed the Commission *may* in its discretion have regard to the degree to which the pre-accident earnings of a self-employed person 'was contributed to by his interest in the capital assets of any business . . .' and the extent to which those assets would enable him to engage or continue to engage in business [Section 114(2)(b)]. That provision is entirely new. It seems clearly designed to function as a *means test on the self-employed* [Italics supplied]. There can be no justification in principle for such a provision in a scheme which applies no such tests to employed persons. The section will function to give the employed person with substantial income and assets a great advantage over the self-employed person who suffers a similar injury. That sort of discrimination seems hard to justify."

[18] Under Section 178 of the Act, the Accident Compensation Commission has the power to appoint a large range of organizations as its agent, including insurance companies, Departments of State and local authorities. This allowed private enterprise insurers to be appointed as agents, but they declined; the State Insurance Office was appointed and remains the Commission's sole agent except for a specialized company which handles seamen's claims. The State Insurance Office had the added advantage of being acceptable to lawyers who felt the experience of the office in settling common law claims would imbue officers with the correct attitude. Palmer, cited above at footnote 2, at 12. According to Professor Palmer, cited above at footnote 2, at 18:

"The State Insurance Office as agent for the Commission never declines a claim. It has no delegated power to do so. Claims which are not granted are referred to the Commission's Compensation Division in Wellington where they are considered afresh. Internal checks exist. When one officer declines a claim that decision must be looked at by his superior. When it is considered that the claim should not be accepted in whole or in part a pre-decision letter is written to the claimant explaining the difficulties and offering to consider any further information which might be available. After a period of 21 days the Commission proceeds to make a decision of which the applicant must be advised in writing. That decision advises the claimant of his right to apply for a review. Thus, prior to the first formal step, the application for review, the Commission has ensured it has full information, has given the applicant every chance, and is applying uniform standards throughout the country. That procedure in itself undoubtedly saves many applications for review being made."

[19] Regional ACC offices are located in Auckland, Hamilton, Palmerston North, Wellington and Christchurch. District ACC offices may be found in Whangarei, Gisborne, Rotorua, Napier, New Plymouth, Nelson, and Invercargill. There is a branch office in Dunedin for ACC headquarters in Wellington.

[20] Annual amendments have conferred more discretion upon the Accident Compensation Commission. See Accident Compensation Amendment Act 1973; Accident Compensation Amendment Act (No. 2) 1973; Accident Compensation Amendment Act 1974; Accident Compensation Amendment Act 1975, for example.

The Commission is a body corporate; its three members are appointed for three-year terms on the recommendation of the Minister of Labour. Its employees are appointed under the Act and

to confirm, modify or reverse the decision of the Commission. *By permission,* a question of law may be appealed to the New Zealand Supreme Court, but only questions of law may be appealed further to the New Zealand Court of Appeal.[21] Professor Palmer of New Zealand in assessing the first two years of the Act's operation concluded:

"It becomes evident looking at the first two years that the old litigatious areas of tort law have almost completely vanished. No one needs to show what caused the accident or whose fault it might have been. The issues revolve around entitlement and even here the room for dispute is limited."[22]

Although the New Zealand Accident Compensation Act appears to have no express application to products liability, there is implicit therein such an extension whenever the Commission so determines. Professor Palmer[23] does pose in his article:

". . . fascinating problems in conflict of laws [that] are created by the Act. For example, a defect in a helicopter manufactured in the United States causing death in New Zealand might give rise to an action for damages in the United States as well as cover under the Act in New England.[23a] It is conceivable too that some actions for damages will still be brought in New Zealand courts as a result of Section 102C which provides cover under the supplementary scheme for a person not ordinarily resident in New Zealand only after he has completed the operation of disembarking from the

---

are not subject to the State Services Act 1962. Officers are paid salaries within scales fixed by the Commission in agreement with the State Services Commission or by the Minister in the absence of agreement. The Minister has power to specify senior positions as special positions for salary purposes (Sections 6 to 42); "The arrangements are clearly designed to give the Commission some independence from Government, especially in relation to the determination of claims. The Commission enjoys wide powers of investment over its substantial funds subject to authorization by the Minister of Finance. The Act lists many matters upon which the Commission is obliged to make recommendations to the Minister. It is required to make an annual report to the Minister which must be laid before Parliament. And in the exercise of its functions and powers . . . 'the Commission shall give effect to the policy of the Government in relation to those functions and powers as communicated to it from time to time in writing by the Minister.' The salary of Chairman appears on the annual Parliamentary estimates in order to allow members to debate the activities of the Commission. In many respects the Commission functions as an ordinary Department of State. It generates policy on accident compensation matters, advises the Minister and Select Committees and prepares Cabinet submissions. Its accounts must be audited by the Audit Office. Yet it is to a considerable degree exempted from restrictions which hem in a Department. The fact that the bulk of the revenue is automatically levied by the statute and is not subject to Parliamentary appropriation means that it is impractical for a Government to control compensation expenditure. In other words, compensation is free from political and bureaucratic horse-trading in a way that other welfare benefits are not." Palmer, cited above at footnote 2, at 10–11.

[21] "For the first 9 months of the operation of the scheme there were 73,750 claims and 73,433 of these claims were approved. Even of the small number rejected one in three were accepted after a further review." Vautier, cited above at footnote 1, at 43. During the first two years, there were about 200 review decisions.

[22] Palmer, cited above at footnote 2, at 19–20.

[23] Palmer, cited above at footnote 2, at 44–45.

[23a] Accident Compensation Act 1972, Section 131. Due to an oversight, this provision applies only to cases where the injury occurs outside New Zealand, so that the Commission would appear to be powerless to prevent double payment.

ship or aircraft or other means of conveyance by which he entered New Zealand. [Accident Compensation Act 1972 Section 102C(1).] Cover ceases when he commences to embark again."

Certainly the Act does not exclude products liaibility, particularly as delineated by Professor Palmer in his comments regarding "medical, surgical, dental or first aid misadventure," which was a 1974 clarifying amendment to the definition of "personal injury by accident." Admittedly, these words were borrowed from the Australian National Compensation Bill 1974 "where they had been included in an attempt to prevent actions for negligence against medical people,"[24] or medical malpractice. The New Zealand Accident Compensation Commission has interpreted the entire phrase cautiously, with the result that doctors have "remained at common law risk" to some extent. In the six examples cited by Professor Palmer,[25] there is one that truly involves products liability questions and then concludes:

"The Commission by its restrictive interpretation seems concerned to avoid sliding down the slippery slope and compensating illness or death every time medical treatment fails. There is a ring of the old tort law in the language used in the review of decisions which talk about the 'risk' and 'remoteness.' The approach seems to me to be misconceived. The aim of extirpating the common law action must be kept in the

---

[24]Palmer, cited above at footnote 2, at 38.

[25]"(i) Claimant had a vasectomy operation performed on him in his doctor's surgery and suffered severe after-effects, including vomiting, severe pain and gross swelling and discoloration of the scrotum resulting from an infected haematoma requiring admission to hospital for treatment. Held: Claim allowed. Claimant had suffered 'personal injury by accident.' 74/R00186.

"(ii) Claimant was admitted to hospital suffering from abdominal pains and vomiting; an appendectomy was performed. The next day claimant died from a heart attack. Post mortem revealed that death was due to heart failure resulting from haemorrhage and shock due to infarction of the small bowel. Held: Claim declined. 'Medical misadventure' did not include an omission in diagnosis and examination in these circumstances. A '. . . failure to diagnose, leading to the true ailment not receiving medical treatment, can rarely, if ever, be the foundation for a claim under the Act, in that the patient's condition remains attributable to the ailment alone.' 74/R00432.

"(iii) Claimant treated by dentist for tooth abscess which he drained. The dentist assumed root filling sound but this was not correct as the abscess reappeared. Held: Claim declined. No dental misadventure or personal injury by accident.

"(iv) Claimant underwent operation for varicose veins. Later suffered pulmonary embolism, which kept him off work for some time. Held: Claim declined. No personal injury by accident or medical misadventure. Embolism merely a manifestation of a known risk. 74/R00408.

"(v) Claimant had an operation on his prostate gland. Capsule of gland accidentally punctured during surgery; surgeon noticed it and made an incision to drain away fluid which had escaped from the bladder. Claimant suffered from paralytic ileus after the operation and underwent a further operation during which claimant found to have gangrenous segment of sigmoid colon and a colostomy was performed. Claimant suffered kidney failure and died. Held: Claim allowed. Personal injury by accident. 75/R0159.

"(vi) Claimant had been fitted with an intra-uterine device. Later she suffered pain and it was found that the device was no longer in the uterus but was embedded in the peritoneum. To reach this position it must have somehow passed through the wall of the uterus. Held: Claim declined. No personal injury by accident or medical misadventure." Palmer, cited above at footnote 2, at 38–39.

forefront of thinking on the subject. Failure to diagnose should therefore be included.

"The proper screening mechanism should be found in the examination of cause-in-fact in each case. It is to be remembered that 'damage to the body or mind caused exclusively by disease, infection, or the aging process' is excluded from the Act. Whether a condition results from disease or from medical misadventure would seem to be a question of factual causation in each case. In the failure of diagnosis cases therefore, the issue becomes whether proper treatment could reasonably be expected to have made any difference to the incapacity. The approach taken by the Commission exhibits the classic vice of drawing a line through the middle of a problem when the sensible solution would be to put the line at one end. It remains to be seen whether the Appeal Authority can rescue the Commission from its own abundance of caution."[26]

A Proposal for an Elective System of Compensation

A modern corporation could offer the Accident Compensation plan to all purchasers and users of consumer products by a statement thereof on the labeling of the consumer product.[27] Advertisements of the products can also carry details of the Accident Compensation plan. Once the injured consumer can substantiate the fact that he or she sustained personal injury, property damage or economic loss, *proximately* caused by the use of or contract with the consumer product, even though the product was misused, he or she should be entitled to *immediate,* basic compensation up to $5,000 to cover medical and hospital expenses and other *provable* out-of-pocket expenditures, including property damage, wage loss, or loss of profits up to a predetermined maximum,[28] rehabilitation expenses, scheduled payments for disabling or permanent injuries or death, and even scheduled attorney's fees (if consultation with an attorney was necessary). Pain and suffering,[29] inconvenience, mental anguish, and

---

[26] Palmer, cited above at footnote 2, at 39.

[27] The following language is recommended:

"Any controversy or claim arising out of or relating to the sale or use of a consumer product and/or products, manufactured and/or distributed by this company, or the breach of any contract of sale or use of consumer product and/or products, manufactured and/or distributed by this company, may be settled under our No-Fault plan with basic payments up to $5,000, and with final, binding arbitration with respect to monies demanded for personal injury, property damage, and/or economic loss in accordance with the rules and practices of the American Arbitration Association. Judgment upon this final and binding award (including basic benefits under the NO-FAULT plan) rendered by the arbitrator and/or arbitrators may be entered in any court having jurisdiction thereof. The voluntary acceptance of this agreement for NO-FAULT consumer product liability, including the agreement to arbitrate, shall constitute a waiver of the right to trial by jury and to a review by trial de novo."

[28] By the same token, there should be *a predetermined minimum* amount as the entitlement of persons not actively or lucratively employed, that is, housewives, children and the poor. The amount would be adjusted periodically in accord with the standard of living.

[29] Section 120 of the New Zealand Accident Compensation Act, however, does provide lump-sum compensation for pain and suffering.

other intangibles would *not* be reimbursable, unless the victim's provable claim for personal injury, property damage, and economic loss *exceeded* $5,000. If the product injury resulted in death, dismemberment, permanent disability or serious disfigurement, pain and suffering and other intangibles would be included. (There should be no difficulty in establishing a schedule of awards for specific injuries, and such awards should be based on demonstrated economic impact caused by the injury.) Excluded, however, from these immediate, basic benefits up to $5,000 (and from benefits in excess of $5,000) is coverage for any intentional or fraudulent conduct on the part of the consumer or user of the product to bring about the injury, damage or loss. For example, knowingly drinking a hair dye product with the intent of injuring one's self or intentionally operating an electrical applicance for the purpose of self-infliction of injury must deprive the injured consumer of all benefits under the No-Fault Accident Compensation plan.

Criteria for Determining the "Compensable Event"

Indeed, what is the "compensable event" entitling the injured consumer to compensation? Certainly it is NOT merely the occurrence of an injury, damage or loss, for the injury, damage or loss may have no causal relationship to the product. Diseases and congenital conditions, perhaps even aggravated by bad *results* of medical and/or hospital treatment, should not be compensable at the hands of the product manufacturer! Havighurst and Tancredi,[30] in discussing their "medical adversity insurance" proposal, offered three criteria for determining the "compensable event" that are also applicable hereto:

(1) RELATIVE AVOIDABILITY, that is, the "compensable event" is within the product manufacturer's general expectations of fairness and certainly within the product manufacturer's control. The essential question is whether the product manufacturer could have perceived and/or prevented the injury, damage or loss. Obviously, the frequency with which the adverse outcome could be expected is crucial. an allergic reaction[31] due to the hypersensitivity of the product user would be compensable; on the other hand, a particular adverse drug reaction, usually tolerable, might be compensated when it occurs in pregnant women, but *not* compensated if that drug is clearly contraindicated during pregnancy, and the pregnant patient is aware of that contraindication;

(2) IMPACT ON QUALITY, that is, the safety of the product will be improved,

[30] Havighurst and Tancredi, "'Medical Adversity Insurance'—A No-Fault Approach to Medical Malpractice and Quality Assurance," 613 INSURANCE LAW JOURNAL 69 (February 1974), at 77–82. The authors point out that "whether a physician is a fit candidate for enterprise liability is no longer an open question, however, since the doctrines of respondeat superior, the 'borrowed servant,' and the 'captain of the ship' all reflect judicial acceptance of non-fault liability for medical practitioners."

[31] See generally Freedman, "Allergy and Products Liability Today," 24 *Ohio State Law Journal* 479 (1963). Also, Freedman, "A Hatband and a Tube of Lipstick: The New Jersey Minority Rule on Allergic Responses," 43 *University of Detroit Law Journal* 355 (February 1966).

for the incentives toward a greater positive effect on quality and performance of the product are mandatory. The "compensable event" bears in mind *that* impact on quality and safety and market feasibility. Of course, the risk may be shifted to the supplier, distributor or vendor, but the *impact* remains; and

(3) ADMINISTRATIVE SIMPLICITY, that is the necessity for compiling an exhaustive list of "compensable events" is self-evident and can hardly be overemphasized. Elements of arbitrariness in attributing or not attributing causation must be eliminated.

Collateral Source Rule Would Be Inapplicable

The "collateral sources of compensation" rule would NOT apply under this "products compensation" proposal, and thereby both the immediate, basic compensation up to $5,000 and any awards or judgments in excess of $5,000 would be reduced by payments received by the injured consumer from collateral sources. However, the product manufacturer would compensate the collateral source *directly,* thereby preventing a windfall to the injured consumer and restoring to such collateral sources at least some of the money paid out as a result of the compensable accident. A further reason for allowing compensation to the collateral sources is that the collateral sources will give full cooperation to the product manufacturer in satisfying the requisites of the "products compensation" proposal.[32]

---

[32] The first test of the collateral source rule under the Florida Automobile Reparation Reform Act was *United Services Automobile Association* v. *Holland,* 283 So2d 381 (Fla. App. 1973), where the first-party insurer claimed that the insured's collateral source of recovery following an automobile accident should be taken into consideration in determining the amount of no-fault benefits to which the insured was entitled. The insured, a Navy flight trainee, continued to receive his normal pay and allowances during the period of his disability and all his medical needs were furnished by the United States Naval Hospital. United Services insisted that Holland suffered no loss of gross income and incurred no medical expenses as a result of his injury; therefore, the trial court erred in applying the collateral source rule so as to allow him to receive reimbursement for his loss of flight pay until such time as he was capable of receiving flight training, finding him entitled to disability benefits until he was able to return to full duty and finding, further, that he was entitled to recover for the benefit of the United States the value of all medical services furnished to him by the Navy as a result of his injuries. The court reviewed the Florida no-fault statute and concluded that:

". . . the collateral source rule, although having its origin in the determination of damages to which an injured person is entitled to recover from his tortfeasor in negligence cases, is equally applicable to damage by insured motorists against their insurance carriers under the Florida Automobile Reparations Reform Act. The same principle is equally applicable to the rights of insured motorists to recover medical benefits furnished by their employers or by some other collateral source. Any contrary conclusion would require all persons whose employers maintain a wage continuation and medical benefits plan for their employees to purchase no-fault automobile insurance but derive practically no benefits from it. Such a result would be both inequitable and unjust."

The Florida court went on to state that the United States was entitled by the terms of its Federal Medical Care Recovery Act to obtain a recovery from a tortfeasor for the reasonable value of the medical treatment furnished to Holland. Therefore, since the United States may in-

Other Aspects of the Proposal

Another aspect of "products compensation" is the necessity for *prompt* payment of compensation to the injured consumer. To deter the product manufacturer from unreasonably resisting payment, a penalty of an added fixed fraction of the total compensation should be allowed the successful claimant.

If the complaining consumer accepts this "No-Fault" system, then he or she must resort to final, binding arbitration for recovery of loss or damage in excess of the immediate, basic $5,000 direct and maximum payment. The American Arbitration Association[33] or similar group can provide the forum and the use of its facilities for quick, economical, impartial, and final binding determination of such consumer products liability claims. Binding compulsory arbitration, however, may not be permissible under some state constitutions which guarantee a jury trial in certain cases, but it can be argued that the consumer voluntarily elected to waive a jury trial. A constitutional amendment might be required to institute a binding compulsory system.[34] There are, of course, no impediments to *voluntary* arbitration through agreement of the parties.[35]

On the other hand, if the injured consumer does *not* subscribe to the Accident Compensation plan, or the "No-Fault" or "products compensation" system, he or she can resort in the first instance, as now, to the court system for relief. It is hoped

---

tervene in a claim against the tortfeasor, it may also intervene in the case brought by Holland against United States and ". . . claim recovery for the value of the medical services furnished by it to [Holland]. The right to reimbursement so vested in the United States may not be extinguished merely because the no-fault insurance law immunizes tortfeasors from liability for claims falling within the limitations of the statute and substitutes the insurer for the tortfeasor as the one from whom recovery must be sought. . . ."

[33] Benjamin R. Schenck, New York State Superintendent of Insurance, promulgated draft regulations under which the American Arbitration Association would administer arbitration cases under the no-fault automobile insurance law that became effective February 1, 1974. Although a primary purpose of no-fault auto insurance is the prompt settlement of personal injury claims without the need for litigation, the legislators considered the possibility that disputes might nevertheless arise between insurance companies and their policyholders. The law, therefore, gives motorists the option of pursuing their claims either in court or through arbitration. The regulations implement the law by establishing a means for quick determination when policyholders who are dissatisfied with the insurance carrier's settlement offer prefer the arbitration route. Several features of the arbitration plan, as presently proposed, as unique. One is that arbitrators appointed by the AAA would be required to attempt conciliation of issues before proceeding to formal arbitration hearings. Another unusual feature of the plan is that no insurer or self insurer, respondents in arbitration cases initiated by policyholders, would be permitted "to seek any other alternative relief or a stay of arbitration in the courts." Moreover, respondents would have to pay amounts set forth in awards, and awards would not have to be "confirmed into judgment."

[34] Such a legislative enactment is found in the Appendix.

[35] *United Aircraft* v. *Greenlandair;* 298 FSupp 1330 (Conn. 1968), *aff'd* 410 F2d 761 (CA-2 1969); the contract covered a quantity of helicopters. One of the helicopters crashed and the buyer instituted suit alleging negligent manufacture. The seller moved for a stay of the action based upon the contractual agreement to arbitrate. The federal district court granted the motion and the Court of Appeals affirmed. The district court said there is "nothing incongruous about permitting arbitrators to resolve a dispute over conduct for which the law provides a remedy."

that most complaining consumers will prefer the NO-FAULT system of "ready cash" for the uncertain reward many years later of possibly greater compensation in a court of law.[36] From the standpoint of the consumer product manufacturer, this no-fault system protects the product manufacturer from being sued for possible negligence or fault; and from the standpoint of the consumer, the NO-FAULT system compensates the injured person immediately for injury, damage or loss sustained.[37] The success of the New Zealand Accident Compensation Act, although government-administered, can serve as a model plan for corporate entities to follow.

[The End]

APPENDIX

Following is the author's proposal for a "Consumer Products Compensation Law" to be enacted by the states:

"Consumer Products Compensation Law

"ARTICLE I

"The Consumer Products Compensation Law has for its purpose the protection of the consumer who has purchased a product and who has sustained (a) personal injuries and/or (b) property damages, and/or (c) economic loss, as the result of the use of the product.

"*SEC. 1* It is the intent of the Legislature that there should be prompt and reasonable compensation for such injuries and/or damages, and/or loss, by reason of the use of the product. The fundamental objective of this Law is to supplant liability at common law or by statute or decisional law, in favor of compensation for the consumer regardless of FAULT. The economic burden and risk of such injury, and/or damage, and/or loss, shall be shifted from the consumer to the product manufacturer.

"*SEC. 2* Every product manufacturer to which the Consumer Products Compensation Law applies (who would otherwise be liable in tort and/or contract) is hereby made exempt from tort and/or contract liability because of bodily injury, sickness, disease, death, property damage, or economic loss, arising out of the purchase and use of the consumer product. But no such exemption from tort and/or contract liability shall apply in the case of an accident occurring *outside* the State.

"*SEC. 3 Definitions:*

"As used in the Consumer Products Compensation Law the following terms are herewith defined:

---

[36] Changes are generally for the legislature to make, not for the judiciary—at least with respect to "greater consumer protection." See generally Freedman, "Six Problem Areas of Products Liability," 42 *Chicago Kent Law Review* 163 (Fall 1965).

[37] For a cogent attack upon the extension of NO-FAULT to Products Liability, see Ford, "The Fault with 'NO-FAULT'," 61 *American Bar Association Journal* 1071 (1975).

"(a) 'Consumer'—One who actually purchases *and* uses a product available for sale 'over the counter.'

"(b) 'Consumer product'—A product available for sale 'over the counter' as distinguished from an industrial product or a prescriptive drug, for example.

"(c) 'Purchase'—The payment of money or kind, as distinguished from the receipt of a product as a donee or beneficiary.

"(d) 'Use of the product'—The use entails actual use or consumption as opposed to merely serving as a conduit for distribution of the product.

"(e) 'Product manufacturer'—Person, firm or corporation who manufactured the product, including the placing of the product initially into the stream of commerce, as opposed to a person, firm or corporation who simply acts as a conduit for the distribution of the product.

"(f) 'Property damages'—Physical damage to personal property, as well as real property, occasioned by the use of the product.

"(g) 'Personal injury'—Accidental injuries to the person arising out of or growing out of the purchase and/or contemplated use of a consumer product.

"(h) 'Economic loss'—Loss in money value occasioned by use of a product.

"(i) 'Compensation'—Money allowance payable to consumer and/or his dependents as provided hereinafter.

"(j) 'Wilful intention'—The deliberate and intentional commission or omission of an act as distinguished from carelessness in acting and/or negligent failure to act.

"(k) 'Non-cooperation'—An intentional act, including the omission or commission to act, based upon knowledge of a reasonable person under the given circumstances.

"ARTICLE II

"Products Compensation shall be payable for personal injury and/or property damage and/or economic loss incurred by a consumer in the use of a consumer product, except that there shall be no liability for compensation when the personal injury, and/or property damage, and/or economic loss has been occasioned by the willful act or intention of the consumer to bring about the injury, and/or damage, and/or loss. However, it shall not be necessary for the injured consumer to plead or prove freedom from fault, nor may the product manufacturer plead as a defense that the injured consumer assumed the risk of injury, and/or damage, and/or loss from the use of the product.

"ARTICLE III

"The liability of the product manufacturer shall be *exclusive* and in lieu of all other liability whatsoever, except that (a) if a Certificate of Reasonable Cause is first obtained, *and* (b) if the value of such claim exceeds the amount of $5,000, then the injured consumer shall be entitled to pursue all other legal remedies against all parties allegedly liable therefor.

"ARTICLE IV

"No products compensation shall be allowed under this Law when the total claim does not exceed the value of $500. Total claims under $500 shall be processed by a special panel appointed by the Consumer Products Compensation Board under accepted administrative procedures.

"ARTICLE V

"A Consumer Products Compensation Board, consisting of 15 members, shall be appointed by the Governor of the State with the consent of the Legislature, and the Governor shall appoint one person of this number to serve as Chairman of the Consumer Products Compensation Board. The Consumer Products Compensation Board shall make its own rules and regulations governing its operations. The Consumer Products Compensation Board shall serve as a court of appeal with respect to decisions of its appointed boards.

"*SEC 1* The Consumer Products Compensation Board shall prepare and establish a schedule or schedules for consumer products compensation, in accord with the principles set forth hereinafter under Article VII.

"*SEC. 2* The Consumer Products Compensation Board shall authorize and appoint various Regional Personal Injury Boards, Regional Property Damage Boards, and Regional Economic Loss Boards, in each County of the State. Membership on a Board shall be limited to twenty-five persons.

"ARTICLE VI

"The Regional Boards, authorized and appointed by the Consumer Products Compensation Board, shall be Regional Personal Injury Boards, Regional Property Damage Boards, and Regional Economic Loss Boards.

"*SEC. 1* A Regional Personal Injury Board in each County of the State shall have authority to issue Personal Injury Certificates of Reasonable Cause. Said Board shall issue its own rules and regulations governing the procedure for issuance and/or denial of such certificates.

"*SEC. 2* A Regional Property Damage Board in each County of the State shall have authority to issue Property Damage Certificates of Reasonable Cause. Said Board shall issue its own rules and regulations governing the procedure for issuance and/or denial of such certificates.

"*SEC. 3* A Regional Economic Loss Board in each County of the State shall have authority to issue Economic Loss Certificates of Reasonable Cause. Said Board shall issue its own rules and regulations governing the procedure for issuance and/or denial of such certificates.

"ARTICLE VII

"The measure of Products Compensation for personal injuries and/or property damages and/or economic loss shall not exceed a total payment or payments of $50,000, nor shall payments extend over a period of time beyond two (2) years from the date of the injury, and/or damage, and/or loss. Such maximum payment or payments shall be reduced by all amounts received from insurance and other collateral sources.

"*SEC. 1* The measure of Products Compensation for Personal Injuries shall be (a) the verified, reasonable and necessary, medical expenses, including but not limited to reasonable and necessary surgical, X-ray and dental services, including prosthetic devices and ambulance, professional nursing and funeral services; (b) verified, reasonable and necessary hospital expenses, including rehabilitation; (c) verified, reasonable and necessary drug expenditures, all related to the Personal Injury; *and* (d) 10% of the total payment or payments as Added Compensation for pain and suffering, which is presumed to have been sustained in every claim made for Personal Injuries.

"*SEC. 2* The measure of Products Compensation for Property Damages shall be the verified, reasonable and necessary monies actually expended to repair and/or replace said property damaged (whichever amount is less) as a result of the use of the product.

"*SEC. 3* The measure of Products Compensation for Economic Loss shall be verified, reasonable and necessary monies which would have been normally earned by the injured consumer but for the Personal Injury and/or Property Damage which incurred as the result of the use of the product. 'Economic Loss' presupposes that the injured person is employed or self-employed at the time of the injury. Payments hereunder may also include payments in fact made to others in obtaining from those others necessary services in lieu of those services that, had he not been injured or damaged, the injured person would have performed, not for income, but for the benefit of himself and/or members of his household.

"ARTICLE VIII

"*SEC. 1* Claims for benefits due under this Law shall be presented to the product manufacturer as soon as practicable after the accident occurs, and in every case within one year from the date of accident.

"*SEC. 2* Claims shall include a written description of the nature and extent of injuries, property damages, and/or economic loss. The data shall include such other information as may assist in determining the amounts due and payable.

"*SEC. 3* If benefits for Economic Loss are claimed, the party presenting such claim shall authorize the product manufacturer to obtain details of all wage or salary payments, or their equivalent, paid to him by any employer in the two years immediately preceding the date of accident, or earned by him, and authorize the product manufacturer to make any reasonable investigation as to whether or not such economic loss may be reduced in whole or in part as the result of any program calling for the continuance of such wage, salary or earnings during absence from work.

"*SEC. 4* If benefits for Personal Injuries are claimed, the injured person shall submit to physical examinations by physicians selected by the product manufacturer as often as may be reasonably required, and shall do all things necessary to enable the product manufacturer to obtain medical reports and other needed information to assist in determining the amount due.

"*SEC. 5* If benefits for Property Damages are claimed, the injured person shall submit verified proofs of loss or damage together with proofs of ownership of the property.

"*SEC. 6* Non-cooperation by the injured consumer shall be a defense to the product manufacturer in any suit for benefits under this Law, and failure of the product manufacturer to pay benefits in the event of such non-cooperation shall in no way affect the exemption from tort and/or contract liability granted herein.

"ARTICLE IX

"Benefits and payments due from a product manufacturer shall be due and payable as the injury, damage and/or loss accrues, upon receipt of reasonable proof of the fact and amount of expenses and loss incurred, but the product manufacturer may agree to a lump sum payment discharging all future liability for such benefits on its own behalf. In any case where benefits due and payable remain unpaid for more than 60 days, any unpaid party shall be deemed a party to a contract with the product manufacturer and shall therefore, have a right to commence an action in contract for payment of amounts therein determined to be due in accordance with the Consumer Products Compensation Liability Law.

"ARTICLE X

"*SEC. 1* The product manufacturer shall have such remedies as are otherwise available to him against his suppliers, fabricators, distributors, assemblers, etc., for any negligence or breach of warranty attributable to the product. Nothing herein shall deprive the product manufacturer of his right to indemnification and/or recompense from such parties with respect to the products.

"*SEC. 2* The product manufacturer is also given the right to make claim for all expenses incurred on account of payments to the consumer, including but not limited to costs of processing claims and expenses of enforcing this right.

"*SEC. 3* Every product manufacturer shall be required to post a bond in a sum equal to 1% of gross sales for the preceding twelve months, thereby guaranteeing its capacity and ability to respond to the claims of users of its products.

"ARTICLE XI

"There shall be an appeal procedure whereby decisions of the Regional Boards are appealable to the Products Compensation Board. Judicial intervention cannot take place until such time as these administrative remedies are exhausted. The sole question for judicial determination shall be whether or not the claim properly arises under the Consumer Products Compensation Law."

Case Index

Subject Index